Paradise and Promises

Chronicles of my life with a self-declared, modern-day Buddha

Paradise and Promises

Chronicles of my life with a self-declared,
modern-day Buddha

A memoir by

Marlowe Sand

BOOKS

Winchester, UK
Washington, USA

First published by O-Books, 2015
O-Books is an imprint of John Hunt Publishing Ltd., Laurel House, Station Approach,
Alresford, Hants, SO24 9JH, UK
office1@jhpbooks.net
www.johnhuntpublishing.com

For distributor details and how to order please visit the 'Ordering' section on our website.

ISBN: 978 1 78279 990 0
Library of Congress Control Number: 2015931104

A CIP catalogue record for this book is available from the British Library.

Design: Stuart Davies

Printed in the USA by Edwards Brothers Malloy

We operate a distinctive and ethical publishing philosophy in all
areas of our business, from our global network of authors to
production and worldwide distribution.

CONTENTS

Preface

Paradise and Promises recalls my experiences in Andrew Cohen's Community from winter of 1986 until 2001. The material is taken from memory, diary entries, letters, video recordings and conversations with family and friends. The identities of nearly all of the characters, except for Andrew, have been changed. Several characters have been merged to simplify the story.

Marlowe Sand

Marlowe Sand is a nom de plume. The author chose to remain anonymous in order not to jeopardize further her life and family. Revealing the toxic dynamics of cult life and modern spiritual bondage of the student-teacher relationship is an important message Marlowe Sand wants to share.

Andrew Cohen is a self-declared modern-day teacher who assembled hundreds of students from all parts of the world around him. The center of activity of his community, EnlightenNext, was a former retreat center near Lennox, MA, USA. In 2015, this community is disassembled and Andrew Cohen is on sabbatical from teaching at an undisclosed location.

Acknowledgements

I want to thank all the people whose wisdom, technical expertise and time over the last twelve years enabled this memoir to emerge. Deepest thanks to my husband for countless hours of editing and for challenging my assumptions, my children for their integrity and gentleness, Debbie Blicher and Sarah Vincent for editing, Sally Bowie for believing in this book and cultivating my interest in complexity, Carin for marketing, Brad Keimach for supporting my independence, Michael Koran—my first writing teacher, and Philip Miller for helping me find inspiration.

I would also like to acknowledge the insight, support and generosity of: Susan Bridle, Nancy Daly, Robin Daly, Andrea Eagles, Janny Heitman, Alison MacArther, Mike McLellen, Peggy Newman, Daniel Orlanski, Elisa Pearmain and Ralf Schmiel. Thanks also to many former students of Andrew Cohen for their deep friendship, and our long discussions together since leaving community.

Andrew Cohen's Five Fundamental Tenets of Enlightenment

The five tenets describe the position that you need to take in order to perfectly cage the ego, and they simultaneously describe the natural state of the inherently free authentic self. If you are enlightened, if you have become one with the pure egoless passion of the authentic self, this is what your actions are going to look like—naturally, spontaneously, and effortlessly. And if you want to become enlightened, if you want to become one with the pure egoless passion of the authentic self, this is what you have to do—through intention, will, and effort. If you are sincere in your desire to become an agent for the evolution of consciousness, these five tenets must be lived without conditions, at all times, in all places, through all circumstances.

The First Tenet: Clarity of Intention
"The first tenet is the foundation of the spiritual life. In order to succeed in liberating yourself from ignorance and self-deception, you have to have no doubt whatsoever that you want to be free more than anything."

The Second Tenet: The Law of Volitionality
"Most of us like to see ourselves as unconscious victims. But in fact, we all know exactly what we are doing."

The Third Tenet: Face Everything and Avoid Nothing
"The third tenet is the ultimate form of spiritual practice. It asks: how awake are you to what is motivating you to make the choices that you make? Because only if you're paying close attention are you going to be able to bring the light of awareness into the darkest corners of your own psyche."

The Fourth Tenet: The Truth of Impersonality

"The fourth tenet states that every aspect of the human experience is a completely impersonal affair. It tells us that the illusion of uniqueness, the narcissistic self-sense that is ego, is created moment by moment through the compulsive and mechanical personalization of almost every thought, feeling, and experience we have."

The Fifth Tenet: For the Sake of the Whole

"The pursuit of enlightenment is for the transformation of the whole world, the enlightenment of the whole universe. It's ultimately for the evolution of consciousness itself."

(Cohen, 2011, The Five Fundamental Tenets of Enlightenment)

Prologue

We raise our arms out of the water reaching towards the sky and cry out, "Face everything!"

We throw ourselves beneath the water in surrender to God and cry out, "And avoid nothing!"

A thicket of ash and brambles runs down to the water's edge. The lake, the hills, and the sky are uniformly gray. The leaves have dropped already, though there are catkin buds on the birch twigs which will stay dormant and survive the winter. It is October in the Berkshire Hills, and a bitter wind bites our skin each time we emerge from the water. We are three women, a lake, and a timer.

We are committed to prostrating ourselves in the water for an hour without stopping. We have each already failed at this self-imposed attempt to atone for offending our guru Andrew Cohen. Two weeks previously, in a group of 25 women, we had been the ones who staggered out of the water before the hour was up. This time there is no one to take us to the hospital, no one to stand on shore and monitor the time.

We stand four feet apart, waist deep in the water. At first, each plunge shocks my whole body and I dread going under the second, third and fourth time. After ten minutes, I am so desperate that it is inconceivable that I could still be here in 50 minutes. My whole body is shaking convulsively, teeth rattling uncontrollably—banging, not chattering.

"Face everything and avoid nothing!"

After 30 minutes, my face shrinks tight against my skull. My brain feels as if it has shriveled inside my head. I can't feel any part of my body. I am afraid.

"Face everything and avoid nothing!"

Time after time, I raise my arms up and out of the water. Time after time, fear grips me as I plunge downwards. I try to

5

convince myself, *It's just the mind that deceives me into believing I have limitations.* I know the power of my own intention. I must go beyond fear.

After a while, the rhythm takes over and I cease to care about pain. I lean into the rhythm, the blessed rhythm, as our bodies swing into action. We chant without pause:

"Face everything and avoid nothing!"

I plunge my head under again. As I rise out, I glance at Erica and Ashley, noses unrecognizable, purple and blue. My God! I see their up-reaching arms, so frail against the pallid sun. I see the fear in their eyes and long to help them. They are thin and weak. They possess such courage to come a second time to this test of zeal.

As the minutes tick away, our fear and doubt grow. We struggle to be worthy, struggle to be accepted in the group, struggle to find confidence inside ourselves.

"Face everything and avoid nothing!"

It had been ten years since my first meeting with Andrew had swept me away with experiences of bliss and intervals of unexpected connection with other students. I fell in love with an ideal of simplicity that was so compelling that it eclipsed all other concerns. I left my life as an English housewife and special needs teacher and, with two small children, followed Andrew first to San Francisco and then to Boston. For the decade before this attempt at purification in the lake, I had lived on the outskirts of Andrew Cohen's Community, struggling to reconcile a monastic life in a cult with good parenting. Recently I had overcome self-doubt and been elevated to a position of status and authority over others.

The goal was "enlightenment," what Andrew called "freedom." To this end, Andrew's students sought destruction of the ego, which he defined as the self-serving part of ourselves. It was an absolute goal, and we believed that only by trusting Andrew to guide us on the path was success possible.

As I plunged into the chilling water, I was not weighing the risks and benefits of being a student of Andrew Cohen: I was already in too deep. It would be 15 years before I would have perspective on how dangerous it is when a powerful and charismatic leader controls others through the creation of a system of values which is impervious to critique from the outside. It would be many years after leaving the Community, with the help of friends and therapists, that I would come to terms with the complexity of my experiences during these years. I would eventually understand that I had sometimes connected with the deepest part of myself and at other times altogether lost track of who I was.

Now, on this October day in the frigid lake, I do not know whether plunging into the lake will strengthen me or harm me. I do not know that I am already allowing other people to determine who I am and that I will soon go over the edge into losing my sense of identity. The most intense roller coaster ride is still ahead.

Part I

A Door Opens

Chapter 1

Healing

My homeopath, Adrian, looked different today; his whole face was smoothed out, fresh instead of jaded. I expected him to probe when I failed to define my recurring, vague sense that there must be something more to life. I glanced up at the ceiling, then out of the Victorian cottage window to the blue delphiniums in the herbaceous border outside. I longed for a miracle to change the stuck quality of my life. I knew that this quality was older than I, shared with my Anglo-Saxon foremothers. We deferred our true selves to men, to poverty, to childbirth. We were deeply conditioned to settle—for the sake of survival and sometimes for convenience. I thought about my daughters. One of us had to break the pattern.

The process of reflecting with the help of this thoughtful, good-looking man had over the last year become comforting. I had grown to enjoy his easy manner, and how he stayed interested even when I told him I was at a low ebb, so low that I might disappear.

Today, instead of asking questions, he smiled as if he had forgotten all about finding the perfect question which might lead me to the perfect homeopathic remedy. Yet I felt that he was engaged directly with me instead of relating to me from behind a wall of reserve.

"Are you OK?" I asked.

"Oh, yes. Better than okay," he said. He told me he had recently met a young New Yorker named Andrew Cohen who had just returned from traveling in India. In Lucknow, Andrew had met a holy man by the name of Poonjaji. In the tradition of spiritual teachers in India, Poonjaji welcomed the visiting students, guided them in their search for spiritual experience, and helped them towards enlightenment. In the presence of his new teacher, Andrew had, in only a few days, undergone a change so radical that Poonjaji declared him profoundly enlightened and acclaimed Andrew the successor of his spiritual legacy.

"He sent him to bring about a revolution in the West!" Adrian exclaimed with a smile. "After just a couple of meetings!"

He paused for a long time, looking at the Buddha statue on the desk between us, sitting comfortably with eyes half-closed. Then he looked at me warmly, not at all the slightly bored professional, but bursting with the urgent desire to get something across. "Listen, Marlowe! It's a miracle. I have been seeking for years and I have never heard of this happening."

"It sounds interesting," I said, happy to encourage him to talk about himself for a change. I knew nothing about enlightenment myself. I certainly didn't hold with nonsense about gurus and spiritual teachers. I did not care that my homeopath was stretching the rules of counseling. Rather, I felt flattered that our one-way conversation had shifted.

"This is more than interesting!" he went on. "I have visited teachers all over the world, yet the moment that I met Andrew and felt his power, I understood all of Krishnamurti's writings for the first time. The meaning just fell into place."

"Who's Krishnamurti?" I asked.

He ignored the question but seemed to have found his tongue now. "This is unheard of! This is like the awakening of the Buddha. It just doesn't happen."

I didn't know much about the Buddha, either. My days revolved around teaching my two-year-old daughter to swim, making sure the baby slept at night, and trying to keep the house in order so that the chaos did not annoy my husband.

"Well, what is it exactly that you are experiencing right now?" I asked.

"Bliss!" He said, "I can hardly talk, I am so happy; it's like being in heaven!"

"Well, I'd like some of that," I said sardonically. "Can you transmit it?"

"I can't, but Andrew can," he said. "If you like, you can come and meet the man."

Two weeks later, Jürgen and I finished a dinner of pork chops, runner beans, and potatoes from my parents' farm in southwest England. Jürgen had changed out of his work clothes so that he could give the baby fingerfuls of mashed food. Slim and tall, he looked equally good in jeans. Elfin, two-year-old Jessica had his dark hair and deep brown eyes. She had recently become assertive about dressing herself, and was therefore wearing the brown velour jumpsuit she insisted on every day. The baby, Becky, looked as if her mass of long curls might stay blond. Six months old, she was clingy and fretful from a long-term chest infection. She fussed when I handed her to her dad.

I showed Jürgen the bottle of breast milk in the fridge and the bookmarked page on the story of *The Little Grey Rabbit* for Jessica.

I had first met Jürgen while eating barbequed salmon in a friend's cottage garden five years before. I repeatedly met his soulful eyes as we shared a bottle of whiskey, and he reminisced about his German national service stationed in Dorset. A few weeks later, when I took him home to the farm, my dad took me aside and, going beyond his suspicion of Germans (common in a post-war generation) he said, "This is a man that it would be easy to hurt." I agreed; I had already seen the honest, steadfast look in Jürgen's eyes. We corresponded and met for occasional weekends, but when a long-distance relationship seemed impractical, I joined him in Munich.

Three years later, I could work and make myself understood in German, but having a small baby increased my homesickness. Jürgen responded by giving up his career in corporate management and moving to England. He now worked as assistant manager at a low-end holiday camp in the fishing village of Brixham.

Jürgen kissed me on the cheek as I walked toward the door and asked what the meeting was about.

"I think it's something about being happy," I said, not sure how to explain the change that I had seen in the homeopath and not sure if Jürgen would see it as a good idea if I could. But I was excited about doing something different. I closed the door behind me.

I drove too fast beneath the medieval walls of Totnes Castle and out into the wooded hills, hurtling between the high, leafy hedges and along the twisting lanes tucked into the hills south of the moor. I hated to be late. Adrian's directions led me along a deep-set valley beside a river. I spotted the little bridge he had told me about and beyond it the stone farmhouse, Beenleigh Manor. Following the instructions, I opened the side door of the house and left my muddy boots in the row with the others.

A rough stone fireplace with an open hearth dominated the living room. But the 17 people in the room, sitting cross-legged and motionless on fat round cushions, focused on a large empty armchair. No one stirred when I arrived. I nodded to Adrian, sitting near the chair, and sat on the floor in the back of the room.

After ten minutes, my knees and back began to hurt. I folded my legs sideways. Then I knelt. Kneeling turned out to be hard on the knees, so I leaned against the wall and hugged my knees. I whispered to the person next to me, not noticing his concentration, "What's everyone waiting for?"

He opened his eyes, scanned my face for something of interest, and then, clearly not finding it, dismissed me. "There's a bunch of people here who are not waiting for anything."

Clearly, I was supposed to know what he meant. I replied, "I don't know what I am doing here. I am just a housewife."

"We are all "just" something!" he said.

I wondered if I should have stayed home and put the kids to bed myself. Then, more kindly, he said, "Andrew will come in soon. I am Pierre." I took his outstretched hand and said, "I am Marlowe."

As if he were invisible, so little did his movements draw attention, Andrew entered, crossed my field of vision, and settled cross-legged into the armchair before I registered that he was there. There was nothing unusual about his freshly ironed beige short-sleeved shirt. No statement of precision nor of anarchy in his black hair, parted in the middle jutting over the edge of his shirt and in definite need of trimming. He walked without self-consciousness, absent from the jarring tension that alerts our senses; yet, for an instant, I registered harshness and arrogance on his face as he cast his eyes around the room. In the powerful jaw there was no room for the casual, yet he was also relaxed and at ease. I recoiled at the fearless, piercing gaze of his black eyes. Yet, in contradiction, the boyish tilt of his head and easy smile gave him an inviting innocence.

No one said anything. I found the long silence uncomfortable and grew suspicious. A young woman with long slender hands sat comfortably on her cushion in front of him. She obviously had been meditating for years. With cynicism, I watched her stare like a child into Andrew's face without blinking. I wondered for a moment if she was developmentally delayed. I was sure I had never looked at anyone like that and I certainly did not intend to. *Why is no one talking?* I thought. *Why do people have their eyes shut? Why is that woman laughing? Why do they look at him as if he were a god?*

People began asking Andrew questions. They asked for guidance in their lives and directions for becoming free. They asked him to describe over and over how he became enlightened. Andrew voiced his conviction that if they only had the courage to let go of everything they would discover "freedom" for themselves. I did not understand what he meant by "freedom." Everyone listened with rapt attention, striving to catch each word.

It had never occurred to me to ask someone else how to live my life. I had assumed that this was something I would figure out for myself as I went along. I wondered, *What kind of teacher is this?*

Andrew met my eyes, smiled, tilted his head to one side, and said by way of introduction, "So you want to change?"

I squirmed. "Well, it depends what you mean by change."

"This teaching is about radical change. Freedom!" he said.

I was intrigued in spite of myself. "Is it permanent?" I asked. He didn't answer.

I asked, "This change that you bring about in people, is it reversible?"

"I heard you," he said. Then, scrunching his brows together, he continued, "No, it is not reversible. You have to be ready to let go and not come back. Are you ready for that?"

"I would like to get rid of some parts of me and keep the rest," I said.

"You have to take a chance. You have to let go of everything and see what happens." And then he laughed for a long time for a reason that I could not understand.

There was silence in the room for a while. Then he asked if I had any more questions.

"Who are all these people?"

He answered, "They want to be here with me. Each day there are more of them. This is my mother," he said, pointing to a gray-haired woman sitting at his feet, looking up at him with her mouth open in apparent adoration.

I thought he was joking.

"You can ask her," he said. "She really is my mother." She was not looking at him as a mother looks at a son. Something didn't make sense to me, but Adrian nodded in amusement.

"Yes," said Andrew. "My mother is one of my students." He laughed again as I wrestled between wanting to run in horror from these unnatural-looking relationships and wanting to take on adventures within a culture beyond my experience.

We sat silently.

After a long time, Andrew asked what I was thinking.

"I wasn't thinking at all," I replied.

I was unable to account for the passage of time. In a strange jump of emotional state, I had lost my desire to scan the room for weird behavior and had stopped evaluating how I fitted in. I found that my fears had been replaced by contentment, even gentleness or joy. The normal emotional chatter of my mind had cleared.

Andrew raised his eyebrows and pressed me further. "What do you mean? Not at all since we last spoke?"

"That's right, not thinking at all," I replied, as if that were the most natural thing in the world.

"Well, that's interesting, isn't it?" he said, spreading his hands wide in amazement. I had no resistance against the tenderness of this moment.

Afterwards, I discovered we had been in meditation. Unlike other teachers, Andrew taught no methodology, used no mantra or focus on breath or sound. He taught that meditation would arise naturally from within, as a result of deep relaxation and attention. These evenings of meditation and dialogue were called Satsang, which in Sanskrit means, "communion with the truth."

In Andrew's presence, my preoccupation with anything outside the room dropped away, and my attention was directed toward a part of me that I had never before noticed, beyond thought and feelings. My preoccupations with unspoken plans for avoiding this and acquiring that separated like strands of silk to reveal a vast expanse beyond. My incessant search for something stopped in its tracks. I was left with a clean empty space, acutely alert to everything going on around me. The flicker of a moth at the window sounded loud but did not disturb the peace. The smell of herb tea brewing in the next room filled my senses. I struggle to find words that will do justice to the ineffable taste, scent, or sound of this experience of being alive beyond the mind's assessment of it.

"Look at her face," Andrew said, pointing at me. "See how beautiful she is."

I had never thought of myself as beautiful but I accepted that he saw beyond physical beauty.

That first night, something in the room, or something transmitted from Andrew Cohen, changed my view of myself and other people. It was a sudden and incomprehensible shift from defending myself to letting go, accompanied by a corresponding shift from suspicion of Andrew Cohen to trust in him, even though I had at first identified him as arrogant and harsh. I did not then try to understand what had caused this shift in my perception.

In a daze, I put on my Wellington boots on my way out of the farmhouse. The stiff rubber of the boot yielded to my heel and my foot slid in without effort, although it had always used to stick. I caught the eye of a woman coming out of the living room. Half a day earlier, I would have checked to see if I had made a mistake by putting my boots on inside the house instead of first carrying them to the door. I would have caught her glance for a second and then turned quickly back to my boots. Now my reticence to connect was diminished, and I flowed into the softness of her eyes, and in them I met the reflection of my own. We smiled a smile of recognition that every problem, every possibility of a problem, had vanished. I felt closer to this stranger than to any friend I had ever had.

In the following weeks, I searched for the familiar sense of me but could not recognize myself. Now, after one evening of meditation, an ancient, ingrained sense that there was something deeply wrong with me had vanished. I noticed the absence of an old gnawing sense under the skin that being alone, even for an hour, meant that no one wanted to be with me. The sense that I was undeserving if I did not excel and receive approval had gone. I was in love. The love radiated outwards but had no object, not even Andrew. It was all the same to me now where I was, what I did, or who I was with. Joy was my companion. This change was sudden, but I had no curiosity about what had happened. I just marveled at it, told anyone who would listen, and relaxed over the next blissful few weeks.

One day, hiking over the hills nearby to the Devon Coast, I reached a hilltop and stood and watched the play of evening sunlight casting deep shadows across the closely cropped sheep fields. I took in the hedges and trees tucked into the folds of the hills. "How incredibly beautiful," I thought. But then there was no more beauty, the definition of beauty disappeared and I could no longer see it from the outside. I became part of the beauty. Marlowe and the landscape in front of me were not separated in any way. I was nothing more than this landscape. Then I thought, "I am nothing at all, I don't exist."

During this period, vivid memories came back to me of my entire life. I remembered sitting on the tapestry footstool in front of my old granny, surprised by the softness of her wrinkled hands while we sewed colored buttons on an old sock. The quality of my new meditation reminded me that as a child I would see a primrose growing in a hedgerow and flow into it, talk to it, and know it understood me.

My mother's love for my brother John and me compensated her for the disappointments of marriage. Sure-footed and steady in every practical and educational detail, she devoted herself to our care while working side by side with my father on the farm. She helped us climb into the fork of the hornbeam tree to see the magpie's stash of glittering treasure: silvery ivy seeds, a silver earring, turquoise beads. She helped us build a tree house in the old oak tree at the edge of the sheep field. She shared with me the thrill of discovering under the walnut tree a broken blue robin's egg which we pieced together and placed in the museum that we had created in the attic.

I was given freedom not to limit myself to what girls did in the fifties. I imitated the accomplishments of boys on the farm as they climbed ropes, drove tractors, and hammered nails. By ten, I had learned to ride horses and had mapped the trails in the woods and surrounding farms. By 15, I followed the hounds, foxhunting, and was learning to break in our own horses.

Mom tried hard to help us socialize, but I found the transition to the world of other children confusing and uncomfortable. Before starting school, I once went into a local shop and stared, amazed, at a little girl carrying a Barbie doll under her arm, begging her mother for hair ribbons and candy. I loathed the acrid taste of candy, and it had never occurred to me to want ribbons for my hair. Barbie dolls, hair clips and girly things were not part of my world; I wore the same green striped tee shirt for an entire summer because I liked the softness of the fabric.

My mother helped me connect with one or two friends at a time. But given a shy and cautious temperament, and an isolated childhood on a remote farm, I did not thrive at school. I was unprepared for the jostling for position among peers and was crushed in the face of even mild bullying. My mother's distress at my distress embellished my pain, so I learned to conceal my wounds. Soon, in collusion against the world, we feared all outsiders. She and I would judge the faults of my boyfriends, and I would reject them, believing that the world was not a safe or happy place.

Though shy and socially anxious, my silence ran side by side with a sense of adventure. Fear prevented me from under-standing either the curriculum or the social dynamics of the schoolyard, but adventure led me to climb rocks and ride horses. Fear caused me to withdraw from making deep friendships, but adventure led me to hitchhike alone around the UK and get a degree in philosophy. My actions suggest that I was not easily led nor readily swayed by other people: not an obvious candidate for a cult. One of my first job references at the age of

18 described me as unafraid to put myself at risk for the sake of speaking out about something I believed in.

For two months after that first Satsang I would wake in the night, my body burning with excitement. Instead of trying to go back to sleep, I would lie there reveling in it, as if a powerful force compelled me to lap up every second of life's intensity. Excitement without cause dominated my experience. The thrill of lying in bed awake, living this moment, was overwhelming.

Two dreams from my early childhood came back to me during this time. One was a nightmare: mountainous masses of dark, oppressive matter slowly moving across the landscape, forming and reforming like molten rock. I would be powerless to move and the mass would finally fill the space, threatening to smother me. In the other dream, I entered a huge room lit with gold, the space filled with jewels and beautiful things. Light radiated from every object. Now I understood the difference between the two dreams: one was my experience before meeting Andrew, the other after.

In retrospect, I wonder if there had been a time earlier in my life when I had sought something like this experience with Andrew. When I look at a photo of myself at the age of seven, I see a face of bemusement, as if I were trying to figure something out. I do remember our middle school English teacher asking if there was anyone who felt that they were looking for something different in life, anyone who had a sense that there was something they needed to find. Breaking my survival strategy of invisibility, from the back row of the class I raised my hand, making public and conscious a desire for some deep change. When the teacher called on me, I looked down at the sketches of horses which filled my school days and replied in a whisper, "I don't know." Perhaps that vague question had stayed with me until now, in 1986 at the age of 33, I had stumbled on the solution: there was nothing to figure out.

Chapter 2

In Love

I did not return to Satsang for six weeks, until the strength of my blissful experiences began to fade. I attended once a week, then twice a week, and then three times. Jürgen grumbled and wanted to know why I wanted to go so often. I tried to explain that I did not want my growth to be superficial, I wanted it to go deep. I explained that if I just spent a little more concentrated time with Andrew then I would be free and not need him anymore.

I would return from Satsang bubbling with energy. Sometimes I tried to talk to Jürgen about it. "It is wonderful," I would say. "Everyone is changing," but Jürgen had been reared to be practical in post-war German austerity. I tried to explain: "It is like what happened to Jesus. He was on fire when he first started teaching after he was baptized." But Jürgen was an atheist. There was nowhere for my words to land.

We had a solid partnership in many ways, but years of my constant demands for emotional connection had created resentment. In response to my appeals for him to work on his moods, Jürgen would reply, "I am all right as I am. This is me. Take me or leave me." We had even tried couples counseling, but after a while the counselor said, "Oh dear, oh dear! You two are so different."

These conflicts notwithstanding, the dynamics of my relationship with Jürgen improved. For a while we became more intimate than even during the tentative love of our first weekend in Berlin. Jürgen noticed the difference and at first encouraged me, saying that the visits to see Andrew seemed to be good for me.

Before meeting Andrew, I used to wait anxiously for Jürgen to get home with my running shoes already on. After a quick peck on the cheek, I would make for the door as fast as I could, jealously guarding my running time as the only time in the day to call my own. But now, one evening when he returned from work—tired from a ten-hour shift, wearing his holiday camp uniform—I stopped. I put the kettle on, and we sat together on the warm doorstep and watched the children pouring sand into the mouths of imaginary teddy bears made out of sticks. He told me about his 60-year-old boss who wanted to marry a 20-year-old visitor to the camp. He told me about the eight-step rule in the cafeteria for cleaning countertops. As he did so, the mundane drudgery of supporting his family in a foreign country became a little easier. This moment of connection after our separate days was all we needed to be together again.

Now, it was satisfying to be together. Before I met Andrew, sex had generally left me wanting more of something: more intimacy, more novelty, more intensity or something, but now I felt full to the brim all day and didn't seek more of anything—the sweetness of connecting with Jürgen was a wonderful thing. I stopped demanding that he make me feel complete. I stopped trying to make him feed the kids tofu dessert instead of ice cream, stopped nagging him for reading the newspaper instead of taking the children to see the boats down at Brixham Harbour. And, as if by a surreptitious miracle, my husband, who had sometimes seemed impenetrable, felt the difference and became sweeter than he had ever been. For the first time in seven years, neither one of us wished that things were different.

By the time I'd known Andrew six months, I felt as if every occurrence had become my teacher. If I made a mistake, then I would learn from it. When my daughter Jessica tried to teach the baby to do somersaults on the bed, I spoke to her harshly; then I saw the impact on her wounded face and softened my voice and took her onto my lap, explaining that babies' bones are still soft.

My mind's machinery had been laid bare. I seemed to see my own mind in action, my understanding of thoughts liberated from distraction, fear, and rationalization. I felt exposed, every emotion strong and visible. I was defenseless but untouchable, for where could I be hurt? There was nothing anyone could say to upset me because I was not trying to conceal anything. For example, I saw that Jürgen became angry at me because I was demanding that he assuage my insecurity with affirmation. I saw now my habit of duplicity when I criticized him for failing to be emotionally connected while not truly available to be intimate with him myself. I could see thoughts running, as they had always run, along railway tracks driving me away from fear and towards ambition. And I could see my choices moment by moment to be on the runaway train or watch it go by.

I had a special notebook with marbleized ink on the cover. I bought many more of them and filled them with responses to Andrew's teachings, because it seemed that all these benefits came directly through Andrew. Many years later I would burn most of these diaries, but one survives from the second year after I met Andrew. I wrote:

April, 1987
Andrew's every gesture is born out of love.

My heart must remain open to the Andrew in all things, wherever I may find him.

Everything that I do must be an expression of Andrew's love; if it isn't, then my ego, my sense of self-importance, is getting in the way.

I lie in the palm of Andrew's hand utterly content, along with 3000 others.

The rest of my life, in every situation, on every occasion, is a prayer to Andrew.

Talking to Andrew, I can be absolutely sure of getting a true response.

My mother taught me that the world was too dangerous a place for me and it was, until I met Andrew.

Life is unbelievably precious, so precious I wouldn't miss a second of it. But it matters not at all whether I die today or in 50 years' time.

I sometimes catch myself unawares and think, "Is there something I've forgotten to worry about? What was it that used to consume me so?"

One day as I was taking my daughter to play group, I saw a man walking down the street—a weighty man limping with a stiff gait. As he came closer, I could see his thick head and greasy neck bulging over the top of his soiled shirt collar. In the past I would have averted my gaze, withdrawn my attention, and taken a step away from him. I would have seen him as a separate species that had nothing to do with me. But instead I saw that he was perfect. It was as if all boundaries between us had vanished.

The only experiences that I had had of such intensity were sexual. Feeling out of control, I said to Andrew that evening in Satsang, "I feel so close to everyone that I wonder if it is dangerous. It's as if I could sleep with anyone. There seems no reason not to be close to everyone."

He said, "This is not dangerous, this is wonderful!"

"I don't understand," I said. "It is confusing."

"Just wait and see," he said. "You have to take a chance!"

I knew he did not mean that I should sleep with strangers. I understood that the unfamiliar connection which I now felt with all people was a natural and wonderful thing that should not be stifled. But I knew also that Jürgen might misconstrue this conversation if I shared it with him.

Totnes, the small, rural town where we lived, drew seekers aspiring to understand themselves, to escape turmoil, to find God, or just to create a lifestyle less hectic than the mainstream. Many people in the surrounding rural villages heard that a newly enlightened teacher had settled in Totnes and were curious to hear him speak. Some were immediately repelled by his radical message. Others saw in him a rare quality and were deeply moved.

For instance, there was a large group of Christians who followed the teachings of Rudolf Steiner and a well-established Buddhist meditation center close to the town. Many people from these two groups came to see Andrew. The intensity of Andrew's meetings took many by surprise. Often the pretense around students' lives fell away spontaneously and they made instant and radical changes. Four or five couples whose children were at the Steiner School broke up after a few meetings with Andrew, and many of the Buddhist students abandoned decades of patient meditation practice for the sake of life in the fast lane with Andrew Cohen. My next-door neighbor found, after one visit to Andrew, that something opened up inside him; and without a desire for a long-term connection to Andrew, he went away deeply grateful for the added dimension to his life. But a growing number, myself included, felt a pull to return, to tap again into the rich pool of understanding and joy that they discovered in Andrew's presence. This group would form his followers.

Poonjaji, Andrew's teacher in India, had sent Andrew to teach in the West, expecting that Andrew would gather students in Totnes, as in the Hindu tradition. Those most interested in his teachings started to spend more and more time together. They rented a house together, beginning a tradition of communal life which would evolve over the next decades. Over the years, Andrew would take increasing interest in his students' living arrangements, daily lives, and practices. He would also create a formal hierarchy, leading eventually to five or six levels of seniority among his students that reflected commitment, depth of understanding, and consistency of expression of his teachings.

Andrew did not teach a doctrine based on religion, not even the Hinduism of his teacher. His teachings came directly from his own experience in India of personal revelation. He told us many times about meeting his teacher. He also described a moment of surrender, when he said to an unknown force, "Let thy will be done." I imagined him alone in a simple stone hut, lying on a reed bed, letting go of all that had made him insecure, all that had limited his early dreams of musical success, all that had made his recent pursuit of martial arts unsatisfying. It seemed that his life was given over, like that of a saint's, to something beyond the goals of this world. I understood him to have given up all seeking for himself and to have dedicated his life to helping others to become free. I believed that Andrew was permanently enlightened, and that if I studied with him I would become like him.

When people asked me how Andrew taught, sometimes I replied that he taught "through silence," sometimes "through question and answer." It seemed as though he saw our under-lying motivations so clearly that speaking with him was like looking into a mirror. Sometimes the mirror reflected something ugly, sometimes something beautiful. In either case, we seemed to be propelled at accelerated speed in one direction or another.

At the start of one evening, a heavyset blond Dutch man sat in the front row of students. Andrew praised his commitment and told him that responsibility meant responding, right now, with purity of motivation. He told us that in order to be free, we had to be deadly serious about freedom, and that immediate surrender was accessible to us all. All distractions, all delays, all relationships that colluded with our procrastination were just excuses. Andrew remained silent as the man announced that he would stay in England as Andrew's student rather than return to Holland to complete his last six months of medical training. I saw that this teaching truly worked if we put freedom first. If we did, then, with a leap, we were free!

I was sitting sideways leaning against the wall—a choice position, close to Andrew and without the dreadful pain of sitting cross-legged without support for hours at a time. I was on

Andrew's left and could see clearly to the back of the hall. I had been aware of some turmoil in a man, with mouse-brown hair and glasses, sitting on a chair at the back. I would later learn his name was Cole. For the first half of the evening he sat in stony silence, then I noticed his stiff, guarded face contort with confusion. His face flushed red at some internal shift in orientation. Andrew was aware of the struggle in Cole too, and drew him into conversation. Cole said that he been practicing Buddhist meditation for 15 years. Andrew said, as he would say to many others, that meditation was a waste of time and was not effective. As he talked to Andrew, Cole's face became stronger and more vigorous, and his posture more upright. I realized that the radiance I saw in Cole and many others who sat with Andrew was a function not of skin and bones, but of the spirit of excitement and wonder that they carried inside. I knew from experience that it was easy in Andrew's presence to allow the boundaries that once held us painfully separate from other people to break down. Cole's relief was my relief and reinforced my own. I shared his pleasure when his pretense at being the perpetual nice guy gave way to bold transparency. Cole would eventually make a commitment so deep that it would inspire him to follow Andrew for the next 15 years, leaving his wife and children, dissipating his family fortune and allowing the family tea importing business to disintegrate.

During one of these early evenings, a worried-looking Frenchman named Pasqual sat at Andrew's left side. I saw him in profile. His hair, tied back in a ponytail, amplified his high forehead and sensitive, soulful eyes. Red-rimmed around the eyes, choking and flushed, he told Andrew that, throughout many years of training as a Buddhist monk, he had been tormented by lack of faith; even now he did not know if his faith was strong enough. Andrew gently told him that contrary to his fear, he had faith so deep that it would not falter "even if his throat were cut with a knife." The Frenchman cried tears of joy, and peace seemed to radiate from him, mirroring the expression on Andrew's face. There was about Andrew's teachings a wonderful simplicity. I noticed time after time that when students became open to him then he tenderly affirmed their direction, and everything in their lives fell into a new clear perspective. Throughout the evening, the Frenchman continued to soften and relax. His face dropped tension, anxiety and grief, and became open and gentle. By the end of the evening, his skin appeared transparent as he sat motionless in deep meditation, unable to move for several hours after Satsang had ended. He would remain with Andrew for more than a decade.

Another evening, there were no questions until I raised my hand. I asked many questions in those days. Andrew looked at me and smiled in loving expectation.

I said, "I have an image of two beautiful trees silhouetted against a red sky. The leaves and branches disintegrate into a formless array. The leaves and branches stop looking like elements of a tree and all the elements are rearranged. I don't understand this image."

He said, "This is beautiful."

"But I don't understand it," I said.

"This image shows you that you do have understanding. It is all in place. Trust this."

Each time he reinforced my insights, I would explode inside as though a time bomb of confidence had been detonated. I felt loved, understood, and affirmed by him. His affirmation was a direct route to my trusting myself even more deeply.

Jürgen came to the teachings once: I desperately wanted him to find something in Andrew for himself. Together we sat on chairs at the back of the hall. There were no questions that night, but the room was bubbling with excitement. Andrew, his eyes sometimes open and sometimes closed, laughed out loud many times. From my own experience on other nights, I knew this to be laughter at the absurdity of our spending years assuming that there was a giant problem with being alive. It was laughter at knowing that we had spent our lives desperate to get away from life when the solution lay in relaxing into life's complexity. We laughed because we saw that there was never a reason to be desperate in the first place. But this night I did not laugh. I felt for Jürgen in his confusion. Andrew didn't say a word all evening.

Afterwards, Jürgen asked me, "Why does he laugh like that? What was he laughing at?"

He saw random, crazy, hysterical laughter. "This is not for me."

The next day, Jessica's kindergarten teacher entered the classroom unexpectedly while I was cleaning the tables. He wanted to know why I was crying. Sobbing, I explained to him that I could not share with my husband 90% of what mattered to me: my relationship with God.

One evening, a beautiful young Israeli woman with a gentle voice said, "Andrew, I have been trying for years to become more loving and accepting towards myself and to heal my inner child. Can you help me with this?"

Andrew replied, "I do not care about healing the inner child. I want to slit its throat." The roomful of people gasped at his use of this image. Undaunted, he continued, "I am engaged in destroying the ego. You have to decide if you want acceptance or if you want to change. Change takes courage and means ruthlessly seeking the truth."

This might have been a trigger for me that something was amiss but instead of reacting to the aggression in his image, I rationalized that Andrew wanted not the incremental change of therapy (which he described as the never-ending obsession with the contents of a garbage bin), nor the pretenses that he saw in the self-improvement community; but for us to boldly set our sights on a radical new understanding of who and what we were. He wanted a deeper kind of love which meant destruction of the ego. And besides, my experience now was of self-generating love. How could that be a bad thing? The word "ego" he would define as the part of us that sought self-interest and was entirely negative. By the second winter, Andrew therefore eschewed the words "acceptance" and "compassion," advocating instead that an investigation of our own motivation would bring us to the truth. He was clear that his love and approval were conditional on our ability to be single-minded in pursuit of freedom. The truth would set us free; the truth would lead us to love one another and our impeccable actions would reveal our understanding. He urged us to abandon every preoccupation with limitation and every belief system or relationship which stood in the way of giving up the ego so that we could become pure vessels for our authentic selves to be expressed.

Andrew had contempt for spiritual teachers whose behavior was corrupt. From the first, he taught that we must uphold an "absolute" standard of behavior in alignment with our understanding, and he insisted that he would hold himself and his students to high standards of honesty and behavior. This emphasis on ethical behavior was at odds with many spiritual paths at this time, which seemed to give seekers—and in particular their gurus—license for extreme behavior, with the apparent justification that realization of truth (or enlightenment) is disconnected from the consequences of action. In those paths, it seemed to Andrew that, once you achieved enlightenment, it no longer mattered what you did.

Andrew went further and was also scathing about teachers who admitted to any imperfections. A decade later, in an interview with the fallen from grace guru Amrit Desai, Andrew (2013) would say, "I've always felt that if it wasn't possible to not have a shadow, then enlightenment really wouldn't mean anything. Whatever it ultimately means to be fully enlightened, I have always assumed that that would imply that the enlightened one was no longer casting a shadow, simply because of their utter purity of motivation." Andrew consistently implied his perfection and encouraged his students to treat him as infallible but this was the closest he came to stating in print that he had no remaining ego. Later in the same interview when challenging Desai to face up to his sexual misconduct Andrew said, "A true guru is declaring to the world that it is possible to be free in this life, to stop creating karma through acting out of ignorance and selfishness, to liberate oneself from the destructive power of the ego to cause pain and suffering."

Andrew's high standards and extensive finger-pointing caused consternation among the spiritual leaders of the area. He delighted in shaking up the status quo. It became common to hear him mock teachers whose message differed from his own. I felt uplifted by the knowledge that he was a fearless warrior teacher who could stand up to the ego, and my own sense of specialness was fed by Andrew's. No wonder, we thought, other leaders cannot sit easily side by side with him. We students celebrated Andrew's growth into a powerful and controversial phenomenon, at first in Totnes and eventually on the international stage of teachers and seekers.

Despite my conflict with Jürgen, I felt so deeply content that nothing disturbed my tranquility. I was unperturbed by attending to Becky's cries each night at 3:00am, or even by nursing her through a fever of 106 degrees. When I thought ahead, I was unafraid of change. I knew that discoveries lay around every corner.

We stayed for a week with Jürgen's family in Augsburg over Easter. I was not afraid now of making mistakes speaking in German, and therefore relating to my in-laws became so much easier. I felt at home now among the passionate South German people and loved sitting in the afternoons around the tiled wood stove eating *küchen* and salami. Other people noticed the change in me too: one of our German friends wanted to know why I looked so peaceful, my cousin commented that my whole face looked smoothed out, and my brother said that I appeared to be so relaxed that he did not know how I would ever get anything done. Often I would disengage and sit in our bedroom, meditating for as long as I could without being thought rude. Once Jürgen caught me at it and demanded angrily what I was doing, fearful that his family would find out.

It made no difference to me now where I lived or even with whom. I do not mean that I felt disloyal to Jürgen; rather, that inside me was a happiness untethered to external circumstances. Jürgen's job prospects in the UK were limited, so we decided to return to Germany where we thought it would be easier for him to find good work. Nothing disturbed my tranquility, not even the prospect of losing my support from Andrew and moving to Germany. Jürgen said goodbye to the children and went ahead to Germany to find work and a house.

During Andrew's second winter of teaching, while Jürgen was job hunting in Germany, I enjoyed Satsang without distractions. And Jessica, who had only ever been cared for by me, Jürgen, and my mother, grew accustomed to babysitters six nights a week.

Each night of Satsang, a few more people crammed into the room, until in this second winter there were sometimes 200 people looking to Andrew to show them the path.

Threaded through Satsang was spontaneous meditation which was so strong that it continued whether our eyes were open or shut. As the months went by, Andrew suggested to people that they meditate more formally every day for an hour. Over the years, his recommendations evolved and the use of long hours of practice, including meditation, would become standard.

There was no apparent pattern to indicate who would become immersed in the teachings and who would take flight and leave. About half of those who stayed had a previous interest in spiritual activities. Of those who stayed, the common thread was that we believed we had found the source of joy and love. We saw that all of us had the same minds, the same tendencies and the same simple emotional machinery driving our choices.

One woman's unhealthy tendency to get attached for the sake of security was the same as mine. The action of my mind or hers was not unique or special. Andrew began to teach that everything is impersonal, formalizing this understanding as the Law of Impersonality: "The illusion of uniqueness, the narcissistic self-sense that is ego, is created moment by moment through the compulsive and mechanical personalization of almost every thought, feeling, and experience we have."

I knew that every profound insight in this room applied to me too. As a result, I searched my soul for excessive and unhealthy attachments. My husband? My parents? My children?

A small woman in the middle of the room talked of her struggle with depression, which she felt was outside of her control. Andrew told her that he believed that everyone knows exactly what they are doing and everyone is responsible for their actions. The woman bristled and angrily told Andrew that this point of view took no account of her illness. Andrew said that, even in the case of severe mental illness, our actions are volitional and within our control. Over the years he became convinced that we are not victims either to circumstances or to the forces inside our own minds; we in fact know what we are doing and have the power to choose otherwise. He therefore believed that we have to take complete responsibility for everything we ever do.

Around this time, we saw the beginning of Andrew's third tenet: Face everything and avoid nothing. One evening, I saw at the back of the meditation hall a slim, curly-haired young man who said in a tremulous voice that he had been to many teachers trying to find relief. In great distress, he said that as a soldier in the Vietnam War he had done things that he deeply regretted. He told Andrew that other spiritual teachers from the Advaita tradition had told him to forget about what he had done because, when he realized that he was only the spirit, his actions would not ultimately matter. They had encouraged him to live fully in the present so he could be free. He said that this approach had left him tortured.

Andrew replied without anger, judgment or sympathy. "We can only be free by taking complete responsibility for our actions."

Emboldened to continue, the young man added, "How can I take responsibility for shooting two innocent babies?"

Andrew was not appalled. He told the man that he had to face what he had done in order to be free. "You can find no freedom by running away from it. If you avoid this, it will torture you forever." The man thanked Andrew for giving him what he needed and said he felt tremendous relief.

I felt I was witnessing the fusion of love and truth in action.

Although Andrew implied that many of his students would become enlightened in this lifetime, there was one student whom he declared had finished her work and become completely free of ego. She is the only student I am aware of whom he said had attained enlightenment. He entered the room one evening carrying in his hand her last letter to him. He had been crying. He had just received news that she had been killed in a car crash while travelling. He read parts of her letter and described that, after he had acknowledged her enlightenment, she had asked him what she should do with the rest of her life. He had replied that it made no difference what she did. He had let her fly free to live her life in complete independence of him. He asked for no allegiance.

I had several private meetings with Andrew for an hour or so at a time. I didn't seek his friendship and was not sexually attracted to him; it just seemed the most normal thing in the world to sit with him. It didn't seem like a "personal" connection, perhaps because he did not need anything from me and was not trying to prove anything. Being with him therefore had a light and effortless quality.

My experiences with Andrew had broken boundaries which separated me from the people I loved and left me open and trusting of him. I wanted him to see me more clearly than I saw myself so that he could help me. I gave him my diary to read, sharing my experiences of intense delight in life. A week later, I realized that I had a lot further to go when he returned it to me saying that he had glanced at it and I was on the right track. I was a little downcast, having believed that each word in this diary represented profound discoveries. Andrew's lack of interest and my own disappointment seemed to show me, not for the last time, that I was hopelessly self-centered. For sure I had not taken in the Law of Impersonality—a guide towards letting go of the desire to make every experience just about me.

In one of our private meetings when I had had a bad week, I said to Andrew that I knew that he was withholding more blissful experiences from me until I gave something more to him. I had unintentionally attributed to him the power of a magician. I watched his face as he hesitated and made a move to disagree with me. However, now, when he might have said to me, "That is not how it is. It does not come from me. When you are no longer in conflict with yourself then you will be at peace," instead he accepted my gift of power and said, "Okay, that's how it is." In my naïveté I had become a conspirator in the co-creation of a charismatic guru.

Soon it was established belief that Andrew was beyond reproach though I remember once a woman told me that Andrew had apologized to her for being too harsh when she was grieving for the recent loss of her husband; he'd still been able to see and acknowledge making a mistake.

During this second winter season of teachings in 1987 to 1988, I accumulated a vocabulary to articulate the changes that had already taken place in my life and the lives of others. I learned how to arrange our experiences within a cognitive framework that Andrew drew from Eastern religions and adapted to fit within his growing experience as a teacher. I do not know the exact origin of his ideas. However, students who had a background in Eastern religions said that the path to enlightenment lay in acceptance of Andrew as a metaphor for perfection or as an external representation of the highest, most sacred part of ourselves: enlightenment would come to those who surrendered to Andrew Cohen. They said there was a distinction between "Andrew Cohen the highest part of oneself" and "Andrew Cohen the man." Andrew later would explain, "through beginning to trust the outer guru... the disciple begins to experience a liberating fullness within themselves... the experience of that fullness within themselves instill(s) in them a sense of confidence and independence that few people ever realize."

I understood that my continued growth depended on accepting that Andrew was myself, though I never really thought or cared about what this meant or in what sense he was myself. I heard this concept of "guru" mentioned, but I did not consider how my gradual acceptance of this principle might trap me in a place without perspective. My experiences were so wonderful in the beginning that I did not attempt to understand what might be implied by submission to Andrew. It seemed obvious that Andrew was helping me to be fully myself.

Chapter 3

Relationship Shifts

One evening, in meditation with about 80 other people, I had been sobbing quietly for about half an hour. Andrew did not say anything to me until towards the end of the evening, though I knew he was aware of me. He gently asked why I was crying.

"It's my daughter," I said. "Today I was sitting at the kitchen table peeling apples and a dark-haired girl of about three walked in from the garden, glanced up at me from the doorway, and smiled with her dark brown eyes. There was an enchanting lightness about her. A split second later, I realized she was my own daughter, Jessica. The child that I saw was more mature, more relaxed, more completely herself than Jessica. I see two different kids: the unknown child in the doorway and my Jessica. When I saw this girl without defining her as Jessica, it was like seeing Jessica for the first time. Recognizing the contrast between the two images made me realize that I am very actively creating Jessica, molding her to be a certain way. I am controlling her by the way that I respond to the person that I hold in my imagination."

"Yes, but why are you crying?" Andrew asked.

"Because I feel so guilty," I said.

"There's no love in guilt," he said lightly without judgment, and then he explained that we were in the business of "allowing" everything that arose in us, that as soon as we denied, judged, or pushed away anything inside ourselves, then we created a problem. "You have to let go of it all," he said.

My thoughts stopped in their tracks. My momentum of self-doubt and self-destructive thoughts dead-ended. I stopped crying and closed my eyes. Pain and guilt floated away. The obstacle to being present dissolved, and I was released into connection with the calm meditation of fellow students. I felt myself lifted up and out of the top of my head to somewhere gentle, without sense of time or place. I returned home feeling more connected to my family than ever.

For the previous four years, I had thrown myself into caring for Jessica and Becky. We were minutely tuned into one another. When I discovered the philosophy of Rudolf Steiner, I shifted from supporting their cognitive development towards supporting their emotional and spiritual development. I sold the TV and filled the house with wet watercolor paintings and wax modeling clay. Each daubed sheet of paper I perceived as having the balance and form of a Japanese masterpiece. I avoided imposing my own images on their drawings, knowing that their innate ability to represent the human form would arrive in its own time. I hung the living room with shrouds of soft pink muslin cloth, conducive to the slow steady inner awakening of a small child. I resolved to invite them gently into the world of reality, offering them a protective cave from which to embark on a world of adventure. They were my project and my life.

Now, after being with Andrew, my relationship with my children expanded and deepened. Before, I'd often feared that if I did not conserve my energy, it would run out. I held back subtly from giving fully to my family for fear that my needs would be swallowed up. I cooked special meals of mashed avocado and tofu instead of baby food out of jars, but seldom did I look quietly into their eyes while they ate it. It was hard for me to join Jessica quietly while she hung ornaments on the Christmas tree. When she asked me to join her in feeding cocoa puffs to her bear, I often pulled away, wanting to be alone. "I have to do the laundry," I would say, or, "First let me finish making the dinner." It was only in retrospect, after meeting Andrew, that the subtle something-missing became apparent to me.

Six nights a week, all through the previous winter, I had sat cross-legged in front of Andrew Cohen in a farmhouse in southwest England. Through association with him I had let go of self-absorption and ambition in my parenting, and connected with my daughters more intimately than before. I no longer felt the old exhaustion that used to make me pull away from them. I didn't need to break off the play and pretend to do the laundry.

On the living room floor, while toddler Becky slept, three-year-old Jessica moved her toy figures to follow the railway tracks to the seaside. I watched as her tiny hands fitted the giraffe in the wooden railway carriage. I helped to keep the monkey secure on top of the smooth concave carriage roof. "The evil witch is coming!" she announced in the voice of the monkey. She handed me the witch.

Furrowing my eyebrows into a mean face, I moved the witch slowly over the mountain of cushions, towards the train. The giraffe screeched and the monkey gasped in fear. The witch banged on the carriage door and said, "Open the door! I'm going to eat you up!"

Jessica seized a magic lamp and said, "This light will shine on your face so you cannot come near the animals inside."

The witch, dazzled by the light, backed away. Jessica chased her far away, to the mountains.

Unaware of the time, we played until Becky woke up. Then we rolled across the bedclothes and sang songs while Becky jumped on the bed, her blond curls bouncing in her eyes.

The ordinariness of this intimacy was new to me, and I did not take it for granted.

Now that I knew what it was to be fully with the children, I was painfully aware of the days when I was not. I wanted to cement what I had learned about being with my daughters before they learned to settle for a minimal connection with others. I wanted them to grow up to be socially stronger than I was. Andrew had helped me to be present with them, and I wanted the whole of our lives to be transformed in this way. I was sure that more of Andrew's teaching would be the very best thing that I could offer my children and myself.

I talked with Jürgen, whenever he would listen, about the extraordinary changes Andrew was bringing about in the people around him. I tried to tell him that if we let in what was happening on a deep level, then it could set us free, we could be transformed; we could find our real potential. I explained to him over and over how different I felt inside. I tried to share it with him. But he shook his head.

After Jürgen had been gone for two months, he returned from Germany for Easter weekend. He looked good in his pale-blue suit even after a 12-hour journey from Munich. When he entered the house, he stood tall and looked at me with a respect I didn't remember. I felt the same attraction to him that I'd felt when I first met him.

Jürgen placed his suitcase against the telephone table and shuffled his way through the wooden blocks, crayons, and pieces of rice cake strewn across the hallway floor. He picked up a corduroy spotted dog from the floor and tried to make it sit upright against the mirror in front of him, but the dog flopped forward onto its face. He left it where it fell. For a moment, as he turned to open his suitcase, I saw deep pain and foreboding in his dark brown eyes, but he brushed off the sadness and greeted Jessica and Rebecca tenderly in German. He unpacked chocolate rabbits, chicks, kittens, lovely animals made from wood, and a huge penguin soft as velvet. He secretly handed me another bag full of chocolate eggs and two little baskets for collecting them lined with green plastic grass. In the morning, we would hide the eggs in the garden for the children to find.

We talked in the kitchen while the children ran in the walled garden in the last light. The breakfast porridge pan soaked in the sink. Scrapings of porridge on little china plates lingered on the counter. Watercolor paintings draped drying over every surface. Being with Andrew had taught me to see energy; as we talked, I saw a three-dimensional stream of energy flowing around us and all around the room. But after we had talked for a while, this stream of energy began to lose the fresh smell of growth and soil. It seemed impeded rather than invigorated by our conversation. My exuberance of the previous weeks fell out of sight. I felt that I could not breathe if I stayed in this room with him. I believed that I had to take care of the fragile opening of my heart, the result of meeting Andrew. I felt something inside me would harden if I did not give it a protective space. I did not know how to be me and stay in the same space as Jürgen.

Jürgen had found work in the city. Our plan had been for the children and me to follow him as soon as he found a house. He was tired from the long journey, but he smiled and said, "I think I have found a place for us to live in Nuremberg. I think you will like it. It has a walled garden like this."

I passed him a cup of tea. For a moment everything seemed normal, even his irritation as he brushed the dust from his blue suit. Then I quietly said, "I am not going."

Andrew had taught me that, in the pursuit of enlightenment, I might have to make radical changes to my life. My standards for a "good enough" relationship had shifted. I could not settle now for a relationship without deep connection and mutual support of growth, and I no longer depended on the security in my marriage to feel at rest. I felt strong inside, and life seemed simple. In an impulsive and unpremeditated bound, I concluded that my marriage to Jürgen was at an end. It seemed so simple to move on.

"What do you mean, you are not going?" Jürgen asked. His eyebrows furrowed in confusion.

"I am not coming with you," I said. A distant part of me observed that the statement sounded unnaturally bland.

Jürgen did not understand what I was saying. He thought I wanted him to stay in England.

"No, Jürgen, I mean, I don't think this can work, you and me."

Jürgen pointed out that things were much better between us.

I acknowledged that when I had stopped being so demanding, the dynamic between us had shifted and we had become closer.

He frowned in disbelief and horror as the seriousness of the situation began to sink in. I saw his pain, and I empathized with his distress, but my vision of what was possible in life eclipsed everything else. I explained once again that my world had opened up and I was in touch with something big that made our old lives seem incredibly limited. I implored him to reach towards change, and tried to convince him that change even of his dark moods was completely possible.

"It's this *verdammte* Cohen, isn't it? He's brainwashed you!" Jürgen slammed the table with his fist. "Did he tell you to leave me?"

"No," I said calmly. "He just wants us to be free and see the truth. He never tells us what to do."

His eyes darkened first in suffering and then with fury, believing that I had deliberately tricked him into going ahead to Germany without any intention of joining him.

When he left the kitchen and went alone upstairs to the bedroom, my thoughts circled in slow motion but refused to add up the result.

He left the following morning.

In the months before Jürgen came home, I had seen in meditation that if I put freedom as the first priority in my life, everything would fall into place. Everything was reduced to simplicity. I was not unaware of the shards of pain which would radiate from taking the girls away from their family, but I was anchored in seeking freedom, and I was learning from Andrew that radical steps might be necessary to guard that passion. My own emotional shock at losing my husband had not yet sunk in.

A month after Jürgen left, I received a phone call from an old friend from university. Jürgen had told them of our separation. He and his wife arrived the next day from London, looking small and neatly dressed. After the children were in bed, I made them tea and we sat on the L-shaped IKEA sofa. With enthusiasm I described to them the power of Andrew's teachings and what a gift I felt it was to have a guide for destruction of the ego. I thought that, if they could grasp the wonder of the teachings, they might even become excited about seeing Andrew themselves.

My friend looked confused, but he tried to understand. "Why would you want to destroy the ego? Without that, you would be crazy."

"That is not what I mean," I said. "I don't mean to destroy the part of me that organizes my sense of identity; I mean 'Ego' the part that drives me to be destructively self-centered. We have to destroy that part."

"It sounds dangerous," he said, glancing at his wife.

"It sounds like trying to get rid of the devil," she said, her face smooth with fear. Knowing that she was an ex-Catholic, I tried to explain that this was the very opposite of an organized religion, that this was a fluid organic expression of the truth without dogma. But they had already placed everything that I said into a box labeled "other."

Without a tear, I told them about my straightforward decision to choose freedom, which meant leaving Jürgen. "I have no choice," I said. "If I do not do this, I will not be me."

"Have you thought about the consequences for the children?" my friend said. He sat on the edge of the couch as if he might leap up in alarm at any minute. He reminded me of a wizened old man.

"If I do the right thing, if I follow my heart, then it has to be the right thing for them too."

They said they couldn't support me in leaving Jürgen. "It would be different if you had a terrible marriage, but things are not that bad." They seemed dismayed that I felt no remorse for ending our marriage, nor sadness for Jürgen.

At college we had slept on beaches in Greece, shared our

heartbreaks, and lived on very cheap curries. Now my friend was headed for success in the civil service while I was joining a cult, though I would never have called it that. Behind our reserve when we said goodbye was a sadness that I never expressed. That was the last time I saw him. Many years after leaving the Community I e-mailed him, but he did not reply.

Jürgen had been gone for six months. The children and I were alone in the little row house in Totnes. The questions formulated themselves all too easily now: "What have I done? What have I created in this unplanned moment of clarity?" I missed Jürgen. I missed the cup of tea he made me in bed every morning. I missed his dark eyes, eagerly sharing jokes about the music he played; I even missed his grumbling about the mess in the kitchen. My family and friends felt that I was mistaken in leaving Jürgen, so I could not talk to them. Even Andrew's followers pulled away, noticing that I was no longer radiant. The experiences of heaven I received in Andrew's presence did not soften the loneliness.

All tasks were beyond me. I didn't know how to write checks or pay the mortgage. The curtain rail in the bedroom fell down. I took a hammer and banged the nail into the wall. The nail fell to the floor. I hunted for it among the bedclothes, found it, and banged it into the wall again. It bruised my finger and the nail fell to the floor again. *I was reared on a farm!* I thought. *I can break a horse; I can sand and paint windows; I can change oil on a car; what is this with a nail?* I took the nail and for a fourth time banged it into the wall. The plaster shattered. Now it would take plastering and an expanding wall anchor to put up the curtain rail. I slammed the hammer into the wall in fury, lay down on the floor, and cried.

Often in the afternoons, I lay in bed. Sometimes I lay on the floor and cried. I could hear my children, two and five, playing in the unfenced garden adjacent to the road, alone for an hour. Some afternoons, my neighbor took them home with her. Eventually I would get up and collect them, pretending that nothing was wrong, pretending that she had needlessly usurped my authority. I distanced another friend.

At bedtime one night, Jessica asked whether it was possible for people to get back together after they separated. I understood that the German stories Jürgen sent her on audiotape could not replace his strong arms lifting her up onto his shoulders for a ride to the top of the stairs or the feel of his kiss good night. I said it was sometimes possible for people to get back together. She asked if I thought Jürgen and I might; I said I thought it was not possible and sometimes people were happier apart. Putting my arms around her, I felt her wish that we could stick everything back together.

Becky seemed too young to understand the separation. Though the next Christmas, she would confuse Santa Claus with her dad when he visited with presents for her. For a while, each time he visited she would call him Santa.

I met with Andrew at the farmhouse for guidance through this time. He invited me in with a big smile and sparkling eyes, his arms spread wide.

Before sitting down, he began, "Congratulations, Marlowe. You have done it!"

I had no idea what he was referring to.

"This is wonderful news," he went on. "I am so impressed!"

"Why would you be impressed?"

"I am proud of you." He gestured towards the couch.

"Why would you be proud of me?"

"I hear that you left your husband."

"It doesn't feel like wonderful news," I said. "It feels awful."

"But you are free now. How could you not be happy?"

"I miss him so much," I said quietly. "I know it was the right thing to leave him, but I feel so torn up and desolate. And I know it is unfair of me, but I noticed that I have been feeling resentful towards you for this pain."

Andrew's face switched from delight to anger. The solid black of his eyes stabbed me. He shouted, "You came to me to set you free, I showed you the way, and now you are resentful and angry with me?"

I was shocked and confused. I had never seen Andrew angry like this.

He continued more quietly, "Your behavior is self-centered and arrogant. You are showing a total lack of respect and gratitude for me. This is not appropriate behavior towards a teacher."

I said, "Andrew, I am grateful to you for the ability to see my life clearly. I am sorry to be aggressive towards you."

As I was leaving, Andrew's close associate smiled broadly and said, "In leaving your husband, you are just cutting away dead wood. You can be free now."

I felt stunned, but also clean and sober. Andrew's reaction banished my sadness and banished my resentment towards him. He had taught me that I could and should avoid certain feelings and reactions. This was different from my earlier experience of accepting everything inside myself, such as my guilt about my children. I did not realize it at the time, but his words forced me to bypass pain and depression and leap back towards meditation and spiritual development. As a result, my momentum to move forward without Jürgen and focus on the profound nature of existence was stronger. I also learned a trick that I would use for years: sidestepping complex emotional turmoil through meditation and focus. It would be another 15 years before I could re-engage with the distress that I had created by leaving Jürgen. The practical result was that I pushed permanently to one side an impulse to follow Jürgen to Germany.

Gradually, I regained confidence. I got a good teaching position in a local school teaching children with dyslexia. I bought a house close to Andrew's students in Totnes and saved my money to visit Andrew when he went on retreats to Rome, Amsterdam, Germany, and the French Alps. A door had opened into spiritual understanding. I felt at home in my little patch of southwest England, more at home than I had ever been before. I felt I could be happy there for the rest of my life.

As a result of meeting Andrew, I found a new and more positive relationship with my father: I suddenly understood his love of farming. Now that the desperate, driven seeking in my life had evaporated, I appreciated his meditation on the soil. Vivid memories came back to me of my early childhood with him, the calm of his movements across the fields, through snow and rain and blistering heat, seldom rushing, seldom faltering. I remembered the scent of sweat as he hoisted hay bales high onto the stack. I remembered my wonder as I jogged to keep pace with him as he checked the night's crop of newborn lambs, feeling the dew from a million feathered grass stalks tingle cool against my legs. He taught me to use the giant needle to sew the bales of wool shorn from the backs of 200 frightened ewes. In summer I would sit on the bonnet of the van as we bounced across the rutted fields and shot rabbits frozen in the glare of headlights. He laid their soft warm bodies beside me and I stroked the velvet ears, which bore just a trace of blood.

In the winter that I met Andrew I inherited from my father his love of the earth. Now, instead of seeing his life as misspent dedication to the land without a chance of concrete success, I suddenly knew for myself the joy of connection with a thousand generations of peasants. Standing in the garden, crumbling the moist black earth through my fingers, I could feel the force of energy in the geranium cuttings that I planted. It seemed then that this same tingling in me, in earth, in cutting, was the essence of everything. I understood the sentient nature of trees and the healing power of the hawthorn up by the pit where the cottages used to be. And I guessed that my father felt the same.

Now when I visited the farm, I worked beside him, thrusting the fork into the tightly packed manure from the pigsties and lifting it to the wheelbarrow with a twist of my wrist. Little by little I felt my muscles move in unison, and I discovered rest in the rhythm of digging the heavy clay earth. I guessed then that there was something sacred in my father's connection with the earth, something he knew but never could have said: that you could work the earth for the rest of your life and desire nothing. As if the act of picking up a spade erased past and future, I took my place amongst a thousand generations of farmers. Even now when I look down at my hands, I see unmistakable farmer's hands in breadth and bulk and strength, waiting only for the scars and calluses which mark the trade. I felt I could live on the farm in peace for the rest of my life.

I came to understand why many spiritual seekers and finders are drawn to a life of manual work and deep meditation. I thought, "I will be a hermit and settle into a quiet life of motherhood, farm work, prayer and contemplation. I will live in this corner of southwest England for the rest of my life." But then I felt another compelling pull: "Perhaps the meaning in life is not in meditation but in action. Andrew promises that I can learn to live what I have seen. I have only just begun to learn how to be with people. I still vacillate between recoiling like a rabbit in the headlights and aping haughty authority. I am still often intro-verted and self-absorbed. Imagine what a gift it would be for my children if I were to go permanently beyond self-preoccupation! I should do it for the children's sake! If I do not want to dodge the ultimate challenge, I will need help to change. Andrew can help me."

I resolved to spend yet more time with him. Already I was not weighing the costs and benefits of this decision. It was as if I was pulled by a magnetic force of the spiritual imperative.

Chapter 4

The Witch

After two winters of teaching in Totnes, Andrew told us with disappointment that the seekers in Devon were fond of the trappings of alternative life—the crystals, the healers, the hippie clothes—but he did not think they were serious enough to receive his message. He and many of his students planned to move to Belchertown, Massachusetts, near New York, where Andrew had spent most of his life. I was proud of Andrew, who was, we said, too radical for Devon, too radical for England. I applauded his search for a home that would embrace his movement.

Jürgen, now living alone in Germany, agreed to look after the children for three weeks so that I could visit Andrew in Belchertown. We travelled by coach for 15 hours to get to the large gothic house Jürgen had borrowed from a friend. When we arrived, Jürgen barely spoke to me. I settled Jessica and Becky into their bedrooms. As I waited for the taxi at the garden gate, I saw Jessica and Jürgen spraying each other with the garden hose while Becky dug holes with a large hoe. I realized that leaving Jürgen and the children alone, without my intervention, would bring them together.

Students were starting to immigrate to the United States to follow Andrew. They rented houses to live in and a meditation hall for Satsang. I planned to stay with some people that I knew from Totnes. The one that I knew best was my homeopath, Adrian. Within the structure of his 45-minute homeopathic session I had begun to talk about my past, my limitations and yearnings. I trusted him to help me explore myself. And he had generously shared with me his experience of meeting Andrew and invited me into his world. But I was not sure if I could handle the shift from this professional relationship to being housemates, as I had begun to feel attracted to him.

Adrian met me at the bus station. As soon as I saw him, I felt a terrible awkwardness and wished I had planned to stay somewhere else. I thought I would give him a casual hug in greeting, but I forgot to remove my backpack. With my arms pinned to my sides by the straps, I couldn't respond to his outstretched arms.

The house was an airy New England clapboard with hardwood floors and a mosquito screen that flapped as we entered. Adrian's wife met me at the door with a bunch of children. They had already been in the house for a couple of weeks. Also living there were an architect from London, his new lover, and her two children. Victoria, who I knew from Amsterdam, joined us and said, "You will love this place. It's heaven on earth." She smiled a deep smile. Looking into her face I knew she was home. "Your face," she said. "It's wide open." These people were so excited about living with and expressing Andrew's teachings that the whole house seemed to glow with energy. But I wondered how in the world I was going to share a house for three weeks with ten people while possessed by a schoolgirl crush on Adrian.

I sat on the bench at the kitchen table watching Yedida, a small, dark Israeli woman, as she reorganized the pans around the kitchen. Offering to help, I started the washing up at the sink. My farmhouse upbringing did not include rinsing dishes. Yedida scolded, "What are you doing? How disgusting! You are leaving all the dirt and soap on them!"

Without answer, I recoiled at her intensity. Although a head shorter than I, and probably weighing less, there was a resolute certainty about every move she made. In her presence I felt as fragile as a leaf. But then she said in her richly accented voice, "I am sorry. Being around you makes me feel like an elephant woman, as if I could knock you over without meaning to. You and I are so different."

"Being around you makes me feel weak, as if I had no substance, as if you were bigger than I am," I replied.

Through acknowledgement of our differences in culture and temperament and our common delight at Andrew's teachings, we immediately became friends.

It was normal for us to meet and connect deeply with people we had never met before because of our common focus. Our interest in looking beneath the surface gave us an automatic intimacy. One evening, as Yedida and I lay in twin beds in the room we shared, we talked about our lives. She told me that past lovers and husbands no longer troubled her. I noticed that her speech speeded up as she spoke; I could hear the vehemence in her voice. It sounded to me as though she were still struggling with her past, so I challenged her to look deeper at what she still had to learn from these relationships. She resisted. I said, "We can stand still, without having to run away, as we look at what we are still carrying. We do not need to judge ourselves for still carrying scars." She saw unfinished things she needed to understand and she was grateful.

This was my first communal living situation. Knowing the children were in good hands with Jürgen, I could immerse myself in this new experience. I discovered that house meetings were the forums in which our interactions were analyzed, discussed, and resolved with seeming ease. At any moment, someone might yell, "House meeting!" and we would drop what we were doing and congregate to sort things out. I was thrilled that this process brought me closer to people.

Also, I seemed to be managing to act normal around Adrian.

At Satsang my first evening in the house, heat and humidity compounded the heady excitement of 200 people, packed cross-legged into the new hall. I was almost overwhelmed by jet lag, excitement and lust, but I lost myself in deep meditation. After ten minutes, I no longer noticed that mosquitoes were biting my arms and neck.

When I woke the next morning, I sat in my bed and, as if a bystander, watched the meditation continue by itself inside my head. I was used to the random arrival of answers to unasked questions. Flashing back to one of my homeopathic sessions, I remembered Adrian's smiling face across the desk asking me to talk about myself, inviting intimate revelations. I saw this invitation as seductive rather than professional. It seemed indisputable to me that he wanted to court my attention and had encouraged my interest in him almost subconsciously. The heat, the intense group process, and the Satsang compounded my jet-lagged spaciness. In a moment of clarity I saw something about Adrian and assumed that I needed to act. It felt suddenly hugely important that I address his low-key flirtatiousness and make it fodder for the group investigation.

"House meeting!" I cried out. All 11 of us filed into the living room. I sat with my back against the light of the window and told them I had seen a pattern in Adrian's behavior: that he took pleasure in encouraging me and other women to open up to him while not giving of himself, that he was seductively feeding off women's vulnerability while staying closed himself. Adrian was shaken by my confrontation. His wife shook her head in disbelief. Someone in the meeting suggested that Adrian and I talk alone together after the meeting.

Adrian and I sat in the window seat upstairs overlooking the maples at the back of the house. He apologized to me. He told me that, although he was not attracted to me, he knew there was something he needed to see in what I was saying. As he talked, I watched his face change color and become softer. He relaxed as if a burden fell away from him. It was marvelous to see him change. He told me he thought we could find a different kind of friendship. Adrian also said that my behavior in confronting him in a meeting was aggressive and manipulative.

Andrew encouraged us to explore under the surface of our

actions; therefore, looking into our motivations was common practice. Sometimes, though, we saw more than we were ready for. This was one of those times.

The word "manipulation" ricocheted around inside me as I walked alone later that day through the New England woods. What had my motivation been? Was it to help Adrian be free or was it to make him look bad in front of the group? I examined my attraction to Adrian as if dissecting the nervous system of a frog; I followed the thin white line of nerve endings to their source: the desire to have him for my own. His rejection of me had triggered my desire to manipulate him into wanting to be with me. When I did not get what I wanted, my next step had been to harm both Adrian and his wife by accusing him in public. As if with a scalpel, I exposed the anger, which motivated my desire to punish him. I also saw that, when I did not have the power to harm either of them, my next step would be to turn my anger on myself. I realized that what had seemed insight into Adrian was largely my own projection. I saw how this series of reactions indicated a lifetime pattern of wanting love, choosing someone who could not give it deeply, attempting to change them out of resentment, and then feeling so angry that I became self-destructive. Calling the house meeting had been the first in what could have been a series of destructive actions. I had found out that I did not have the power to destroy anyone but there still remained the possibility of self-destruction.

Initially, revealing the machinery of my mind was refreshing and made me feel liberated. Then I felt ashamed and shocked by the discovery of so much destructive force of which I had previously not been aware.

By the following afternoon, my third day in the house, I felt I had more essential information, this time about myself. I once again announced, "House meeting!" This time, with great melodrama about my own manipulation of Adrian, I told everyone what I had seen about myself and that I felt ashamed and wrong and that I had seen how destructive I was.

Yedida said, "There is a place between avoidance and condemnation which allows you to be real." I must have looked puzzled, for she added firmly, "Yesterday you did not want to face your dark side at all, which was one form of arrogance. Today you turn against yourself with shame and judgment. This is just another form of arrogance!"

I only half-understood, but I knew what Yedida said was important. It would be several terrible days before I could begin to let in what she meant. I had seen that a powerful force of greed and destruction drove me. As this pattern of behavior unraveled in front of my mind's eye, I understood that this was how I worked as a woman and always would. I knew that I could repeat this pattern a million times. I understood that this was the pattern of all women's destruction everywhere. We, his female students, believed that Andrew wanted to free us from this darkness and that he alone had no dark side.

In psychoanalysis, the unknown motivation of the client is regarded as a form of defense, because it may be serving a protective purpose. Helping clients to see their motivation takes place slowly, over years. I had just been through an accelerated discovery process. It was faster than I was ready for.

The next morning, I joined a group of students swimming in the lake. I got out onto the jetty beside my architect housemate. Effortlessly reading his mind, I felt his insincerity. I had never felt the energy of a man from the inside before. It was raw and aggressive; but it was my rawness and aggression, no longer his. I felt the arrogant self-centeredness a man feels when, in athletic competition with other men, he dives elegantly into the water. At that time I could swim but I had been too afraid to dive. Now I dove repeatedly into the water without fear.

I have never dived since.

For several days, I continued to feel other people's feelings as if the boundaries of my physical body had disappeared. It felt as if I was them instead of me. This feeling, though, was not blissful and strengthening as it had been in Totnes. Instead, it was accompanied by vulnerability of a negative kind. It felt dangerous.

I had once heard Andrew say that if you become enlightened and don't have a stable sense of self, you will go crazy. He called this madness the other side of the coin: mirroring enlightenment, but actually the opposite. An enlightened person, independent and confident, fearlessly engages with life; but on the other side of the coin, there is no one to do the connecting. I felt a dreadful void where I used to be and was therefore drifting, anchorless, in other people's feelings.

I remembered how a student had said to me in Totnes, two years previously, "You are one of the most closed and introverted people I have ever met."

I had replied, hurt but realistic, "That is why I am here."

Now, here in Belchertown, I had dropped my guard and become open, but to the point where boundaries between me and other people did not exist. My veil of illusion that I was a nice, kind person had fallen away far faster than I could cope with. My will to play my part in life had seeped away. I wanted to abdicate being me.

There was a buffet lunch on the riverbank. Taking a paper plate from the pile on the linen tablecloth, I lined up behind Erica to get salad. I remembered how, two years previously, I'd felt her warmth each time we waited in line for our children to come out of preschool. Petite and elf-like, she had fitted easily on the children's benches. Now she turned around, and I looked into her eyes. There was no one there. She was walking, talking, but not there. With a shock, I realized that I was seeing my own reflection. I was close to crazy, and so was she.

Frightened, I left the lunch line and lay on the riverbank, looking up through the trees. Perhaps from a past life, perhaps a hallucination, I felt myself tied with thick ropes to a chair made of roughly-hewn logs, 500 years ago. I felt my head jerk backwards as the chair was lifted. I was being lowered into the river as a punishment for being a witch. I heard the crowd jeering as they watched the slow winching of the chair towards the pond. I welcomed the punishment. I wanted to drown.

That July evening, Satsang was very, very hot. I sat in the middle of a mass of hundreds of people packed so close that we touched knees. There was no room to get out. People asked Andrew questions that went to the most searing challenges of their lives. I tuned in to each person who spoke; their distress was my distress, their search my search, their questions my questions. Andrew, the person asking, and myself were one being.

I understood and took personally every word Andrew said. It was overwhelming. I collapsed onto the floor in a faint or just a refusal to accept a burden so great. I must have been unconscious for a short while, but then I could hear everything even though I could not move. A woman sitting next to me put her arm around me. I was desperate for her support, but Andrew, across the throng of people and—I thought—unaware of me, said, "Don't touch her! She is getting everything she needs from me."

I could not move. I wanted to give up, could have given up, had already half given up. Then a fundamental, binding choice crystallized, the choice between being Marlowe and being led to where madness would take hold.

Andrew repeated, "She is getting all the support that she needs from me, but she just doesn't believe it."

I understood that he was reaching out to me. I heard a voice say, "I do believe it," and realized it was my own voice, but so quiet that I wondered if I had actually lost the power to make any sound.

Andrew didn't respond.

In urgency, I struggled to make my voice louder. This time it was definitely me that said again, loudly, "I do believe it! It is enough!"

Andrew said, "I heard you the first time!"

His acknowledgement seemed to jump-start the beating of my heart. I sat up.

In the meditation that followed, I learned that I could find deep peace even while knowing myself capable of tremendous aggression and destruction. I saw with a certainty that has never left me that I was on the edge of being crazy because I had too little humility to accept what I was. I found peace in the discovery that I could choose not to go mad even under great internal pressure. This was what Andrew meant by saying that everything is volitional. I knew then that I could engage with life while knowing about myself, and that there was nothing unusual about what I had seen. I had also seen that this Community offered a safe situation in which to learn more and more about myself, to learn and let go, learn and let go.

I made space for these thoughts during the remainder of my stay in Belchertown. I would need this understanding in the years ahead.

I felt deeply grateful to Andrew, believing that he had saved me from falling apart. It would be a long time before I could see that he had bound me closer to him by saying that he was giving me everything I needed, instead of saying that everything I needed was within me.

Chapter 5

The Decision

A couple of years after Jürgen had left and a year or so after Andrew had moved to America, I left Andrew a phone message asking whether I might join his Community which was now established in California. A senior student returned my call and told me that Andrew knew I loved him very much but did not think it right for me to come. She said that Andrew had told her to stay on the phone with me until I understood this was not a rejection. Upset by the response, I persisted in my appeals so that he would understand how important being with him was for me. It was only after several requests that I was told I could join the Community in America.

It felt simple: I had found meaning in my life and we were moving to America. The children and I gave away our fat ginger cat. I gave notice at my job and took my kids out of school.

When I first met Andrew, my mom told me that she felt she had lost her daughter. She said that all the ways she and I had understood each other had vanished overnight. But now I was unafraid. Many of the things we used to share revolved around finding out what was wrong with other people or how to do better ourselves in relationship to other people. I agreed that we could not understand one another, but I thought it was a good thing because I was less afraid of the future, less critical of others, and less inclined to compare myself to them. Now, when I said I was moving to America, my mother feared that she would never see us again. She begged me not to go. She promised that, if I stayed in England, she would look after the children every summer so I could go to Andrew's retreats.

My dad said nothing. Only my brother John said, "I do not pretend to understand you, but I trust your conviction. I trust you'll do what is right for you. You just have to budget to return to the UK every year." He was the only person who supported me. I would indeed follow his instruction and visit England at least once a year for the next two decades.

Meanwhile Jürgen, desperate and angry, believed Andrew had brainwashed me.

When I look back at my decision to leave England, part of me is awed at the passion that inspired me to follow my intuition. Another part of me is chilled to see the cost of my single-mindedness. I suspect now that I dislocated myself from my family's pain because of several ideas in Andrew's teachings. Firstly, Andrew taught that if I became free, it would serve my children and the world because I would no longer be a destructive person. Secondly, "compassion" was a word Andrew abhorred; he taught that the resistance of people around me was a function of their ignorance, which suggested to me that I could legitimately dismiss their views and feelings. Thirdly, I knew that my success in being free depended on being one-pointed. As Andrew said, "clarity of intention" was the only way to live a spiritual life. I unconsciously assumed that clarity of intention meant that some emotional conflicts needed to be shelved or driven underground.

Two weeks before I left, my dad shattered his left leg with a bush cutter. Three days of ceaseless rain had made the clay soil slippery on the side of the ditch where he had been trimming nettles. Normally agile and surefooted, but now preoccupied, he had lost his footing and slid towards the ditch. The spinning metal blade severed the arteries, sliced through tendons, and shattered bone. On the phone that night, my mother told me the story of how prone, dragging the useless leg behind him, my father inched the quarter mile home. He called for help but no one heard. Then, weakened by blood loss, he laid his head on the ground.

My mother was walking up to the farmyard when she spotted

his unconscious body. Seeing the blood, she darted to the chicken shed, tore at the straw bales to release a length of baler twine, and, hands nimble with desperation, twisted it into a tourniquet. Then she rushed for help. The doctors debated cutting the leg off above the ankle: they thought there was only an outside chance that it might mend.

I went home. For the two weeks Dad was in the hospital, I fed chickens and picked tomatoes. I visited him one last time in the hospital before the children and I left for America, surreptitiously giving him matches so he could smoke under the blankets while his leg was suspended from the ceiling. Never good with words, he didn't say anything about our leaving the country, and I did not mention it either. I guessed that he would not have fallen in the ditch if he had not been distressed about my leaving, but I don't recall feeling any conflict about leaving him. I remember only thinking that I had been guided to pack and be ready to leave two weeks in advance so that I could spend this time with him. When I tried to hug him without disrupting the tubes leading into his nose, he said, "You will always have a place to live here. You can come home any time."

I let our house in Totnes to a woman who could see auras. She told me that whenever I talked about Andrew Cohen, my aura lit up like a rainbow. As we chatted and drank tea together at the kitchen table, she kept looking over my shoulder. "It's behind your right shoulder," she said, "hovering like a protective angel."

I was leaving behind everything I knew; I might be glad of an angel.

Part II

The First Seven Years in America: 1991

Chapter 6

Finding My Place in the Community

Six-year-old Becky had the window seat on the plane. "Where are we going, Mom?" she asked for the tenth time.

"Mummy told you! We are going to live in San Francisco," eight-year-old Jessica answered, covering her insecurity with a thin layer of knowledge. She was drawing scenes of tropical jungles inhabited by dogs and elephants. Brightly colored flowers and creepers framed the page.

I repeated to Jessica what I'd told myself in my more inspired moments: "This is our life now. We are going to make a new life in America, and we will be with our Community friends. You will realize when you're older that this is the greatest gift I could possibly give you." But my voice didn't sound as convinced as I thought it was supposed to. Andrew's first tenet, *Clarity of Intention*, quavered.

"Can Gran come and visit?" Jessica asked.

"Of course she can," I answered, but I wondered secretly whether visitors were allowed in Andrew's Community. In a year, when my mother came to stay, I would have to find her a bed and breakfast because it would be "unnatural" for someone outside the Community to live in our houses.

As the airplane flew over the Atlantic, I felt as if half of me were left behind. I drove away the memory of Jürgen's tortured face when he last saw the children and my mother's anxiety when I had no answer to her questions about how I would support them or where we would live. I was taking the girls away from their father, their grandparents, their uncle and aunt, their school, and my income. I pushed away the feelings of foreboding and recalled how happy the children and I felt when I lived in the present moment. I reminded myself that, at those times, the course I'd chosen seemed so compelling that I did not feel the need to weigh the pros and cons.

We made our first home in Mill Valley, north of San Francisco, in a small cellar beneath someone's house. The only window looked out onto a redwood forest, darkening our view. There was a microwave but no stove. I had always believed that microwaves destroyed the energy in food and left it lacking in something vital, but I convinced myself that the higher purpose of my life justified serving my children dead baked potatoes. The kids' bunks just barely fitted in the hallway to the bathroom, where there was a shower but no bath. We shared this bathroom with spiders, silverfish, and woodlice. One day, we found a tarantula under Becky's bed. We put it in the woodpile in the yard. But I couldn't be concerned about material issues: I had to make this situation work.

I had trouble finding my footing among Andrew's students because there was no support network for new arrivals. The family who owned our basement lived upstairs, and their teenagers babysat for us. Leaving the children with them, I spent my evenings in meditation at the teachings. I talked occasionally and superficially to my family because they thought I was making a mistake. I concealed the challenges of my life from the other students because they seemed to expect that I should be positive all the time, not full of anxiety and regret. The sinking feeling in my gut, I learned, was "doubt." The blight of Andrew's students, it should be looked in the eye and told to run as if it were the devil himself. Gone were the days of "accept everything and deny nothing."

There was now an official and elitist hierarchy among Andrew's students. "Formal students" were accepted as having a more serious commitment to him; the more casually committed were called "lay students." Those I knew from Totnes were now grouped in houses around Mill Valley with others of the same rank. My friend Victoria, whom I had met at a retreat in

Amsterdam, was about to become a formal student. She and her daughter were moving to a house that was already furnished, so she gave me much of her old furniture. However, Victoria's new status meant that I would seldom see her. She would live and eat and go to meetings with other formal students and be too busy to spend time with me. The Community, which had begun as a blind, headlong adventure into the unknown, was becoming an established highway with a philosophy, rules, and expectations.

A consequence of Andrew's responsibility for increasing numbers of students was that contact with him became infrequent. Except for his formal teaching evenings, he became more remote, available personally only by special appointment or to a select few. Yet, even though he had many new students, Andrew's influence over our daily lives increased and his expectations became more exacting. Senior students said proudly that Andrew kept raising the bar.

I was alarmed to see some of the other students accumulating debts in their attempts to stay in America long after their funds had run out. I had saved up enough money to keep my family for a couple of months. I bought an old Honda Accord for $900, which served me well until the brakes failed as I was driving down a steep hill. Skilled at driving beaten-up vehicles from an early age, I used the gears to navigate to safety. The children and I would often sit at an outdoor café in Mill Valley, but I didn't dare spend money on coffee. I brought sandwiches for the children, which they nibbled at while watching children at the next table downing milk shakes and croissants. I regarded as extravagant a student of Andrew's who took her son to eat pizza once a week.

Despite my savings, the first year was tough on all three of us. In the privacy of our apartment, I was short-tempered and irritable, as if the children were responsible for my failure to thrive. I yelled at Jessica when she made Becky cry and I resented Becky when she cried. I wanted the girls to be strong and self-sufficient; I wanted the same for myself. Once, the mother upstairs confided to me that their teenagers loved the girls but feared for their safety when they heard me shouting at them.

After our first meal with American children, who laughed at us for eating pizza with a knife and fork, six-year-old Becky's survival strategy was to look and talk like the other children. Becky convinced me to buy her silvery socks and blue sneakers to match those of her classmates, and she refused to wear the sweaters we had brought with us. She dropped all British English from her vocabulary and lost her accent. "It's not a 'pavement,' Mom," she would tell me. "It's a 'sidewalk.'" And, "Don't say 'boot,' say, 'trunk.'" I was a poor student. In fact, now, after 22 years in America, I still have difficulties using colloquial American English and have never changed my accent. No questions were asked when, still on a tourist visa, I enrolled the children in school.

Becky's teachers told me she was learning to read but was unable to sit in the chair. At home she changed from being an exuberant, energetic little girl who loved to laugh to an anxious child who had increasing problems with organization and attention. Picking her up at day care one afternoon, I found her sitting alone in the corner, not playing, not talking. The caregiver said she always behaved that way. I felt awful that I had not known how sad she was. Eventually, she would develop a friendship at daycare that would become a vital connection over the next six years.

Jessica relied on her good organizational skills and excellent memory for mastering her academic work, but she was too shy to break into the established peer group of girls at school. A second challenge for her was breaking into the group of girls in Andrew's Community, who, like Andrew, did not welcome introverts. An outgoing nature was highly valued both in the culture of California and in Andrew's Community. The girls and I had many strengths, but even by English standards we were quiet.

Andrew said that he thought it was good for the English to spend time in California; I knew that the expectation was that we would change. Andrew's second tenet, The Law of Volitionality, states, "We are all at some level aware of what we are doing and act deliberately." The suggestion was that change was in our own hands. I became fearful that my children would be too shy to speak to Community members and therefore expose me as not being a good parent.

Celebrations were the worst-case scenario for all three of us. One hot Saturday after we had been in America for a couple of years, we joined the rest of the Community for a picnic at Stinson Beach in celebration of Guru Purnima day, an Indian holiday for honoring spiritual teachers. When I first heard the name, I'd felt a little shock: It was the first time I had really registered that Andrew was a "guru."

The girls were now nine and seven. As I prepared them for the event, they surely must have picked up on my anxiety.

"Jessica," I coached. "It's really important that you respond when people talk to you. It's a way of giving. One-word answers are not enough." But Jessica was as unlikely to converse as I was to be Queen.

"Becky," I said. "There will be lots of other children. You can have fun with them when we are talking. You have your new kite with you; maybe someone will help you with it." Becky was the youngest of the kids. The other girls had so far seemed unrelenting in their refusal to accept this small, plump, intense girl, and the adults deemed her shyness rude and disrespectful.

We helped to carry the iceboxes down to the beach and joined a dozen other people in blowing up balloons. Over the previous six hours, a team of ten people had been arranging rugs and carpets on the sand and assembling awnings to shade a hundred people. We unwrapped and arranged the food on tables draped with Indian fabrics: quiches, mushroom pâtés, Middle Eastern pastries, mango relish, glazed fruit tarts, cheesecakes; everything handmade with great care over the previous days.

The children were supposed to play by themselves while the adults celebrated. For Jessica, Becky, and myself, this plan was not a possibility because the girls needed my support to be social. I saw a big boy running across the sand, flying Becky's kite, while Becky sat alone playing with sand, watching out of the corner of her eye. I wanted to say to the boy, "You are doing a great job flying that kite. I had no idea they went so high! I was wondering if you could show Becky how to do that." But I thought someone might detect my underlying message, which was more like, "You bastard bully! Becky has never even flown that kite herself. You give it back and ask if you can help her fly it!" But I said nothing. Instead I attempted a conversation with some other students, meanwhile listening to Becky's pain. I felt fundamentally divided. I would be stalled within this contradiction for the next years.

My daily anxious search for work stood in stark contrast to the delightful meditation of Satsang. In Satsang, I once again knew that I was whole. I felt buoyed up from inside by a massive, liquid rock of faith which threw the daytime struggles with doubt, insecurity and loneliness into perspective. I knew without doubt that the only way out of my family's unhappiness was to throw myself into the teachings.

Each night, about a hundred of us would make an orderly line on the dusty road outside the meeting hall, carrying our meditation cushions and wearing shawls. We would enter respectfully and sit silently, without moving. In front of us on a low platform would be many letters to Andrew, each accompanied by a huge bunch of flowers. Students wrote personal letters that revealed secrets, asked for help, shared new understanding. For my own letters, sometimes I would spend an hour choosing a bouquet of flowers, as if the perfect choice of bloom would cement my destiny. Many people began, "Beloved Master" or "Dearest Beloved Master" but I could not bring myself to use the word "Master" for at least six years, having grown up as a left-leaning feminist sympathizer. When Andrew entered the hall, sometimes we sat in silence for two hours, and sometimes he took questions and challenged us to understand his words. Either way, I left the room radiant with happiness and feeling at home in the Community.

Back in Totnes, I had tasted a way of being with myself which was temporarily astounding and transformative. I had no doubt that it was the highest form of existence. Here in America, when I closed my eyes at Satsang, the nectar of meditation connected me with Andrew and all the people in the room. I knew it would keep me going whether or not I also had to make effort.

While I was mastering the practicalities of survival in California, Andrew's teachings were evolving. In the first few years, he had set much store in the depth of his students' realizations and suggested that these alone would propel them to the completion of their work with little effort and much cause for celebration. After a while he saw that, unlike in his own case, his students were not catapulted to permanent enlightenment by deep realizations. He noticed that their understanding and experiences would fluctuate, and their actions would not always line up with their understanding. We came to believe that while Andrew had become permanently enlightened from one series of experiences, the rest of us would need to work rigorously. Andrew taught that, if our intention was strong enough, we could become enlightened; but that there was an unknown element of "grace" involved which made the outcome impossible to predict.

My English teaching qualifications were not recognized in California's state schools, and I had no work permit or green card. I spent many afternoons at the living room table looking up private schools in the Bay Area Yellow Pages: special needs, gifted, kindergarten, elementary, secondary, even schools that taught English as a foreign language. I sent letters, made phone calls, and walked into schools to request interviews. After six weeks I had nothing. It was clearly going to take me time to get a teaching job, but I needed an income now. I put up fliers for cleaning jobs on all the community notice boards I could find. I wrote on the fliers, "European attention to detail." I never knew what image that conjured up, but it seemed to work. I got a few calls and soon was able to work every day cleaning houses.

One of the first families who hired me asked for my references, so I showed them my file, which included a degree in philosophy, teaching diplomas, and accolades for working with emotionally disturbed teenagers. The woman looked so embarrassed that I knew I had made a mistake. After that, I didn't tell people about my background.

The farmhouse in which I grew up had flagstone floors which absorbed much of the dirt from cats, dogs, and the occasional sick lamb. Although my mother mostly succeeded at keeping our Wellington boots out of the kitchen, there was often a trail of mud, straw, and hayseeds brought in on the turn-ups of trousers and the backs of woolen sweaters. No one ran their hands behind the couch cushions in our house, for fear of the unknown. I knew how to break in a colt, poultice a swollen fetlock, creosote a wooden gate, and drive a tractor, but I had never really cleaned a house.

For example, I did not know that you have to vacuum a bathroom floor before you wash it. The wife and children in one particular family had beautiful long black hair. I tried to mop the white marble bathroom floor, but before long there were wet, black hairs stuck all over it. I could wipe them around the floor with a sponge, but there was no way they were coming up. The mother decided to walk her two-year-old twins in the stroller while I covered the worst of the downstairs dirt; I had about 20 minutes before they came back. Dismayed by the persistence of the black hairs, I took a break from the bathroom to tackle the living room. It took me longer than I expected to assemble the attachments of the vacuum cleaner, and longer still to find out that none of these attachments could suck out chewed-up cookies from the creases in the couch. I had barely got to the second chair when the mom returned with hungry, crying twins. She pointed with disdain to the Dustbuster in the closet, which was an unknown appliance to me and apparently is what everyone uses for couches. She stomped off yet again, pushing her twins before her. She fired me when she came back.

My friend Victoria explained to me the usefulness of the greenback sponge and that the most important part about house cleaning is to make it look good. "Even if you don't have time to clean it, you have to straighten things up, make it look like you've been there, arrange the bottles in the bathroom, straighten the magazines," she said. Over the next six months I cleaned many houses, but I suspect I never delivered on "European attention to detail."

After losing many cleaning jobs, I finally got an interview for the position of lead teacher at a pioneering school for children with autism. As I crossed the dusty dry schoolyard, I noticed the classrooms. It looked as if this school was planning to grow beyond the eight children currently enrolled. I was greeted in the hall by a lovely Indonesian girl with long braids. I assumed she was a staff member and later found out that she was a pupil.

"I'll take you to see Kit," she said.

"Who's Kit?" I asked.

No answer.

Kit was the director. She was perhaps 40 years old, with long bedraggled hair, wearing baggy sweatpants. I noticed immediately an animal cunning in her eyes.

"Fan'as'ic!" she said. "Ha am hooking for shhomhue ho un my school." It took me a moment to realize that she had lost her teeth and was not wearing dentures. With great difficulty, I translated to myself, Fantastic! I am looking for someone to run my school.

"But I have never met a child with autism," I said.

70

"Don whorry, ah wirlh heach you." (Don't worry, I will teach you.)

"What's the school called?" I asked.

"The chha oo whoo," she said.

"I'm sorry," I said. "I didn't quite catch that."

The Indonesian girl chimed in, "The Can Do School. She named it that so all the children could pronounce it."

"Oh, right, I see." I said. "There's one other thing. I don't have a work permit or green card."

Without hesitation, even before I had handed her my references, she told me she would get me a "hurk hwermit" and "gee chard." And, thinking that this was the answer to my current predicament, I disregarded the cunning in her eyes and took the job.

I had walked in on the opening month of an extraordinary experimental school. Kit took me on as her protégé. From her, I learned how to enter the worldview of a child with autism. I was, as she kept telling me, like a "schkonge" (sponge). She shadowed me for two months, critiquing my every interaction with the children. When 150 pound Amy bit into her own hand and drew blood, Kit showed me how to restrain her by wrapping my arms around her without fear. When I asked a highly intelligent child to spell a three-letter word, Kit told me angrily that she knew he could spell but that our contract with him was to progress one small step at a time so that he could build confidence. And when I helped Alex spread butter on his own sandwich, she threw the bread in the trash and made him do it again by himself, explaining that once a child masters a skill we must hold them to it or they will regress and never get the skill back. Kit adored the kids, sharing their food and kissing them lovingly on the forehead. They, in return, never took their eyes off her, wondering what she was going to do next.

Kit showed me that if I used effect, ritual and anticipation I could hold the attention of six kids with autism. After a while, building rhythm into every part of the day became second nature for me. The rhythm of language in *The Three Little Pigs*, the movement rhythm of horseback riding, the kinesthetic rhythm of singing while sweeping the floor or rolling pastry. The staff and the children were running, climbing, cooking, jumping, acting, and chanting, for six hours a day. The children loved it; the aides hated the amount of physical work. Music, meanwhile, jump-started their speech and reinforced learning. It helped them reorganize when their bodies were agitated to the point of frenzy. The lead behaviorist was a black rock musician from Oakland. In addition to restraining 15-year-olds when they were out of control, he wrote songs—about toilet training, chewing one's food, and even cleaning the guinea pig cage.

The toilet training in particular was an important milestone. At frequent intervals throughout the day, everyone in the room who could demonstrate keeping their pants dry (including adults) would be rewarded with the tantalizing shake of a huge can of jelly beans and our rock musician's *Dry Pants* song. It was a blues tune with the following words: "Dry pants are really great. Dry pants are really great, when they're wet it is too late, dry pants are really great." At the end of the song, the child would beam with pleasure and dip his hand into the jelly beans accompanied by applause from everyone in the room. The children loved the song so much that if their pants were wet and they were deprived of it, they would cry miserably. Before long, they were nearly all toilet trained.

Kit was a brilliant teacher, but she had very poor math skills. Within a year, the school started to run up debt. A woman from the local restaurant where we often fed the kids came one day in great distress and said she wouldn't leave until she was paid. A six-foot taxi driver from Oakland barged into the school and threatened to kill me if I didn't pay him what he was owed. I had to send him away empty-handed. Over a period of six months, the arrival of all of our paychecks became increasingly unpredictable. Despite her math deficit, Kit was skilled at calculating how little she could pay each person and still keep us working. She relied on our affection for the children to keep us coming back.

She also admitted to me one day that she liked having employees without green cards because it gave her more power.

Kit paid all the employees of color, but not me or the other white employees. Her logic was, "You have the protection of the law behind you; and besides, I've trained you so well you can get work anywhere in the world." I had hired some of the staff myself from Andrew's Community. Feeling responsible for their missing paychecks, I loaned Kit the money to pay them. Even though I was halfway through my green card application process, I quit when Kit owed me $12,000. Five court cases later I recovered half the money from her, which I had to split with my lawyer.

My children and I had been in Mill Valley a year when we left the apartment in the redwoods and joined a house of lay students on a suburban Mill Valley estate a little north of San Francisco. Our housemates were two other women and four kids. Eventually another couple and their toddler would sleep in the garage.

We learned to share space. The three of us women quickly became accustomed to showering in one bathroom in less than twenty minutes, each stepping into the shower as the other stepped out. I have always hated jarred pasta sauce, but I got used to it now, though when one of my housemates mixed together and reheated three different kinds of leftover pasta, I drew the line. But the children had a harder time adjusting. Becky, age 8 and Julie, age 6, shared a ten-foot-square room. Becky read avidly, and was very quiet and somewhat fearful. Julie was larger than life, had a beautiful singing voice and was intensely loud and excitable. At their first meeting, Julie bounced into the room, her ankle length pink skirt fluffed out around her and Becky hid behind my legs. Becky insisted that she needed a barrier to divide their room in half. The adults talked about whether we should use this opportunity to teach them about being together, but after much discussion we agreed that we should put up a sheet dividing the room. Within a month, Becky and Julie had become so close that they had taken the sheet down. It stayed in a crumpled heap at the end of their beds for the rest of their time together. Ten-year-old Jessica was kind and attentive to the younger children, becoming like a second mother to them. Once a visitor told the adults, "I can't believe what I just heard. Jessica said to the little children 'If I am being too bossy just tell me.' My children have never said anything like that." We had founded a family together, and the children fitted together like siblings of different ages.

Our first Christmas Eve together, we were arranging the stockings under the fireplace when we discovered that English traditions are very different from American ones. Father Christmas in England brings a stocking full of small fascinating items: puzzles and individually wrapped candies, a pack of cards, an ornament, a small stuffed toy. Parents give the larger presents. In the United States, Santa Claus gives huge lavish gifts that fill the fireplace and parents do the same. As we arranged the presents under the tree, it became clear that the youngest little girl—the only American—was getting ten times more presents, of greater value and greater appeal, than the other three kids put together. So we unwrapped all the presents and shared them equally among them.

Our favorite babysitter failed to turn up one day. We discovered, months later, that she had gone to jail. Some of the teenage babysitters were kind and generous to the children, but others stole from us or went partying to friends' next door. Sometimes we searched for professional babysitters rather than use Community teenagers. One day a new sitter arrived, her smile half-covered by her long blond hair. We introduced her to the children, and 11-year-old Jessica followed me out to the car as we got ready to leave. Jessica was compliant and normally stoical. She almost never gave a strong opinion, but now she said, "Don't go! I don't like her. She is not good." Thinking that she was just complaining about having to deal with yet another new face, I brushed aside her fears, but she continued to protest. My housemates and I drove off, thinking nothing much could happen in one evening, and as usual we switched off our cell phones so as not to disturb the teachings. Later, I learned that Becky had cried that evening and been unable to sleep, and the babysitter had threatened to smash her face in.

Slowly I came to love and trust my companions among the lay students. We enjoyed being together so much that we started businesses together. A Chilean guy started a jewelry-making business; six other people started making fountains; a small group began a graphic design business; another six people opened a café. I brought more and more people to work at the Can Do School before it closed, one as a masseur, another to teach bike riding, another to teach cooking. There seemed no limit to how much we would learn from being together, nor how much joy there was in being together.

Little by little, as lay students not closely involved with Andrew himself, we discovered the ability to deal with conflict. Throughout their childhood, Becky and Jessica witnessed adults communicating without anger or disrespect when issues arose. One of the benefits of the authoritarian regime that guided us was to give the children this extraordinary model of civility. They grew up without the "normal" disrespect and expressions of frustration that characterize so many interactions in nuclear families.

There were many good things about the situation, but Andrew's behavior was evolving, and the contradictions deepened. Although Andrew talked constantly about the "Law of Love," we noticed his callous dismissal of anyone who left the

Community and his attitude of indifference to family members who were not in the Community. It was as if "Love" was reserved for Andrew and his closest associates. This inconsistency was not something we talked about.

In Totnes, a loose collection of individuals were caught off-guard by the pure expression that poured from a vulnerable young teacher; in California, a more systematic organization was growing around the passionate charisma of an authority figure. Students constantly showered accolades on Andrew for his perfection and his teaching. Poonjaji had instructed that everything that came from Andrew's lips should be recorded. Many people were therefore engaged in recording, by videotape or notes, everything he said. Some of these notes were written up and sold as books; the videos sold as VHS tapes. I did not consider the effect that this kind of adulation might have had on him.

The increasing number of students made greater degrees of organization necessary. A hierarchy of rank developed which would change many times over the next decade or so. The ranking included lay students, novice students, formal students, committed students, and senior students. These last held the most responsibility for supporting Andrew's teachings.

The number of meetings also increased. Their purpose, like that of everything else, was twofold: to support the evolution of individual and collective expression of the teachings, and to promote their dissemination. There were meetings for women, men, planning, finance, celebrations, spreading the teachings, and networking with other spiritual organizations. People living together held house meetings to address the issues of individuals. Little by little, scrutiny of our actions both small and large revealed underlying aggression and defensiveness. Everything that arose in our actions or minds became fodder for meetings, enabling us to see our motivation.

We were now told to take on our conditioning rather than

accept ourselves as we were. When Andrew spoke during Satsangs, it was often about tackling our fundamental resistance to change and our unwillingness to face ourselves. Andrew felt that women had a harder time than men in living a spiritual life. Women, he told us, were particularly stubborn about dropping their defenses, and becoming open and intimate with others. Women's meetings were begun to investigate how women's conditioning appeared to be a hindrance to becoming enlightened.

The microscope under which we lived sometimes brought us closely together and sometimes felt overwhelming. At first, I looked forward to meetings as a chance to become more vulnerable, to see myself more clearly, and to understand the teachings more deeply. Some of our meetings were led by senior students who reported directly to Andrew. My nervousness increased because I heard that students sometimes screamed at each other and threw people out of the meetings or stayed up all night to get a response from stubborn students. I heard that men and women often had reduced each other to tears in their attempts to trigger change. Senior students said that the Community had now changed and that "feedback" had become more subtle and nuanced than in the early days but this did not seem to allay my anxiety. Each week, someone from the group wrote notes about the meetings to Andrew. As the years went by, my anxiety about performance increased. If I had to write the notes, I might be up most of the night consulting with several people to make sure I got them right. There would be trouble if the notes lacked accuracy or passion.

During one of the meetings, we heard that the lay students' housing arrangements would be changed. The 60 or 70 lay students grouped together in a dozen or so houses around Mill Valley would be reshuffled. The accusation was made that, in our house, relationships were too comfortable. It was said by someone close to Andrew that we colluded with rather than

77

challenged one another; and so it was "suggested" that the house be disbanded. We met with the other lay students; and taking account of the "suggestions," arranged ourselves into new houses.

Many times over the next few years, the hierarchy of students was renamed or reshuffled and individuals were moved up or down in rank. Therefore, there was a constant rotation of new arrivals and invisible departures among the different ranks. Soon, moving ceased to be a shock, as every year or so students were reshuffled into new housing configurations.

I don't recall the considerations for these changes, but the needs or preferences of Jessica and Becky were not among them. They would never again feel like they had a family group. They would feel instead as though they lived with a constantly changing set of peers. Jessica would one day describe her childhood as having been like living in ever-changing foster homes with minimal supervision.

Becky was very sensitive. There was one house in which five or six children slept in the basement. Becky sometimes found it hard to be with the older children, but even worse for her were the ghosts that she saw in the basement. For the six months that we lived in that house, she never went downstairs on her own. For fear of being teased, she also never admitted to the other children that she saw ghosts. She pretended a strength she did not feel. At school she pretended to have a normal family for fear that the authorities would take her away if they knew the truth.

Her artwork reflected her fears. She illustrated monsters eating people and fighter planes bombing cities. She drew solitary space-people on planets isolated by millions of miles. I understood her fears, but my own life was also packed with ghosts, so I did not have the resources to support her.

On the positive side, Becky was an outstanding artist and a strong student. She developed a subtle sense of humor, which endeared her to her teacher, who assured me that, given time,

Becky would have a lot to offer her peers. The teacher revealed that other girls bullied Becky, who began to protect herself by taunting them before they got to her. These were the years when, in spite of the California sun, she wore nothing but baggy track-suits as if she could disappear in their dark folds.

Distressed that I had been unable to intuit her distress, I tried to help. I worked with the teachers to offer Becky a series of play therapy meetings in the company of her worst attacker. Then, knowing she was at risk both at school and at home, I defied her teachers and the principal and insisted she repeat second grade. Becky was angry with me at the time, but she established good friends and became settled at school the following year.

The next time we moved, we were in a house with three boys older than Becky, one of whom was a bully. I asked this boy to imagine what it would be like to be Becky when he was unkind to her. He replied angrily that he hated weakness and Becky was weak. The trickle-down effect from a hierarchy that rewarded aggression and power was reaching Becky. I did not yet know the extent to which the tone was dictated by Andrew himself.

My family, 3000 miles away, were steadfast. Jürgen visited the children every year. He sent presents and cards which arrived every birthday, Easter and Christmas for 18 years. My parents welcomed the children for extended visits every summer and sometimes for Christmas. My dad taught them how to make pets of goslings, hunt for tadpoles, and paint eggs. My mom took them to museums and taught them to grow flowers and climb trees. My brother never gave up building a connection with them even during the five years when they answered in monosyl-lables.

They also never gave up on me. I knew that my taciturn father loved me. My mom's heartbreak at losing me to a guru was an open wound for her. My brother, aware that I was pulled by something all-consuming, once gently said that he was aware that he was for me "out of sight out of mind." In contrast, I knew that in our absence he would hold us in mind with affection.

Once in a while, my conscience told me it was wrong that my loved ones should feel so much pain because of my choices.

Over the next few years, the standard of housing within the Community went up, and students pooled their living expenses. Instead of a rundown ranch, we rented well-kept large houses. Soon we lived in a house with new carpets and nicely appointed kitchens. But it was the people more than the surroundings that made me glad. I had never been so comfortable with people, and I wondered why I used to think that I needed time alone. What did I do in that alone time? Was it just for worrying, for self-absorbed contemplation? Now I had no time for myself at all, and I was very happy. These feelings gave me hope for meeting the goal of connection that had inspired me to get on a plane for America. In the evenings, during meditation at Satsang, I would allow myself to escape into the dream of otherworldly bliss.

But Andrew's expectations for us were constantly changing: he was raising the bar. He told us that the goals of this Community were not just connection and intimacy and blissful meditation in Satsang. In a brochure promoting his audiotapes, he wrote, "The course of my life as a teacher has been defined by my continuous insistence that the experience of love and bliss is meaningless when it is not supported by a life lived with true integrity." He expected each of us to undertake a personal investigation more rigorous, more demanding, more evolutionary than we had imagined. And he seemed to be trying new ways of getting people to change and be free. He had one woman wear a blindfold in public; others were not allowed to speak for months at a time. One woman was kicked hard in the backside, and another was tickled until she screamed. One man had to meditate for hours in a graveyard; another was required to do hundreds of hours of rebirthing.

During one of these waves of zeal for accelerated change, Andrew invited all lay students to move up the ranks to become formal students. Dozens of people moved house in one weekend. For most of them, including myself, this elevation was short-lived. I was soon informed that I was not meeting the standard in my new house and was instructed to leave. Normally when people were asked to leave, they were gone that same evening. Because I had children, my housemates gave me the weekend to find somewhere. When they noticed that I looked relaxed— relieved, even—at the prospect of moving out, they were outraged, and they took back this special leniency. I had no furniture, not even knives and forks. Normally I did not mention my home life to outsiders, but one of my bosses was particularly perceptive, and she offered to let me stay in her apartment. On the face of it she appeared to possess more open-heartedness than those in the Community, but I told myself that she lacked the perspective and understanding of the higher goals by which we lived.

As he raised the bar, Andrew raised his expectation of obedience. I saw this expectation literally when he ordered a student to take his new luxury Saab to the scrap yard and watch it be crushed in order to destroy his attachment to worldly possessions. Andrew once said that he was the most jealous lover of all, and his students needed to love him more than any partner. I assumed he meant "loyalty to me" as a metaphor for "an undivided response to life" and that we should value our spiritual life more than our closest relationships. In retrospect, I see something different in those words.

Even though I was learning about myself and how to get on with people, I was not "going for it" enough to be a good student. I kept being reminded that, if I could "give more to the teachings," my children would benefit; if I could become free of the fear and doubt that dogged me, then the girls would benefit. The "more" always implied looking towards Andrew Cohen and never seemed to include looking towards my children.

After their school day, the girls went to day care until I

finished cleaning houses and picked them up. Then I left them all evening with babysitters so that I could attend the teachings. Even though my former parenting beliefs indicated that I was failing my children, I was told by the Community that my enlightenment would be the highest gift to Becky, Jessica and the world.

Andrew showed little interest in children "Children: should never think they are the most important thing in your life." "Children are just ego." "What possible reason could you have for wanting to have children?" Nonetheless, we took every word he said about children as gospel.

Andrew saw my children in the distance at picnics and had spoken to them only once. When Becky was 11 and Jessica 13, he invited all the children to his house for milk shakes. Becky told me afterwards that "a servant" had opened the door for them and let them in to an immaculately clean and tidy house. Another servant had made the milk shakes and served all the children while Andrew sat on the couch. Becky wondered at the time why Andrew did not pour the drinks himself.

Once, the girls and I met him accidentally at the bike depot in Mill Valley. Andrew was sitting at a table drinking coffee. I did not know whether to greet him or to pretend not to see him. I felt awkward, fearing that he would see something bad about my parenting. When I introduced him to the girls none of us had anything to say beyond, "Hello." He seemed embarrassed, and I felt sure he had not wanted to meet us.

Later I told John, my brother, about this meeting. He responded, "What do you mean he does not know your children? I assumed he had a connection with them!"

For a moment, seeing the Community as my brother saw it, I asked myself why Andrew took so little interest in the children. This conscious questioning stands out in my mind because it was so rare. Why, I wondered, did he not appear to care about them? But I did not take any additional step to question his overall motivation.

I heard one day that Andrew was shocked by the fact that the children in the Community talked of him with fear. I strove to knock the timidity out of my girls so that I would not be shown up as having raised insecure children. Nonetheless, at our frequent house meetings, I often received feedback for my "overprotective" parenting style. My housemates said I should not allow my children to whine or behave in ways they thought disrespectful; that they were too introverted; and that their attitude was not sufficiently "giving." I was told to "take on" my children. Luckily I would not learn until years later that Andrew had given parents the green light to use corporal punishment on their children. But the girls would wait in fear for me to come back from meetings. One day an impromptu house meeting delayed their promised outing to the redwoods. After the meeting, instead of gathering together the bike helmets and picnic, I sat the children down on their bedroom floor and berated them, demanding a change in their attitude. Demanding that they drop their whining and disrespect. Their apologies did not end my tirade borne of self-loathing. After episodes like this, I would feel so guilty that, a day or two later, I would try to make amends. My unpredictable emotional responses became the norm for Becky and Jessica.

It appeared that Andrew seemed to regard children as a nuisance that got in the way of our living the Community life. He said many times that he could see no unselfish motivation for having children. I knew that my children and others needed more than they were getting, especially the children with special needs who did not get the homework help they needed. I suggested that we organize hikes for the children every Saturday, but the conversation turned to my motivation for bringing up the topic. I asked whether there was a woman in the Community who could be a "big sister" for Becky: I was told that everyone was too busy. Once, I suggested that we have meetings for the children so that they could talk about the teachings too, but I was told that I would not be the right person to do it.

I half-understood that, by accepting the premise that my vision was clouded and Andrew's was clear, I had become incapable of independently evaluating what was going on. It crossed my mind that I was losing my ability to draw conclusions for myself, but I decided this would only be a problem if Andrew were imperfect. We students were aware of the risks of the guru system and talked with pity about the consequences for students who had given their trust to corrupt teachers. We wrapped ourselves in the certainty that Andrew stood alone in defiance of the ego; our system was of a different order. I therefore absorbed the hierarchical structure and the value system believing it supported my growth.

My initial pleasure at dynamic exchanges with Andrew in Totnes was slowly being overridden by anxiety at the unpredictability and severity of his disapproval and that of senior students. I sometimes thought Andrew's challenges and methods overzealous, but I knew they were driven by genuine desire to help students grow. I did not question whether there might be a less stringent path to growth, perhaps because Andrew discredited less stringent paths as being less effective. I had been raised to work hard and always did so. I had finished every course I had ever started. I did not expect life to be easy. Now, as always, I assumed that, if I worked harder, I would be successful.

I had been in the Community for five years, and was neither fully surrendered to my guru nor trusting my old self. I had heard so much about the pressure among women formal students that the prospect of joining them both inspired and terrified me. I had no way of knowing whether I felt ambivalent because there really was something wrong in the Community or because I was simply resistant to change; after all, the guru system only works if students surrender.

My early sense of freedom became tainted by a deep fear of

rejection by Andrew and his students. In Totnes, I had seen great beauty and deep love in Andrew. I would melt with tenderness just looking at his photo. Now in Satsang, I looked into his face and saw anger. Probably my projection, I thought. A reflection of my own anger. How dreadful that I look at my teacher and see anger.

I often questioned silently what I observed, but I learned to explain it away. I saw that the people around Andrew were sometimes cruel, but I was learning that often it took a strong response to get people to change. I felt it wrong that my roommate stayed up all night to arrange decorations for an event and then cleaned houses all day, but I assumed I felt that way because I did not understand the concept of service myself. I wondered whether the student recently banished to New Zealand had really done something bad or whether Andrew might simply have felt threatened by him, but I assumed that I was in no position to judge. I wondered at the fact that Andrew now accepted gifts of expensive Italian shirts from people who cleaned houses for a living, but I assumed that I was too selfish to do the same. These thoughts flitted under the radar of my mind. I banished them almost before they reached awareness, to a sealed box called "DOUBT."

After I left the Can Do School, I found that Kit was right about some things: she had trained me so well that I could get work anywhere. I started to work for families who had children with special needs, and before long I had built up a successful private practice. I combined teaching communication, motor planning, and horseback riding for children with autism.

Little by little I expanded my skills in working with children with autism and adopted more structured behavioral methods which I added to my repertoire from the Can Do School. Over the eight years we spent in California, I was able to increase my fees from 15 dollars an hour to 50 dollars. I learned that, with enough repetition, children with autism could learn one skill at a time.

At age six, one little boy could say three words, and they kept changing. I spent hours every week sitting with him at a table. Using his favorite corn chips as rewards, I would demand, "Touch your nose," and if he did not respond I would help him with a touch on his hand. I would repeat the same instruction many times to make sure he really mastered it. Once he mastered "touch your nose" I would move on to "stand up," "give me book," "touch your head," and so on. When, out of boredom and inactivity, the little boy hit me I would turn him around, pin his arms to his sides, and hold him in a lock for several minutes after he stopped protesting.

This method of instruction mirrored the stringent, unforgiving tone of the Community more than the humor and rhythm of the Can Do School.

Beginning to find my place in the network of students, I lived at one time in a lovely house with six children and five adults that had floral curtains and fitted carpets. This house, we were told, had once housed the Grateful Dead, and they had used the living room for their recording studio. There was a shortage of bedrooms, so we made the unusual decision for one of the male students—Tony—to share a long narrow bedroom with a female student named Ashley and myself. Tony was a new student, but he had quickly become a formal student and then had been demoted shortly afterwards. He was a slightly overweight, dark-haired man, practical and skilled at bodywork but inclined to self-doubt, which made him the focus of many men's meetings. It was hard for him to gain respect among the men.

I began to look forward to returning home late at night after the women's meetings to "accidentally" linger with him in the kitchen until the other adults had gone to bed. Defying exhaustion, we would drink herb tea and talk. The shine of his eyes alerted me to the knowledge that he enjoyed my company. Ashley's bed was between Tony's and mine. I would lie listening for his breathing, wondering what it would be like if Ashley were away for the night.

Most couples who entered the Community split up soon afterwards. Sometimes if two people were of the same status and both were "doing well" Andrew would approve their request to become a couple; and then, without courtship, the couple might spend a night or two in a hotel before returning to their communal life. They would be expected to respond to all their brothers and sisters with intimacy and connection without favoring their partner, except at night, if energy allowed.

There were few new couples in this Community. Andrew had lectured at length on the danger of dependence and attachment, which he saw as inherent risks of special relationships. He clarified the mechanism of desire, hooking the unwary with a delusory promise of perfection. Too often, he taught, the desire to sustain a relationship led to compromise and lack of commitment to freedom. He mocked seekers who believed that through relationships self-awareness can grow. He mocked most of all Tantra teachers who believed that sexual union could lead to enlightenment.

For many years in the Community, I was too tired to think about sex or romance. Besides, I knew that because I was a lay student, it would be very unlikely that I would be allowed a relationship. On the rare occasions that my desire for sex became conscious, I thought of it as a reward, awaiting me a long way down the road if I became a better student. Now I was ready to defy the risk of failure and probable pain, so I phoned Andrew's house. One of his students received my request for permission to ask Tony to join me in a relationship. I waited a couple of weeks for the answer, during which dreams of sensuous moments of connection flashed irreverently to the surface of my mind, wrapped in pious packages. Hand in hand, we would be more effective warriors for Andrew's teachings than we would singly. We would be senior students in a far-off land, helping to carry

Andrew's teachings of happiness and liberation to thousands of people locked in ignorance!

I believed Andrew's motivation to help us to be free was pure. When I doubted him, I berated myself for not trusting him fully. But looking back, I wonder how any man could have stood such blind adulation as to be asked for permission in affairs of the heart. How did it impact Andrew's sense of self that he was given unquestioning authority over hundreds of lives? How did it impact him to represent, for decades, the purest part of ourselves? At what point did he claim to be perfect, or did we seduce him into it? Did a change take place in this once simple, apparently holy man, or was the arrogance I first saw always there?

The answer to my request came a couple of weeks later. A senior student called me back with a message: "Andrew says you have only just started to live his teachings, and he would like you to gather more confidence before risking the distraction of getting into a relationship. Just keep on going." Disappointment sank before it became a thought. Without registering rebellion I clutched the faint praise, and rearranged my priorities to avoid distraction and build confidence. Tony, meanwhile, continued doing well. He was soon sent to Germany for a few months to help with a new enterprise there.

I had been living in the Community for seven years, gradually finding a footing among the other students, when a meeting was called for all Andrew's students in Marin County. One of the senior students sat cross-legged in front of us at the yoga studio where we usually held meetings, and told us with excitement that the long search for a permanent home for Andrew's teachings was over. He told us that since the population on the West Coast were superficial and were not ready for Andrew's radical teachings, we would move East where people were more real. A large estate had been found in the Berkshires with a mansion, multiple buildings, and land.

The crowd all cheered. "That's incredible!" "Fantastic!" "This is going to be the start of a real revolution!" "When do we leave?"

Excited at the idea of the new center, I gladly paid the financial donation to make it happen. A month later, in a large warehouse, the possessions of 120 people were organized into uniform boxes, sealed by an army of packers, and loaded into three Community containers leaving for Boston. While closing and sealing hundreds of boxes, I wondered whether I should be packing my own possessions. I surveyed my life. My identity was now bound up with being a student of Andrew's, and I found life outside the Community increasingly irrelevant. I loved living in houses of many people. I had satisfying friendships with women and men. I understood that I could not see and destroy the selfishness inside myself without the help of Andrew and his Community; it was only when I allowed them to see me that true change was possible. Yet my hesitation to live a spiritual life to the full was a tangled mixture of resistance to change, and a deep fear and suspicion of the actions of formal and senior students. I told myself that while mistakes might be made by individuals, I could trust in the overall evolution that was taking place. Most of all, I trusted Andrew.

I thought about the children. Becky had started middle school; Jessica was settled into high school. Leaving now would mean interrupting their school year. Meanwhile, the green card process had already cost me $28,000 and taken six years. The card was due to arrive any day, but I might not receive it if I moved out of state.

I decided to let the Community go ahead without me and join them as soon as the card arrived. I did not know that it would take more than two years. Soon, I waved goodbye to the car convoys leaving California and became the unofficial saleswoman for the cars left behind. I knew that my delay would be seen as lack of commitment to the teachings.

I took an apartment with my children, living alone with them for the first time in seven years. I enjoyed being closer to them, but from their point of view the situation was a mixed blessing. Our increased time together resulted in tension as well as cohesion, particularly for Jessica. She had spent seven years learning how to manage her own life without much intervention or advice from me. Now 14, she had struggled to find her place in the social order at school and was starting to enjoy the freedom of Community life with little supervision. She met my new attempts to be a hands-on parent with resentment and increasing secrecy. Meanwhile, 12-year-old Becky had found a supportive group of friends at school, but she resented my efforts to limit her access to friends that I regarded as a bad influence.

I kept in contact with Andrew's activities; and a year or so later attended a weekend retreat with him in Boulder. The chance to talk with him privately came, as always, after Satsang. I waited for an hour in the corridor. When I entered the room with Andrew, I found him as alert and interested as if I were the only person in the world. It was as easy and natural to be with him as it had been in Totnes. I spoke freely about the challenges of bringing up children in the Community and my reservations about moving to the East Coast. During our short conversation, he seemed genuinely surprised to hear me explain why parents are responsible for spending a lot of time with their children on a regular basis. He thanked me and said that what I was saying would help him understand other parents in the Community too. I felt so good about this conversation believing that this would lead to changes in the conditions for families with children in the Community, that I wondered why I had never talked things through with him before. I left Boulder somewhat relieved of my concerns and decided to travel East even though the green card had not yet arrived.

A short time later, in 1998, as Jessica neared the end of her second year in high school, we planned to move. Both girls had been awarded full scholarships to a good private school in Boston. When we talked in detail about the move, I was unprepared for the children's reaction. Becky was clear that she wanted to live only as a single family, and did not want to return to the Community. She had established friends in her first year at middle school and was sick of moving house. Jessica had very good friends, loved the drama program, and wanted to stay. She felt it would be impossible to find friendships among the teenagers in Andrew's Community and was convinced she would be excluded, even unwelcome, on the East Coast. She said she would rather move back to England or Germany than go to Boston. I tried to reassure them. I don't remember if I really listened to the girls. My parenting style was already an authoritarian imitation of Andrew's style as a teacher. Besides, I had made up my mind and sent everything we owned to the East Coast. Not for the last time, Jessica would be deeply angry that she had no choice about the changes imposed on her.

Jessica and Becky went to my parents' farm for the summer and then to Germany to visit their father. I scaled down my work, giving myself time to examine my internal demons. Way back in the farmhouse in Devon, my heart had opened up in unexpected delight and connection with Andrew, people, and the energy of life. I had followed this dream in hopes that I would integrate these tastes of awareness and love into my whole life. I recalled a recent conversation with Jürgen during one of his visits to see the children. He had asked me if I now thought I had done the right thing by taking the children to the US. I answered in Community jargon, "It depends on whether I follow through." I tried to explain, "If I follow through in being free, the children will benefit. I will set an example to them of going beyond fear." If I had been totally honest with Jürgen I would have added, "But I have no idea how to live beyond fear and I don't seem to be getting any closer."

Although I had completed plans to move East, I took a stark

look at the situation. In disappointment, I faced the reality that I had lived in Andrew Cohen's Community in San Francisco for years but I was not living life to the full. Holding myself back from being truly part of the action, I often felt that I was on the outside looking in. My sense of isolation had increased because our connectedness was scrutinized and tested. Now I said to myself, "It is pointless to go to Boston to live in the Community in the same old way. I am not going to disrupt our lives again for the sake of being an outsider. I must either throw myself in with everything I've got or else I shouldn't go. I have to find out now, not later, if I should stay here."

Chapter 7

Through My Body to Heaven

San Francisco in June was so lovely. I thought to myself, "I am alone. I don't have to be an example to the kids; everyone in the Community has already moved to Boston; what if I do exactly as I please? I mean exactly? If I abandoned every 'should,' and in particular every 'should not,' who would I be? What do I really want to do? This is the moment to stop pretending." So I stopped altogether. Stopped trying. Stopped attending to the unfinished planning lists in my head. Stopped thinking about how to get it right.

My attention was drawn not to what I thought or even what I felt, but to a stream of something richer that runs through it all. I began to listen not to the contents of my mind but to a constant refrain of music that runs beneath the surface. It was like a stream of joy that is always present in between the thoughts and feelings. The movement of the mind had separated itself out, into distinct events arising from a field of phosphorescence. The knowledge of what lay beyond my mind changed me. And because of this shift in attention the future started to take care of itself, as if I was guided by a larger impulse than before.

One Saturday night, I was in my apartment and wanted to go out. I knew people I could spend time with, but I was thrilled at the thought of going out on my own. I put on sophisticated eye makeup to complement my green eyes, tight black leggings and a clingy knitted dress and took myself to dinner. I sat alone eating lobster ravioli at a table set for two at the most expensive restaurant in San Rafael. I did not distract myself from the sensation of being lonely; instead, I let the fear of being alone evaporate into excitement. I gave myself the gift of a date just for the fun of it, not to make myself feel better or to make a claim for independence. It seemed to make no difference now whether I sat meditating in my apartment—bare now except for a bed and some boxes—or whether I went to R-rated movies on my own.

For a while I had been visiting an acupuncturist, Dr. Li, for exhaustion and headaches. I admired his strict professionalism in the way he didn't watch me dress, nor let his hand stray; though once, I was almost sure, it wasn't absent-mindedness that had let it linger on my belly. I began looking forward to the sting of his needles in every tender part of me. I began to shave my legs before my treatments, and I even began to use the expensive scent that I'd put away for so long, though I hoped he didn't notice that I hadn't worn scent before. When he added a back massage to the acupuncture, I wished that his firm expert touch would not stop at the back. He began to visit my home for treatments to save me the drive, and his considerate nature moved him to check with me on occasion to make sure I could manage his fee.

Little by little, I allowed myself to think about the possibility of getting involved with Dr. Li. I would cook apple pie with custard for him and he would teach me how to make Korean noodle soup. Late in the evenings I would join him in his apartment, which I imagined was bare of luxuries but was surely as neat and carefully organized as his office. I would not distract him from his research on herbs with beautiful names like Angelica and Euphrasia. While he mixed herbs from the hundreds of jars lining the shelves, I would quietly read *The Ending of Time* and *Journey Toward the Heart*. I would borrow my uncle's canoe and delight Dr. Li with a trip across Belvedere Lagoon. I dreamt that he would allow me to row him out into the middle of the lagoon and then gently take the oars from me and kiss me.

It was ironic that I should meet such a caring and spiritually aware man, after ten years of reluctant abstinence, at this juncture in my life, when I was planning to move, and it made no sense to allow myself to want this connection. What if I or he fell in love? I wondered. How would it be possible to leave him? It would be so inconvenient, especially as my entire household had already been shipped to Boston.

To share my confusion, I had coffee with a psychologist friend. "I don't know what to do," I told her. "I am on my way to Boston. I shouldn't get involved now. It's crazy, and it wouldn't be fair!"

"You should go ahead," she said.

"You don't think it's selfish?" I asked.

"No!"

"So you think I could just go for it?"

"Of course," she said. "Who knows what the outcome will be?" She added, "I've been watching you over the last few months. You have been getting stronger; your career is going well, and you've started to trust yourself."

I felt she was really saying, Being without the Community has helped you. I replied, "Thank you. But I have to follow this thread." I wished that for once I could get someone outside the Community to understand my reasons for being in it. She could not understand my commitment. I only knew that I had to travel East.

She said, "I hope it works out for you, wherever you end up. If it doesn't, you can always come back. There's no dishonor in coming back."

I hugged her and said, "Thank you," but I knew I wasn't coming back to San Francisco.

I let loose my growing appetite for intensity, now that I could do so without criticism from the Community. I gave myself over to the delicious sensation of desire. Relishing the thrill of obsession.

After nine months of acupuncture and Chinese herbs I was more energetic than I had been at 21. Soon, I wouldn't need Dr. Li's treatments any longer. And I would be leaving, so if there was to be an adventure it had better start soon.

"You smell so fresh," he said one day when I lay down on the table. "You'll be spending July 4th with your boyfriend?" he asked in his boyish way. Today he had his bicycle pants on, and I watched the tight small muscles of his calves. His feet, still in bicycle shoes, tipped up as if in heels. His body was small and perfect, hardened by Kung Fu training. (He'd given up Kung Fu because he said it was taking him down a road towards aggression.) I recognized his bodily intelligence long before I learned that he taught Tai Chi and Chi Gung; his restrained intensity both excited and scared me. I wished he were more substantial, taller or less delicate, but I was drawn to the silent, efficient focus in the way he moved. Ignoring his question, I replied in my polite English way, "I was wondering if you would like to go out together sometime."

And so two days later, he came to my apartment. He looked so shocked as I ushered him into the living room—empty except for a couch and a TV—that I explained, "It's because all the furniture has already been shipped." Then he wandered into the kitchen and helped himself to a glass of wine. He handed his cup first to me for a sip. I felt pleased that he seemed to be so at home in my house.

He put his arms around me as if he had known me for years, and I wondered at the lack of something subtle between us. Where was the romance? The sense of wonder? As we sat close together on the couch, he unceremoniously stuffed pieces of ripe mango into my mouth, more as if he were feeding a bird, then tempting a lover. But then as his hands addressed the loneliness in me, reaching under the waistband of my cotton khaki pants, I dismissed his graceless ways as lack of practice.

He pushed me gently back to lie down. It felt so good to feel a man's touch after so many years that I sighed a long satisfied sigh of relaxation.

"Yes," he replied. "That's good, breathe out."

I responded by letting my hands explore and so did he. I was hungry and curious, even though I wished some detail of my body would hold his attention so that he would want to linger longer. I wished that I could tell him that I wanted his hands to be firmer and his mouth softer, but I hadn't yet learned enough about my own body. I wished that he would open his eyes. I politely averted my own eyes when he turned away to organized protection, relieved that he was keeping me safe. Then as he lay on top of me, my intense determination to understand sexuality burst open. Suddenly my yearning for the man of my imagination vanished; and I saw him not as a sophisticated, evolved teacher, but as a simple man with limited experience. My fantasy future with him was replaced by the reality of two ordinary selfish human beings. Instead of romantic significance there was only the bed beneath us, and pleasure; but instead of craving, I felt only peace. This was not the common disillusionment of finding out that my lover did not meet up to my fantasy expectations but something deeper. This shift was borne of looking clearly without my own desires getting in the way.

I thought, "It's a joke to think that I was looking to him to make me whole. The search for another person to bring me fulfillment is a delusion. Desire is wanting something from another that cannot be given. My wholeness lies in this understanding. My freedom lies in knowing that it is all down to me."

As I pulled on my khakis and did up the button on my blue top, I wanted to burst out laughing. Instead, I said his name. Misunderstanding, he said, "Yes, it was wonderful for me, too." I felt tenderness towards him because he did not know I had left the game.

As we drank tea downstairs, I invited him to drive across the country with me, knowing that he would turn me down. I asked because I felt he would be disappointed if my desire for him suddenly vanished; a soft desire to take care of him had replaced my tortured wanting. We parted with a brief hug in the hallway and he left without much of a farewell.

I seldom laugh a full-bodied laugh from the belly even with close friends. But when he had gone, I laughed uncontrollably. *What a joke*, I thought, *that when I decided to follow my every wish and search to find out whether I seek God or man, I find freedom through sex itself.*

After a few days, my thoughts returned to Dr. Li. This interest, I knew now, was lust pure and simple. I felt the urge once more to own him and the devious neediness that would try to reel him in. But it's hard to manipulate with your eyes open. He called wanting to say goodbye to me. When I went to his office, he invited me into his therapy room and put his arms around me. I resisted the urge to hold him tight and feel for his desire of me. I walked away smiling in triumph that I had not even tried to seduce him again.

Afterwards, romance lost its hold on me. Now, something more raw called me, and it was still three weeks before I would leave San Francisco. I wondered how I could continue my discoveries about sex without creating a tragedy. But it was not sex itself that I sought; I needed to find out something about sex, and I did not even know what the question was. If I moved before I had found out, then I would never be able to rejoin Andrew's Community wholeheartedly. So, I reasoned, if it was sexual experience that I needed to understand, this was my chance.

I didn't notice Paul when he first arrived at my garage sale. An overweight, balding accountant, I thought, when I first set eyes on him. He wanted the dining room table. It was a nice pine table; but as he rightly said, it needed resurfacing and wasn't worth the $80 that I was asking.

"How about $40 and a massage?" he offered.

I was on time, as always. I thought I had the wrong house for a moment because the garden was beautifully kept. The house, nestled into a rock face and skillfully angled around a giant redwood, was not what I had expected. Inside, it felt like a temple. In the miniature garden in the living room, water gurgled up, moistened a moss-covered rock, and trickled away through polished stones. My nostrils alerted to the sweetness of a burning incense candle. From another room, a woman's voice chanted softly to Indian music. I felt as if the house were breathing softly, inviting me to tread with loving care and feel the secret of its beauty.

Paul invited me to sit beside him on the couch and offered me some tea. "You can have whatever kind of massage you would like. It's good that you have no time deadlines so we can take the time we need."

"I don't know what I want," I said quickly, with embarrassment.

He asked, "Would you like this massage to be sexual?"

I answered, "Yes," excruciated by my honesty.

"Would you like me to keep my clothes on?" he asked.

Shocked, I very quickly said, "Yes."

"Try to tell me what you would really like. You can tell me at any time. You also have to pay me; not a lot, only $10. This is so that the relationship is one in which you are in charge. It will free you to receive and not have to give back, and to ask for whatever you want except intercourse."

No ordinary massage, this! Slowly, for perhaps an hour, his hands traveled over my body, powerful and deep, leisurely softening all the muscles of my limbs, my back, and my head. My resistance yielded to the strength of his hands. My muscles relaxed, until movement ceased and agitation vanished and embarrassment receded. Then the touch changed, his fingers caressing every inch of my skin more and more softly. I gave myself up into his care. I opened my eyes for a moment and took in the design of woven flowers in the rug on the floor under the table and my cream woolen jacket, which had fallen on the floor. Noticing my glance, he picked up the jacket and folded it carefully and placed it safely on the back of the chair. How nice to be cared for, I thought.

My skin came alert to his touch, listened for his next move. As I lay on my front, hands by my sides, his slow, steady touch flowed over my body, caressing my back and buttocks, ever softer.

"You're teasing me!" I declared in mock horror.

"Is it all right to be teased?" he said.

"Oh, yes!"

Something soft touched my skin. I could not name the something. I could not name the exquisite sensation on my skin. "It is wonderful!" There was no defining it. This was pure sensation before taking hold of it, taming it, and stabling it in the known. I let myself go into the instantaneous rawness of sensation before the dilution of thought.

"What is that?" I asked.

"Rabbit fur."

"Oh, my God," I said, shocked at the animal in myself when interpretation kicked in.

He asked if I would like to open my legs, and his hands enquiringly wandered lower, ever nearer to the center. Gently, he taught me how to ask for touch where and when I wanted it.

I turned to lie on my back, and he asked permission to touch my breasts. The music changed to an African drumbeat. The scent of incense was mixed with that of the delicate oil on his hands. This massage was more intimate than any intercourse I had known. His tongue dwelt long on the scar on my toes, which I had always thought so ugly. I realized that this man was caring about every inch of me.

"No part of me is unworthy!" I slowly gasped.

He said, "No part of you, inside or out, physical or on any other level."

He rested his hand on my pubic bone and said, "Breathe in slowly, from here. Breathe out slowly, making sounds, whatever sounds you like. Sounds are good." As I breathed, the sensations expanded and moved. My hands began to tingle, and then the whole arms; energy ran up and down the length of them. Then I felt a pulsating energy all over my body and the table began to shake as if it were driven by a motor.

"Turn the vibrating machine off," I said.

"There is no machine," he said. "This is your life force."

"It is the grace of God!" I said.

"No," he said. "It is the Goddess. It is you the Goddess."

I began to allow him, and even ask him for more and more sensation, on every part of me. I began to experience tiny distinctions in quality of sensation. We began to discover a rich and varied landscape, shared through his hands and tongue and my body.

I had no idea I could feel this much. I wondered why I had never on my own explored my body to find this much subtlety of sensation, and also knew that from now on I would.

Probably, I thought, *he would rather not be here with me doing this. Probably he thinks I am being greedy. Probably he thinks I am no lady at all.* But looking into his eyes, I knew that my pleasure was also his, even though he did not seem aroused. Probably I should stop now, I thought, but when I asked myself why, there was no answer. *What sort of woman anyway would seek this much pleasure? Not nice? Not good?*

He answered my unspoken question. "Do you dare to break the taboos, do you dare to go beyond 'ought' and 'should'?"

This must be too much pleasure, I thought. *But who decides "too much"? Who is measuring?* Slowly, the most unthinkable question formed itself: *Maybe it isn't true that I don't deserve everything?* This question challenged my fundamental assumption that I only deserved a limited reward, that I was not "good" enough to have very much of what I wanted. *If it is not true that I don't deserve everything, then maybe it is OK to receive deeply and fully and to open up to a stranger and to allow myself to be loved.* I felt the ground of my life shift to quicksand.

I was freed by our financial deal to ask as I had never before dared. I was allowed to find my own full depth of expression, given the freedom to be uncensored and the invitation to go beyond shame. I was touched so deeply that the only desire I had left was that one day I would have the chance to give more than I had received.

I noticed now the smell of his faint clean sweat. I looked at his sturdy thighs and wondered how heavy he would feel, but intercourse was excluded. I discovered that he would meet me in whatever intensity of desire I chose, using hands and tongue alone. Secrets unfolded. Laughter was out of control. Tenderness sustained between the two of us until time vanished and there was only now. There was no one to confirm my old ideas that a woman shouldn't be too extreme. There was no one to say what was appropriate. Sensation exploded outwards until there was an endless streaming of energy, of him, of me, flowing, no beginning and no end to it. This was more than I knew was possible. I rode waves of intensity, blasting away the conception of how much I could stand. It was more than I had dreamed of, more than I could imagine.

I hesitated, then saw that the only question was how much of this I would allow. What would happen if I kept on going? I let go. I became aware of a horizontal beam of light. I was drawn into the light and became light. The light was the only thing that existed. Could it be true that we are nothing but light? I found that I was composed of an endless stream of light and in that light was energy of infinite power.

I had thought that to be touched intimately by a stranger, he had to have no face. I had planned never to look Paul in the eye, so neither of us would get attached. But I found that I loved looking into his eyes and seeing the man there. He looked back. His face was beautiful; his whole body was beautiful.

"I do believe you are falling in love with me," he said.

I froze in panic. "But no! That cannot be the outcome!"

"It's okay," he said, holding my gaze calmly in his blue eyes. "Don't stop breathing. Breathe from here." His hand was almost motionless, deep inside me.

"Slowly now," I said. I met his gaze longer and longer until there was no tearing myself away, until just looking into his eyes was the sweetest union of all.

Sensing my need for space, Paul moved a step back from the table, smiling, lightly watching my naked body on the massage table, relaxed and unhurried. He did not seem to need to do anything, did not need to make conversation. He glanced out of the window into the garden. I heard the birds singing and the water fountain trickling across rocks. The scent of the oils still filled the room; I picked out the low drumbeat from the CD playing in the background. I was speechless as vibrations ran by themselves from my torso, the length of my limbs and into my head over and over again. I had opened myself to the knowledge that I was indistinguishable from this endless force. How terrible that I had denied it all my life. I had found not just sex but surrender of more than body, surrender of even my most closely guarded secrets. In surrendering to my own desire, had I wakened in the arms of God?

"It's so sad," I said, "that so few people know about this."

"This is yours now; you will always have this. This is the tantric secret. Practice taking yourself to this level of energy often. Play with it. Use your knowledge of how you like to be touched."

Three weeks later, I began the drive to the East Coast. This might have been a moment to reconsider my decision to move. I might have thought deeply about what was best for my children. I might have seen the ego present in the impulsive act of jumping in my car. I might have had the courage to stop and consider whether the future really was taking care of itself. I loved being alone. I had not travelled in the States, so I picked a route that would take me through the deserts of Utah. I put up my tent in one of the red canyons, lay down on the grass, and reflected on my discoveries about sexuality and love. Sexuality, I had seen, could be a doorway into understanding everything about myself. I wrote two letters:

Dear Li,

I think, but I'm not sure, that you are a catalyst. I wake this morning still burning up. But the passion has no object anymore. It is directed outwards towards everyone. I deny nothing. I'm overwhelmed by the love of all the people that I meet. I thank you with all my heart for the care and devotion which you gave me.

Dear Paul,

Thank you with all my heart
For sharing my secrets,
For making me laugh,
For receiving every part of me and for teaching me how to receive.
For the exhilaration of entering the unknown together with you.
For the freedom to be uncensored.
For the almost unbearable ecstasy, which still endures.
For tenderness.
For everything that could ever be given to any human being. It is more than I knew was possible. I am deeply, deeply earthed, deeply connected to myself. I'm alone in the desert of nothingness.

Early in the morning I left my hilltop campsite and walked down a cliff path into the canyon. It was very hot, even at seven in the morning. The leaves on the bushes hardly moved. My legs felt powerful, my muscles strong. I felt as if I could walk forever on the bare rock pavements. Whenever I stopped, I listened, but I could pick out no sound of movement.

I was searching for something. Under an overhanging rock ledge, halfway down the cliff, I stumbled across the curved ruins of a Hopi dwelling, abandoned 800 years before. I ran my hand over a soft cushion of moss growing on the moist rock and pushed the spiky bushes apart with my hands, revealing a tiny spring nearby. The path led through undergrowth. The soft rustling of birch trees called my attention to another path leading deeper into the canyon.

I wanted more of the sublime energy of connection with the earth. Red cliffs soared above me and the sound of scattering earth from my footfall echoed down the canyon. I thought about my ceaseless search for something ever since I was a teenager. I thought about finding peace within spiritual experiences with Andrew Cohen; I thought about finding some combination of sexual and spiritual experience with Paul. I realized that even at that moment I was craving more experiences in this desert. From somewhere then came the question, "Why do you think you need more?"

It stunned me. I knew that I didn't need to look for more. I knew that I was part of the energy of the canyon, that I had everything that I was looking for, that I didn't need more of anything to know who I was—not more experience, not more bliss, not more excitement. I realized that to continue seeking "more" was a form of slavery. I thought, *There is no need to engineer my life in any way!*

And then I felt peace. There was no "me" that I could identify. I saw that the old me was merely the sum of my quests for "more," that when I stopped wanting anything more for myself, then I was left without anything that defined me. When I took away my desires and cravings and searching and grabbing, even for God, there was nothing left. The "old" Marlowe, therefore, was nothing more than a **huge** bundle of cravings. *Why*, I asked myself, *would I want to perpetuate that?*

At the bottom of the canyon, it was quiet. I stretched my head back and back to follow the huge arch of rock that grew upwards and stretched like the limb of a giant to span the canyon. I felt its power. I was not sure if I could stand anything that bold. I backed away from the archway and sat on a rock ledge where it was not so hot. The sky was cloudless and turquoise. I liked the red of the rock, my favorite color, rust red. The dazzling contrast of colors invaded my eyes. I sat cross-legged, absorbing tingling rock energy through my spine. I felt rooted to the earth in meditation.

All day I sat motionless in the shade at the bottom of the sandstone canyon. The cheese in my lunch melted and seeped into the bottom of my backpack. I felt inseparable from each sedimentary layer of the mountains. I knew then that I was guided from within, but all around me I saw God in sky and air and felt God in the rocks. My thoughts drifted slowly. I had no momentum at all. Any movement would have been in search of something, so I did not move.

I closed my eyes and my attention drifted back to Paul. How strange. Miraculously I had loved intimately but without the mechanism of attachment binding me to him. I had said goodbye to him with an open heart, and yet saying goodbye was painless. I didn't want anything from him or anyone. I received his gifts and walked free. My nervous system was altered so that I was aligned with the energy in other people and in the rocks themselves. Meditation had become a default state.

I had been traveling alone for a couple of weeks, settling into the Utah desert. The people I met on the road were softened by my openness; that was new. Whereas before, people would feel a slight discomfort around me, now they wanted to be in my presence. They sought my eyes instead of moving quickly away. This was particularly true of children, who followed me when I was sightseeing.

I thought about the construction worker I had met at Mesa Verde who shared his beans and rice with me as we sat one evening in his tent. He had said that, when I talked about Andrew Cohen, my face lit up. He said, "When you are like that, then nobody can do anything to you, can they?"

"I guess that's true," I replied.

He was gray-haired and looked tired, though he couldn't have been more than 50. Then he said, "I used to want to become a monk, but I haven't talked with anyone about these things for 20 years," and all of sudden he started to cry. "I am a selfish, withdrawn man, and I have been this way to my wife all these years."

As I watched, his face fell backwards in time, and the 50-year-old man became 40 years old, and then he was 30, and then he was 20, and then he was just a boy.

I said to him, "This is most wonderful. Trust this that is happening now."

The next morning, he drove for two hours to buy me a book about Native Americans who had once lived in the hills of Utah.

The intense Utah sun shifted around to invade the shade provided by the sandstone wall above me. I drained my water bottle, tilted one shoulder into my backpack and headed up the cliff path towards my tent. I started to think about where I was headed. I thought, *I can trust myself. I don't need an external guru to tell me if I am on the right path. Maybe I have some special quality, maybe I am turning into a teacher. Maybe this is enlightenment?*

As I continued up the cliff, I thought, *But what does it mean to still have these thoughts? Perhaps I am more arrogant than ever! Is awareness of these thoughts enough for them not to be dangerous? How far have I gone? Andrew Cohen could answer my questions. Andrew has been my guru for 13 years; he is the only genuinely enlightened person that I know. I have to find him. And I will see if, as I have planned, I should rejoin his Community or if I am ready to be my own guide.* I was sure that when I arrived in the Community I was strong enough to trust my intuition about whether reentering the Community was the right decision.

I disconnected the gas canister from the burner standing on the patch of earth I used as a kitchen, slid the tent poles into the bag beside the flysheet. It was time to leave the desert. I drew a line on my map across the country to Andrew's center in the Berkshires. I reckoned it might take five days if I didn't rush.

On the way, I wrote to Andrew projecting onto him the qualities that I most wanted in him. In spite of the fact that by striking out on my own path and breaking Community taboos, I had discovered more freedom than in the previous years, I still referred to Andrew as the source of my understanding:

Thank you. I've been given so, so much love in the last two months and by the grace of God, I've been able to open my heart and receive. Thank you, thank you, Andrew, for your teachings of wisdom and understanding which steer me towards a straight path, always aiming towards humility, always pointing away from narcissism and self-indulgence. Your teachings steer me to put every experience in the context of giving to the whole. You point the way towards love rather than fascism, surrender rather than egocentrism, sanity rather than madness. You encourage in me that which is human rather than elitist.

When I left Utah, it was late afternoon. I crossed over the mountains at the top of Monarch Pass, and then the road dropped abruptly down into Denver. Just over the rise, I saw a huge expanse of Colorado. My chattering mind paused. The plain stretched out interminably without a ripple. What I saw outside and what I experienced inside fell into alignment. I was excited, thrilled and simultaneously at peace. I saw that, if I let go, every future scenario fanned out into infinite space. I saw how every one of my beliefs tried to fix and control the future. My mind was empty and clear.

The sky slowly filled with billowing cloud formations, glowing with fluorescent streaks of sunlight. The next minute, they turned to looming black and gray masses. Detailed mountain silhouettes made the backdrop for a double rainbow, which I followed for ten miles downhill into Denver city.

I drove the long, flat, monotonous drive across Colorado and Kansas for ten hours straight. When I looked in the mirror in the campsite bathroom, I silently asked my reflection, *Who is this? Happy/unhappy? Kind/unkind? Beautiful/ugly? Dangerous/loving? I don't know who or what it is looking back at me.*

"I am drinking deep, very deep from every experience now," I wrote in my journal. "It's as if I've never really tasted life before, never before been committed to being alive. I am filled to overflowing. Today I saw that my body is sacred and I am nothing more than a vehicle for the expression of light."

When I got to Illinois, the only campsite I could find was close beside a truck stop on the edge of the highway. I would generally consider that too dangerous for solo camping so I checked into a motel. I wrote again to Andrew:

> Your teachings have been my anchor throughout these last intense few weeks. The only clear thread that I had was that it was absolutely important to do the right thing and that I had to understand what was true. This is what I learned from you; otherwise I would have been at the mercy of every whim of my own and those around me. Without you, I would never know that there is still pride, and I would believe my arrogant thoughts about how special I am.

Mosquitoes swarmed aggressively at the next campsite in Ohio. I swam lazily in the water there, warm as tea. I wrote again, "Every second, by allowing what is, I discover my own passion and power, sexuality, sensuality, the undeniable source of life. I cannot deny them."

The next night I camped on a farm in Amish country, my tent resting on thick green grass. I bought raspberries from a ten-year-old girl wearing a headscarf and a blue-and-white, knee-length gingham dress. She picked them while I waited. I photographed horses tied up outside a church beside neat rows of buggies. Bearded men in topcoats and white collars came out first after worship, then women dressed down to the ankles. I wrote again to Andrew: "Whatever is happening to me, I do not want it to stop, I want to go deeper and deeper in experience and understanding (I come to you for the understanding not for affirmation), yet still I feel a faint concern that it may be about me."

In New York, I stayed near the Finger Lakes. I would reach Foxhollow the next day. The journey felt over. Instead of swimming and exploring the nature reserves, I sat quietly in my tent, wondering if my response to Andrew would be different. *For sure*, I thought, *I will find out how far I have really gone. But Andrew is a true Master. If I have not taken the wrong path, then I have nothing to fear from him except the death of my ego.* Yet I really had no idea what kind of reception awaited me. Andrew had talked with derision about tantric spiritual masters who used sexual experience as a path to spiritual growth. Although I had come to understand his scorn for the delusory promise of perfection that ensnares couples when they are attracted to each other, I wondered if they would throw me out for delusions of grandeur. Would they accuse me of false claims, or would I be welcomed as changed?

Part III

Success and Failure in Shadowland

Chapter 8

Success?

For the first time, I drove between the mature white pines of Foxhollow. Ahead of me, I saw the red front door of the mansion. There were numerous condos and cottages, a large barn, a large acreage of land. Major reconstruction was in progress: the swimming pool was being filled in, and sash windows lay on the ground, stripped and in the process of sanding. In the distance I saw a beautiful lake.

Walking through the front door of Andrew's Massachusetts mansion was like walking into a force field of emptiness: the agitation of the outside world that I normally carried in my body disappeared. I recognized in passersby the absence of superfluous thought. I had traveled across America deep in meditation, yet entering these doors, feeling the emptiness of this house, I felt I'd come home.

In the kitchen, I saw for the first time the row of gleaming stainless steel commercial ovens and the sinks and refrigerators designed to cater for hundreds of people. Eight people were making lunch, so I joined them. The chef—one of Andrew's senior students—explained how to cut burdock stalks evenly and at exactly the right thickness. She showed me how to roast peppers over the gas flame, to blacken the skin perfectly so that when you ran it under a tap, the skin would peel off and leave the succulent flesh. I was delighted by the focus on making each salad as close to perfect as possible. I felt immediately at home. It felt like balm.

I was excited to see friends that I had not seen in two years and thrilled to tell them about my travels. However, soon I found that I couldn't connect with anyone. I was unware that Andrew's students and in particular the women were at this time under intense pressure from Andrew to "come through" and give up their destructive conditioning.

"I can't believe how much love I felt in people I met on this journey," I told a woman I used to know. "I am overwhelmed with gratitude towards all the people behind me, surrounding me, buoying me up."

"This sounds very good," she said, with suspicion in her eyes, "But I hear nothing about Andrew in what you are saying. Where is the gratitude to Andrew in all of this?"

"Of course I appreciate Andrew!" I said. "These experiences were the result of my listening to Andrew's tapes about relationships over and over again and the result of meeting other people."

"But Andrew is the source of it all," she said firmly.

Her friend added, "There is perhaps something superior about the way you're telling us. I think you need to look at this tendency. Like the rest of us."

I was open and undefended with everyone around me, and I was met by fear. As I talked to one person after another, each one added words of caution, comparison, or advice. One told me, "We have to be really careful not to make too much of our experiences. It's a mistake to draw too many conclusions about them." Another said, "You are going to learn so much when you settle into life here. It's incredible what's happening for everyone, it's beautiful. It has changed so much."

Their words sounded like clichés. I suspected they could not value a new response to the teachings. I wondered whether they were afraid to acknowledge anything that did not come directly from Andrew. It was as if their perspective had closed in tightly around them and they no longer saw the beauty of what we had once known in Totnes.

Horrified that these lay students could not see what had happened to me, I feared that they would pull me down. *Where is the fire in these people?* I asked myself. *This is depressing; I felt* more fire in the Mormons in Salt Lake City and the truck driver at Mesa Verde. Maybe, I thought, there is something wrong and I do not belong here.

And then it was time to meditate. We filed slowly and silently into the great room. Rather than sitting on the floor like in Totnes, we sat on fine office chairs with our feet on the ground. The moldings of the tall windows were visible above the folded velvet curtains. The walls were bare. A single vase of flowers stood before us. For three hours we chanted:

The fire of your heart must burn brightly,
That fire will give you all the energy, strength and presence of mind
To bear with, understand, and ultimately see through your own mind,
That fire will be your meditation
And in that fire your ignorance
Which is all your wrong ideas
Will burn...

Until the words burned into us.

Despite my earlier misgivings, I left the meditation room crying, moved by these words. I thought, Anyone who could write those words must be trustworthy. I long to meet Andrew where he is, permanently. I am so lucky that here we can meditate for three hours a day on our own true nature, which is fire. I want to see all there is to see in me and I long for the fire to burn up all my wrong ideas. This organization IS where the fire is. Maybe it is a good place for me after all.

After meditation, we filed silently out of the room, put on our shoes, and wandered down the hall. I walked over to a group of formal students and told them, with tears in my eyes, that the fire in this meditation resonated with my own soul. They nodded their heads—cautiously, it seemed to me. I knew they were not feeling the fire right then, and for a moment I considered taking a step back and trying to fit in, but I did not doubt the fire in my heart. I continued, "These words that Andrew has written are incredible. This fire is our own true nature." And, redirecting me, they said, "Andrew's really only interested in how we express the teachings in action now." I was confused, we had chanted about fire. The fire resulted in action. Yet these students seemed nervous at my mention of it.

"I see," I said, feeling crestfallen. A voice in my mind whispered an ancient, destructive strategy: *Perhaps they are right. Perhaps it would be better to try to fit in and not talk about what I have learned on my own.* But another voice argued, *These people are not the authority just because they have been mouthing Andrew's words for the last decade! Nothing will lessen the fire that I know.*

The Community seemed like a minefield waiting to threaten my newfound spirit. Not knowing which way to turn among these students for safety, I held onto the beacon that was Andrew.

I offered to help a group of formal students make seitan (wheat protein) stew in the kitchen. Their cursory glances revealed their indifference. As the cook's hands, deep in the sink, rinsed and massaged huge bowls of flour into gelatinous balls, I realized that these people thought I was the person I used to be, but I knew I was not that same person. Suddenly I did not feel safe. By reacting to me as they imagined me to be, they would pull me—knead me—into an old shape if I let them. If I conformed to their expectation, I would lose the confidence I had gained.

Just then, the cook stopped kneading dough, looked up, and said, "Wait a minute, Marlowe. I just reacted to you in the way that I always used to because I thought I knew who you were. And then you moved in a way that made me realize that I have no idea who you are." She asked me what had happened to me. She saw that the old Marlowe full of fears and doubt had gone.

Grateful for this momentary recognition, I felt a little better.

When it was dark, I sat on the bench near the remains of the swimming pool with my wise friend Kristin. She was older than the rest of us by a decade, and the depth of her smile warmed me. Once accustomed to wearing bright kaftans from her travels, she now dressed like the other women in a tailored jacket and slacks. She took off her blue headscarf to let me stroke the rough stubble underneath. The shaved head showed her commitment to her new practice of celibacy. Andrew used celibacy to punish students, eliminate distractions or to enhance commitment. One of their goals was to understand sexuality more deeply as a result of their abstinence.

Finally, I had found someone who could hear me.

"How is it possible," I asked, "that through a couple of erotic encounters I have come to see that everything is spiritual: music, sex, laughter, clouds, the big rigs on the highway, a McDonald's hamburger?"

She listened, without saying a word, as I talked for a long time. Then she said, "This is wonderful, but there is no hurry. You can relax now."

She smiled and put her arms around me, and I cried with relief at finally being understood.

The girls were still in the UK. I had a week or two before they would join me, and I wanted to sort out whether we should even be here before they came. When we spoke by phone, I heard that they were well.

It was urgent that I talk with Andrew before I was pulled down by his students. Though I felt the place was dangerous, I believed that Andrew himself could be trusted. I perceived that his presence was everywhere but it was rare to actually see him. On the rare occasions when I saw him walk down a corridor, I saw students scuttling to rearrange their demeanor and give him space.

One of Andrew's closest students told me that Andrew wanted to talk to me. After waiting an interminable two weeks, I was given a time to meet him. I welcomed whatever reflection he had for me. I calmly walked up to the second floor and entered his beautiful office. Andrew said, without any particular emotion, that most people took off their shoes when they entered his office. I took off my shoes and set them at the door because he had asked me to do it but I felt no shame that I had done something wrong. I was meeting him without fear, at least for the moment.

With a generous smile, he opened his arms wide and gestured for me to sit on the huge soft couch. "It's fantastic!" he said. "I only have to look at your face to know that you are a completely different person. The old Marlowe is gone." And then he wanted to know every detail of how I had changed and what I had understood and how I thought that a sexual connection could have been a catalyst. "I was very impressed with the letter that you sent me about relationships," he said.

Knowing that I could trust him because he recognized the truth in my experience, I felt safe in his company. "It was your teachings, Andrew," I said. "I was listening to your teachings on relationship and sexuality, the same ones over and over, because I knew there was something in them that I had to figure out."

Andrew nodded and motioned for me to continue.

"And then when I was with a man, it all fell into place. I saw so much, in one instant that illusion fell away. One minute I was completely infatuated and the next I could see everything exactly as it is."

He said that there was not anyone among the celibate students who had understood to this depth what I was saying about sexuality.

"Let's continue later," he said. "Fantastic! You are a completely different person," he repeated.

A day later, Andrew called for me to return and he listened eagerly as I explained that I never used to understand why he saw relationships in such black-and-white terms, that it had seemed harsh, but now I understood: "Either we stand leaning into freedom or we are leaning in the opposite direction. There is no in-between."

I sank into the deep cushions of the sofa while Andrew sat at his desk, his eyes bright with curiosity as if I were a new toy that he could not figure out.

I told him I could see how negative and undermining of freedom I had once been, and I understood the challenge he faced in helping people to be free. "I am sorry for how I have been for 13 years. I see now how so many of your students are pulling down the revolution you are trying to bring about."

Andrew was shocked when I told him about the reception I had had when I arrived and how I had felt undermined. He wanted to know the name of each student I had encountered. His face revealed his deep concern. As if I were an equal he dropped his guard and asked, "What should I do about them? How can I bring about change amongst those people? Why don't they get it?"

"It's time now for me to give something back," I said. "I will help you if I can. I can perhaps be like your sheepdog, herding people towards your teachings."

He smiled warmly and said, "I need people like you."

I warmed inside at the implication of his trust in me. I felt closer to him now than ever before.

"What do you want to do now?" he asked. "Why haven't you asked to be a formal student?" I was taken aback by this invitation. When I lived in California, becoming a formal student seemed like a distant and formidable dream attained by students of a different and rare breed with more courage than I had. I had not even been sure that I wanted to be a formal student. Now the prospect seemed an effortless and obvious next step. The lay Community no longer felt safe to me. The closer I got to Andrew, it seemed, the safer I would be.

"I will," I said.

"We will talk more," he said. "Everything that is happening to you is wonderful."

I went back downstairs and entered the dining room bustling with a hundred students, some formal, some not, some resident, some visiting. A large-framed man at my table poked at his linguine with puttanesca sauce and searched for some pine nuts. "Is this the protein?" he muttered under his breath.

Word silently spread that, on two consecutive days, I had spent hours talking with Andrew. Now, everyone wanted to know what had happened to me. Andrew's approval had strengthened my confidence; mirrored back to me now from two dozen expectant faces was appreciation and interest.

I talked to many women. "You see, I discovered that every single woman has literally unlimited power. We all can make the choice to admit this to ourselves. Imagine what would happen if every woman knew that she was the source of unlimited power!

What would happen if we allowed what is there, allowed the vast extent of our own sexuality and energy, dynamism and ecstasy, denied nothing. Do we dare to even talk about it? Do any of us dare to believe it?"

And then they were quiet, as if that were too much.

I talked with men and women about being in the desert, about finding that I was nothing more than cravings for experience. And I told them how, on my travels across the country, I discovered that swimming in the cool mountain lakes before Monarch Pass or standing in the blistering heat trying to contact my immigration lawyer at a truck stop in Kansas it is fundamentally all the same. Whether I am gripping the steering wheel, slotted between four unheeding big rigs, tearing 80 miles an hour across the expansive Nevada desert, or lying on my back feeling the energy of the rocks in Capitol Reef Canyons, my experience remained essentially the same. There was something in all the experiences which never changed, which was so powerful that the ups and downs didn't matter very much. And I explained one of the things I saw was that, when I am in bliss, it is obvious that my breath is the breath of God. One day I didn't feel blissful, but I said to myself, "Who am I to doubt that this too is the breath of God?" And it was clear to me that all breaths, whatever the sensation, whether we feel good or lousy, are equally God's breath.

I had arrived on the East Coast with my heart wide open to all the people around me. My sensation was of love towards people irrespective of their place in the hierarchy. This love was amplified by affirmation from Andrew.

After a couple of days, I noticed a change. The woman next to me at breakfast had asked the day before if I would tell her about my travels. Today I felt her pull away a fraction rather than share the honey with me. It must be my imagination, I thought. I began to tell her about my experiences in the desert. She replied curtly that Andrew said it was more than experiences and changed the subject.

All of a sudden, the questions and the respect stopped. One day everyone was fascinated by my story; and the next minute, if I mentioned it, they changed the subject. Years later I would learn that Andrew had made sure of this. Finding my feet within the group might not be easy.

That evening, I met with 15 other women to discuss the teachings. Someone asked what the topic should be.

"I would like to talk about surrender," I said.

"Do you really think that is appropriate?" someone asked, staring directly at me. "I propose we talk about renunciation."

One of the women asked me why I was wearing eye makeup, another pointed out that now the formal women wore neatly cut suits in somber colors. She said it was not a rule that we should not show our upper arms, but no one did it any more. I felt indignant at the insinuation about my lacy blue sleeveless top. One woman told me with pride how gently Andrew had guided her to manicure her fingernails and have electrolysis on her face.

I guessed that these students would find it hard to receive

someone whose understanding had come about not through sitting in front of Andrew, but through Tantric experience. From him I had felt no such prejudice; therefore I felt resilient enough to weather their disapproval, confident in my knowledge that they did not understand me. I felt sure that Andrew would help them to understand a bigger perspective when he got the chance.

A month after arriving from the West Coast, I settled into a house in Cambridge with two lay students—Victoria and Ziggy—and their two children. Both women had been separated from their husbands by Andrew and had been elevated to the level of formal student and demoted again multiple times but there the resemblance ended. Victoria had been a steadfast friend in Mill Valley even when we were of different ranks. Her light brown hair was nearly always elegantly blow-dried, showing off her wide-set, brilliant hazel eyes. Her college teaching background made her more inclined than most to think and say what she thought. This had caused her to rise and fall like a yo-yo in the Community. In spite of mourning for her husband, she met everyone with a smile that was both generous and sad. From my first meeting with Ziggy when we lived together in Mill Valley, I found her quickness to read intentions and eagerness to please endearing and yet incongruous for a trained lawyer. Eventually her inclination to second-guess every decision she made overwhelmed her. Sometimes I longed to suggest that she let her long dark hair fall freely and untidily to her shoulders but it was nearly always tied tightly back. Now separated from her husband, it was with an effort that she remained chipper. She had once had an eating disorder and I wondered if she might take the same path again. My girls returned from visiting Europe at the end of that summer. Neither was happy at the private school. Thirteen-year-old Becky, small and round for her age, had not found a sport or club activity that suited her. She had abandoned art because it was "not cool" and had not found another interest. She had shaved parts of her long blond hair and dyed the front locks pink. Fifteen-year-old Jessica again succeeded at figuring out a new set of academic expectations, but she was deeply unhappy about having moved. She had always struggled to integrate into a succession of Community peer groups and had always felt marginalized. Now, the Community group of children had had two years to strengthen their bond without her. Looking for a radical way out, Jessica applied to international boarding schools and was accepted to the United World College in Wales. She was devastated to discover she had applied too late for the financial aid that would make it feasible. She had no choice but to stay in Boston. She turned inward, becoming more distant from me. She was by choice strictly vegetarian, but she still did not like many vegetables, so her diet was limited in calories and nutrition. Her sensitivity to the texture of clothing was acute; even in the New England winters she seldom wore a coat. She was therefore cold, thin, withdrawn, and often sick.

Victoria and Ziggy had been very good friends of mine for many years. But our connection was deeper now because I was holding back less. I settled into life within the household but soon I saw a disconcerting fact about myself. As we cooked pasta for dinner one night, Victoria told me gently, "I know that you are feeling overwhelming love inside, but sometimes I feel somewhat distant from you." Because I felt her love as she was talking, I asked her to tell me more. She went on, "Sometimes we feel that you are unusually loving, and sometimes we don't. Sometimes it seems to be just in your head. It is really about expressing this oneness and not keeping it to yourself."

This feedback, given without threat, sparked my curiosity, resonated with what I knew to be true inside myself, and brought us closer. I appreciated being shown how easily I could fall into old habits.

I still felt the energetic flow inside my body, but when I did, it was hard to pay attention to practicalities. I would live in bliss and then realize, for example, that I had forgotten to attend Becky's parent-teacher night.

One night I got home from job hunting, the kitchen counters were covered in trash, the children were pushing each other around, and Ziggy told me to get dinner ready. I retorted by saying I had gotten up at 5:30 and had been job hunting all day and anyway it was her turn to cook. Soon we were in a full-blown row... As we crossed swords, I recognized my aggression. I had believed that it had dropped away, but instead it seemed to have vanished only temporarily. Now I saw that I could meet aggression with aggression just as easily as always. I had no reason to congratulate myself.

I wrote to Andrew: "Today I responded to a moment of aggression from Ziggy with aggression in turn. I have not changed. I have the same mechanism working in my mind. If each of us continues to meet aggression with aggression, then we each perpetuate world suffering. In small ways or large, we are all equally responsible. I need to become a formal student, since as a formal student I will learn to live without this aggression." I discussed my request to be a formal student with my house-mates, then sealed it up in an envelope.

The reply came back the next day from a senior student that Andrew was very happy to hear that I was just starting to acquire some humility and that, because of this, I was now a formal student. I felt wonderful but also sad to leave my two friends. On our last final evening together, I told them, "Even when I am a formal student, I will still want your feedback. You are my friends, and that is what friends do." It made no sense to me that my status as a formal student should make me unaccountable to my old friends. But I had underestimated the hierarchy in Andrew's Community.

Every lay student aspired to be a formal student. Given that I was such an unlikely candidate for success, they could now believe that anything was possible. My children and I were swept up in a whirlwind. A team of lay students carefully packed and moved everything we owned; I didn't even touch a box. Even the beds were made. It was like being treated as royalty. When I walked into our new home for the first time, I was moved by an extraordinary sight: the dining room table was covered in huge bunches of flowers from every lay student house and many individuals. There were handmade cards expressing hope, thanks, wonder, and amazement in celebration of my becoming a formal student.

I felt a great responsibility to succeed and knew I would feel a temptation to feed the most basic human appetite: to feel superior. Andrew was right about that. The exquisite gratification of public acknowledgement by Andrew and therefore by the whole Community was powerful.

Stephanie was a senior student of Andrew's and the leader of the Boston Community. She sat down with me privately on the couch in the living room, her hands stiffly beside her and said, "I am very relieved that you finally started to look at yourself. You are in such a perfect place to begin destruction of the ego."

Her straight blond hair was parted exactly on the side. Her cream blouse perfectly ironed in spite of the humidity. I felt a faint chill in my back but welcomed the chance to examine my pride. However, I knew that the world was beautiful and that I only had to be deeply positive and everything would be fine. I forgot the chilliness and became very excited when she told me that my formal practice would be 600 prostrations a day, meditation for one hour a day, and chanting.

Every morning at 4am, the three women in the house cleared the living room of sofas, lay down our eight-foot wooden boards, and placed a picture of Andrew Cohen in front of us. We stood up straight, raised our arms to the sky in prayer, fell to the ground, and stretched the full length of our bodies out on the wooden board, and slid up again to standing. We did this 600 times. With every movement we chanted:

To be free means to have nothing
To be free means to know nothing
To be free means to be nobody.

It was a hot September in Boston. Even at five o'clock in the morning, the sweat poured down my face. Halfway through the practice we stopped to sit on our fat round cushions and write in our journals. We limited our writing to listing the challenges that we were facing at the time. I welcomed this practice to protect myself: I wasn't sure I could trust myself with transcendental experiences. I wrote:

Dear Andrew,
When Stephanie first told me what my practice was, I realized I had put my life in your hands and that that was good. When I started doing the practice, I experienced joy at being on my knees before God 600 times a day. My desire to be someone is so pervasive; the prostrations are my guide. I love them because they remind me of the force of my desire to be special. They are my chance to crush this force 600 times a day. I am so grateful for this practice. I feel that if I do this there is some hope of being forced into humility.

I wrote in my neatest handwriting on a pad of handmade, cream-colored parchment and addressed it to Andrew. And then I added in my diary, "I am facing my own arrogance in thinking that I am someone special for having written these lines to Andrew. How the hell do I stop thinking like this?"

The next day, I wrote to him again:

Leaping with joy and delight, like a dolphin, far clear of the water, in one perpetual timeless leap without motion.

Being at ease is a metaphor for letting everything be as it is. Every time I say these words, I know again that I don't need to hold on to any experience in order to be free. That was the answer to the

question that I never asked you of how to stay in the unknown. I see
that my potential for impacting the world for good or evil has multi-
plied, and I could be an egomaniac. Therefore, this Community is a
safe place for me to be.

A few days later I wrote again, believing—as I had been told—
that Andrew read every letter.

Letting everything be as it is... leaves me with nothing but love
Paying attention... leaves me with nothing but love
Meditation on the fire... leaves me with nothing but love
Holding onto nothing... leaves me with nothing but love
Being present... leaves me with nothing but love
Being in the unknown... leaves me with nothing but love.

A couple of days after sending that letter, as the whole household
sat down to a flavorful dinner of mushroom barley soup, I got a
phone call from the person at the desk at Foxhollow. She said in
a neutral voice, as if someone were behind her checking her
delivery, "Andrew has a message for you. He says that you
should not write any more letters to him."

"Thank you," I said.

I sat back down at the table. A familiar mask plastered itself
across my face, and a hand that I could not feel spooned tasteless
soup into my mouth until my bowl was empty. No one asked me
what was said, though without a doubt I would have told them.
And I would have been "comforted" by the knowledge that I
would be better able to learn to live the teachings if I did not
write to him.

One of Andrew's tenets, "Face everything and avoid nothing,"
spelled out the instruction to look openly and relentlessly into all
aspects of ourselves that came to light. During the weekly group
meetings, women and men met separately to discuss individual
issues. When students became stuck in their spiritual journey and

were unable to face aspects of themselves, then a question, a loving phrase, encouragement, or intense pressure from the group sometimes led to cathartic and accelerated movement. The tenets expressed the direction; the group context of our houses provided the context for learning how to live them, and the meetings pushed things forward. Sometimes Andrew met with the formal students. On one of these meetings I remember he asked me about the teachings and I talked openly with him for quite a while. Afterwards one of the women said that I had not put a foot wrong when Andrew had tested me in the meeting. I was totally surprised. I had no idea I was being tested; I thought merely that Andrew and I had been having an interesting conversation!

A woman who had been there later described me as having talked with Andrew at length. She had at the time been delighted because she felt that finally someone had made it and even more delighted that it was a woman. She had perceived that I was the same as Andrew but without the hardness and instead a glowing and very light lovingness. She had been unable to understand why Andrew had tested my understanding over and over again in the meetings.

On my fifth night as a formal student, I went to my first Boston women's meeting. Five of us sat cross-legged in a circle. My new roommate Heidi sat wrapped in a thick woolen shawl, looking pale and upset. I watched as the three other women addressed her.

"How dare you behave this way!" Justice screamed. Having always seen Justice smiling, it shocked me to see her so angry. What, I wondered, could Heidi have done to make her react like this?

"I am sorry," Heidi whispered.

"You have manipulated us all. You say you are sorry; you say you want to change; and yet you keep doing the same thing over and over again!" Shirley, the fifth formal woman in Boston, provided the follow-up.

Heidi started to reply but was cut short.

"This is no way to show your love for Andrew," Shirley continued, perhaps thinking that appealing to Heidi's devotion might bring about a shift.

"I have always loved Andrew," Heidi said without any expression whatever. Her eyes stared at the carpet in front of her.

"I don't understand why you don't see that what you are doing is volitional," said Justice, harking back to Andrew's tenet that each of us is "responsible," without exception, for every one of our actions, irrespective of context, conditioning, mental illness, or individual differences.

Heidi did not reply. She seemed to have shut down.

Shirley finished the job. "You've just been doing the same thing over and over again."

Still in touch with my conscience, I was shocked by the cruelty towards this woman. I asked whether I could speak to the three women privately.

We moved across the hallway into the other bedroom. Sitting down on the floor, I said, "I do not know what Heidi has done, but I am not at all sure this is the right way to respond to a woman locked in fear."

"We are not sure either," one of them replied. "But what else can we do? She's not responding. We've tried everything else."

Someone else said, "We all feel insecurity sometimes. We all know that her shutdown mode is just defensiveness. She's being aggressive. She's just trying to make us back off."

I said, "I do not see how this is supposed to help her want to investigate her lack of initiative."

Justice replied, "We realize it will take you a while to settle into how things are as a formal student. Give yourself time." Then, to all of us, "We'd better get back to the meeting."

On the way home, alone in the car with me, Heidi said, "It wouldn't be right for me to draw you into this. You are new here."

I told her it was OK with me.

She said, "I know that what I am doing is volitional, but I don't know how to change,"

"What is it, exactly, that they want you to change?" I asked.

"It's about me not giving."

"What are you not giving?" I asked.

"I am not sure, really. Oh, that is terrible! I should know. I should be able to explain it clearly!"

A week later, Heidi left the Community.

I heard that Victoria had also gone. No one knew why she left. Victoria—a successful college lecturer until transcendental experiences with Andrew led her to leave her career and her husband, and immigrate to America with her daughter. She had never wavered in devotion to Andrew.

I called her cell phone immediately. "Where are you?" I asked.

In tears, she answered, "I am moving out. I can't go on. It's enough,"

I went over to the Duck Street house we'd shared. No one answered when I rang the bell, but the door was unlocked, so I went upstairs to Victoria's room. It was strewn with clothes. She stood looking at a picture of Andrew, her head bowed, rocking slightly, her arms wrapped around herself. "What are you doing here?" she said. "Don't let anyone see you. You shouldn't be helping me!"

"I will help you," I said, folding a red, woolen sweater into a box. "What happened?"

Victoria's hazel eyes were swollen and her normally made-up face was blotchy. She told me that the senior students had been angry with her when they found out she had given me feedback on a letter to Andrew. She said, "They said that your letter was very beautiful and how dare I criticize you."

Andrew had pitched us against one another. He had used me

to hurt her and destroy our friendship.

Victoria randomly bundled heaps of papers and little bags of makeup into a moving box. The box collapsed when she moved it across the room.

I unfolded another box, placed a strip of tape securely across the bottom, and started packing books. I told her that nothing could change the friendship that we had had for the last ten years.

She replied, "It's as if you were suddenly infallible and I was blind. I love you, but I knew that you were not perfect, so I couldn't hold back. It's so black and white here. One person is up and another is down."

I thought about my strange experience of arrival on the East Coast. At first, everyone treated me like I was the same very introverted person that I used to be even though I knew I wasn't. *Now they treat me as if I were infallible, and I know I am not that, either.*

We hugged and sat on the edge of her bed, which by tomorrow would be someone else's. I could feel her thin shoulders through the light fabric of her mohair sweater. In Amsterdam, 15 years before, we had shared ecstatic experiences of our first meditations. Each of us understood the other's experience as if it was our own. She had comforted me when I left my Jürgen. She had given me furniture when I arrived in America. She had explained how to use greenback sponges to clean houses when I started my first job. She had gently reflected that I could show more love to my parents when they called rather than sounding cold and hard. And she was one of two or three people in the whole Community who had found the energy to woo my shy children into a relationship. And now I felt my shoulder warm and wet from her crying.

"I can't stand it anymore," she was saying. "Something has changed. Andrew is not teaching love now. He wants something else from us." It was the first time I had ever heard her express a doubt in the integrity of the Community, and now she was doubting Andrew himself. Sometimes people new to the Community questioned what was going on, but the rest of us had learned that thoughts such as these were the work of the ego trying to swerve us from the true path. We never voiced thoughts that questioned the integrity of the Community or of Andrew.

"What is this change?" I asked.

"Ever since he started talking about impersonal enlightenment, I don't know why, but the love isn't there anymore. It's as if he has shifted directions."

I agreed with her, remembering Heidi's miserable treatment in the women's meeting. "But," I said, "I trust Andrew. Maybe he doesn't know what is going on. Maybe the change comes from people closer to him than we are." I knew that Victoria had always been deeply trusting of Andrew.

"I used to think that too," she said. "I used to think that he just believes what people tell him and he never has the whole picture, but now I am not so sure." Then she added, "It's so good that you are a formal student. At least now someone can set about changing things. Don't let them get to you."

"Don't worry," I said. "I am strong." But it was not a hard strength.

More importantly, I felt empathy for these two suffering women. In another few months, that empathy would be replaced with an acceptance of collateral damage and a strange unspoken assumption that "care" was reserved for Andrew and those closest to him. Women in this situation, even my personal friend Victoria, would become less than nothing.

We started carrying boxes downstairs to her car. I was shocked by the extreme fear that I had seen in Heidi and now Victoria, but I wondered whether Andrew had understood something about them which would lead him to be so severe. Then I remembered Andrew's conversations with me in his office. I had felt, or thought I felt, his genuine puzzlement about how best to help people change. Seeing two students in such pain did not make sense to me.

Chapter 9

Rishikesh—Silence and Solitude

Day 1

On a warm February morning, the bus pulled up outside a bustling café in the sacred city of Rishikesh, for centuries a pilgrimage site and center for saints, sages, and gurus. I had travelled alone to Andrew's annual three-week retreat in India. Groups of Europeans in silk shawls were scattered among the Indians, drinking chai at rough-hewn wooden benches. Not tourists, exactly, but seekers, drawn by one or another of the Western or Eastern gurus offering retreats in this holy town on the Ganges. Hopeful bead merchants, chai sellers, and beggars threaded their way through the tables.

I found a phone booth where I spoke briefly to Jessica and left a message for Becky, telling them I had arrived.

I had endured the sensual onslaught at Delhi airport. The sweet, rich smell of sugar, sweat and urban earth; the bewildering bustle and noise; and the beggars who pulled at my clothes. I had at first spurned the nasty trays of sickly looking candy covered in flies, and turned down the offers of sweet tea. I had battled an opportunistic youngster who had taken my shoe hostage, cleaned it, and insisted that I pay him an outrageous sum of money. His once-eager face had contorted into a snarl as he threw the shoe onto the ground and vanished into the crowd. I had jostled my way through a dozen men harrying me for attention, beckoning me towards rickshaws, taxis, and scooters.

I stayed overnight in a hotel that was grimy all the way up to the high ceilings. The sheets were brown on both sides. The squat toilet in the bedroom was caked in dirt. I rolled my pant legs high and took care to touch no part of it. Light bulb wires hung empty from the ceiling. The door to my room didn't have a catch and swung perpetually open to the hallway where two Indians slept stretched across the entrance to my room. I climbed over their sleeping bodies to ask the receptionist for a wakeup call, but he was already asleep under the counter with six or seven other men. I lay down on the bed, nervously clutching my purse in one hand and pepper spray in the other.

At 3:00am, I walked to the station, which was the bedroom of 300 homeless people. One man briefly roused himself to shout at me as my shawl brushed his face. The people who were awake stared at me in disbelief. In my haste, I had taken the wrong train—a small, slow, local one which lurched to a stop at every village in the dusty, rural, populous landscape. I sank into my role within this desperate and beautiful drama of life and death acted out in public view. Mile after mile of cultivated crops. Young men tending lumbering buffalo with heads hanging low from the weight of their horns. Groups of women in bright blue saris walking the dusty tracks hauling water and wood. Women with hammers breaking rocks and carrying bricks on their heads.

Peddlers squeezed through the packed corridors, bringing hot spiced tea and sweetmeats made of boiled milk and cardamom. I finished my last PowerBar; then, abandoning the rules for staying healthy, bought tiny clay cups of tea like everyone else and drank the sweet liquid of fresh sugar cane. I had given up my intention never to touch the layers of grime built up on the wooden pallet train seats. I leaned comfortably against the dirt obscuring the light from the window. As the train trundled slowly into the night, I dozed off, comfortably sharing a pallet with half a dozen people.

Darkness faded early. The night mist lifted and the sun warned of coming heat. The train paused at a station. For 11 hours, I witnessed the station people's private lives. Slowly, as I sat on the wooden pallet in the third class train carriage, my horror turned to appreciation and my fear to openness. I glimpsed out the window the easy, perfect movement of wiry men in polyester pants carrying heavy baskets on their shoulders towards the train. Women carried loaded baskets on their heads with stately grace. Night and day, folds of cloth like shrouds encased bundled figures lying on the platform. Children ran beside the train, their upturned faces full of eagerness, smiling in excitement and in random hope.

I was no one special. As I looked out the window of the train I realized that this long journey and this great country had eased away my desire for control. The train was no longer a mass of threatening chaos but a finely woven, thousand-year-old, orderly tapestry of human patterns. It was perfect that every passerby and homeless family had their place on the platform. I stopped fighting. I felt as comfortable and secure as if India had been my home for a thousand years already and I was just revisiting an ancient scene from my past.

I changed trains several times and eventually arrived in Rishikesh by bus. I hired a rickshaw when I arrived at the station. The driver's bulky, practiced calves showed that he had enough to eat. After his first couple of strenuous pedals, the momentum of the bike picked up, and we rapidly left the train station behind. As we approached the retreat, I cast my mind back over the many retreats I had attended with Andrew. Amsterdam, Rome, Switzerland, Bodhgaya, Boulder, London. This was my first silent retreat. Having loved the solitude of the Utah desert, I looked forward to hours of blissful meditation, when I would not have to worry about making mistakes relating to other people.

The air smelled fresher here, 1000 feet up. I ascended the steps between tall stone pillars into the courtyard of the ashram. The dirt yard was tidy, but the flowerbeds were untended, the blooms sparse. Everything was prepared to accommodate 250 students from all over the world. The huge rented space was populated on one side by many small buildings where students would sleep. I recognized that the high awning of the meditation tent was new, and was already prepared with colorful cushions for tonight's teachings. I knew that many of Andrew's students would have been here for weeks, even months, setting up water purifying systems, organizing the kitchen, hiring help, putting up tents, cleaning toilets, and picking up trash.

The methods Andrew used to help us change had evolved since the days in Totnes more than a decade ago. They now included meditation, formal talks by Andrew, question and answer sessions, discussion groups, and readings. During the retreats, the organization of hundreds of people was meticulous. Nearly 200 new and lay students would attend the teachings in the big open space and be divided into teams to help with the cooking and cleaning. The novice students would help with the organization and have their own group meetings. The formal students, myself included, had our own silent retreat. I do not know what retreat was offered to the senior and committed students.

Dozens of students, chattering loudly, gathered around the walled enclave, their faces eager and intense. I cast around for friends from Europe whom I had not seen for years. I noticed the absence of many faces. A group of women who were once formal or senior students in the Community were not in the courtyard. They had once been labeled "The No Women." Segregated, they would meet for many hours a day in hopes of mustering "a deeper intention to be free." They were under pressure to "come through." I did not know where they were, nor that they had been profoundly mistreated at previous retreats. Nonetheless, I felt sorry for them. I hid the sympathy in case someone said, "Are you leaving yourself space to pull yourself back?" Indeed, secretly I knew that at any moment I might fail to find the resources to live this life. I knew from experience that each time we became complacent, we stopped leaning forward into the unknown and lost the edge. I still believed that Andrew supported us to live with confidence on the knife edge.

This year, 60 formal students from centers around the world, including myself, would be in silence except for chanting and conversation with Andrew. We would slip off our shoes and file silently up steep stone steps into the small loft, where, for ten hours a day, we would sit motionless. The room was empty: exposed wooden rafters above us, bare walls beside us, light woolen rugs beneath us. I placed my cushion three rows from the front, no longer worried about whether my knees would hurt. Yet at the back of my mind was the nagging fear that around Andrew the unexpected often happened. Like a mantra to ward off a lurking fear, I told myself, *I must face everything and avoid nothing.*

Andrew arrived and moved silently, without scanning us, to the embroidered cushion at the front. His black hair, cut shorter than usual, revealed a drawn look on his face. I thought back to the early days when he looked vulnerable and kind. His Italian silk shirt and Western pants were perfectly ironed as usual. He once said that, if he dressed impeccably, anyone seeing a problem with him would find it was their own problem, not his. I wondered at the long painful years I had spent trying to regain confidence after my move to California. I relished the good feeling now of being one of his formal students.

Without a word, Andrew closed his eyes. I closed mine and felt effortless love for this place. I retreated to a state where all felt fuzzy and warm, and thought fell aside, revealing enormous space. Suddenly our Master said, "I want you to meditate with your eyes open for the rest of the retreat." I thought of him as "Master" now; even the word "guru" had lost its alien ring. Annoyed, deprived of my residence of easy bliss, I felt anger building inside. I had taken time off work, spent a lot of money, and travelled halfway round the world to be here. I didn't even know how to meditate with my eyes open. I suspected that it would not feel blissful.

My focus fell lightly on Lori's sitting back, shawl wrapped

around her shoulders, motionless in my field of view. I noticed her haircut; so inferior to my hairdresser Miguel's deft hand on my head. What a relief it was to know that for three weeks it made no difference at all whether I had this superior thought or not. I would do no damage. I remembered Lori's self-righteous tone last year when she said I was a parasite on the Community because I talked so little. Her hips were wider now than when she was working out regularly; they solidly spread onto the small cushion supporting her pear-shaped trunk. I noticed in myself a mixture of satisfaction and sadness at her growing bulk. But her complex personality and my response to it fell away and became irrelevant. The importance of what she did or did not do became a distant fiction in my head. I watched as her neck softened and relaxed, becoming a gentle blur of color and pattern, form and space no longer a shawl, no longer Lori, no longer a person, nothing that I recognized. I was entranced by the scene. *Only this matters. Only what is. And I have been so mistaken about that. Does my past interpretation of Lori have anything at all to do with what is real?*

"Anyone have anything to say?" my longtime Master asked without a smile, without any emotion that I could identify.

"Yes," I said. "When you asked us to open our eyes, at first I felt a sense of loss because the bliss that I had when my eyes were shut had gone. I resented that my experience was very average. I wasn't particularly happy. Then I began to just see what was in the room in a very ordinary, simple way. Ordinary things began to be transformed into something extraordinary. It was as if I started to see things not with my old ideas but in a new way. It's so simple; it's like going through the mundane into something beautiful."

I suspected that what I had said was deeper than what anyone else around here had realized so early in the retreat. I wrapped myself up in the knowledge that, unlike the others, I was easily in touch with truth. I saw a flicker of my desires over the years.

"If you're going to have an experience like that, you're going to have to start living it," Andrew said.

"Yes, I know," I replied a little too quickly, meeting the shining blackness in his eyes without flinching. I had no idea if he really was severe or if I had projected severity. I had no idea whether my response was arrogant or whether I imagined that, too. Since I had become a formal student my Master had been asking me to leave behind the bliss that came so easily to me. Not because there was anything wrong with it, but because my interest in it was a distraction from being present and in touch with other people. "It's not about experience," he would say. Anything profoundly understood made no sense to him unless he saw the result in the way we interacted with other people.

I wondered at this revelation. I knew that I had understood something crucial, but did I distance myself from Andrew in the way that I thought about it? Had I made that, too, into a clever conclusion? I wondered if I could distinguish insight from delight at having been insightful.

Some people asked about writing diaries during the retreat.

Our Master considered the idea.

I said, "I find writing to be very helpful in allowing me to let go of experiences. Could I please write too?"

Master said, "Definitely not **you**, Marlowe. I didn't mean you." My Master forbade me to write anything so that I could learn to just "be."

But in deep down disobedience, I decided to memorize every detail of the day so that I could write about it later. Then, framed in the doorway on his way out of the loft, Master turned and said—it seemed as if to me, **"For the next three weeks, hold on to nothing. Don't try to work anything out."**

And I held on to these blessed words as my main guidance for the next three weeks, even when things got tough.

Day 2

We got up at 5:30. In our spacious stone bungalow, my roommate Jody and I carefully boiled water to clean our teeth but did not let the toothbrush touch the pitted concrete sink for fear of parasites. The only thing I knew about Jody was that she was Australian, because I overheard her voice in the dinner line on the first evening. After our first day of silence, I trusted her. At first I used mime to establish permission to borrow her nail file. She asked me for a candle when hers went out. I asked her for the loan of her insect repellent. But soon, without glance, hesitation, or permission, we shared our handful of possessions.

I felt more grounded if I did something physical, so today and every day I did 100 push-ups on the cold concrete floor. Then, wrapped in a thick woolen blanket to ward off the morning chill, I walked slowly in darkness, through the gardens, to the loft. Each day was to be the same. One hour meditation, breakfast, chanting, meditation, chanting, meditation, lunch, meeting with Andrew, meditation, chanting, meditation, chanting, dinner, chanting, meditation. The routine seemed so natural. I had a growing sense that I could actually decide to "Let everything be as it is." I was excited to find the tools of the teachings had become concrete and usable. Andrew had given me everything I needed in order to be free. But then the second I thought, "See! This is wonderful, what I have," the joy was gone and I felt empty-handed, reaching for something.

At meeting time, I saw that not everyone was thriving. A small woman with gray hair was sitting in front of me, and I was aware that she was shifting in her seat and trying to avoid a direct line between herself and Andrew. He cast his eye among the students and asked, "Where is Elaine?" She shifted her seat, unable to prolong concealment. I don't remember Andrew's exact words, but I remember the uncompromising harshness in his voice. He berated her for her weakness and lack of spirit. He challenged her sincerity. He accused her of undermining her peers. I guessed that she had done something terribly wrong before this meeting and wondered what it could have been for her to deserve such public humiliation. She trembled. She lost energy like a tulip flower, drained of life force, beyond the possibility of rehydrating before the petals fall. I was sure she would not be able to take any more. Stunned at the cruelty in Andrew's voice, I feared for her. But, since trying to defend Heidi from the formal women, I had learned that I was powerless to change the course of action. Shortly, we would file out of the loft into the warm night, and Elaine would vanish into the darkness and be gone in a minute. No one would stand up for her.

In pain at her pain, I wanted to help, but I was afraid. I scrawled on a piece of paper, "My support and care go with you. I am here if you need anything." Too little to be of any use. She took the note and was gone.

I never saw her again.

Day 3

On the first morning, there was tea at 5:30, before meditation. This morning there was no tea. I stood dejected by the empty tea urn. Food and drink became an obsession. As soon as one meal was over, I started to think about the flavors and textures of the next.

I thought briefly about Elaine, distraught and shocked. I told myself it was not my place to interfere. I had months ago lost the conscience that might once have spurred me to action.

With my shawl wrapped tightly around me, I fell in line with others walking in a silent stream towards the steps that led to the loft. I looked for a place to put my cushion. I paused by Kimberley, but felt the history of sexual abuse that ran through her cells and feared that if I sat beside her it would run through my cells too. Then I felt her soft, vulnerable sistership. I sat cross-legged close beside her in the front row and secretly sent her strength.

The first chant of the day began: "What was your relationship to thought, before you believed there was a problem?" I tried to figure out what it meant. What are the various possible relationships to thought? *Do I have a relationship to thought? Or do I just think? And "before" what? What kind of problem?*

"What was your relationship to thought, before you believed there was a problem?"

I weakened, hearing only the rhythm of the chant, not the words. The blissful void begin to reclaim me; I could get there now without shutting my eyes.

"What was your relationship to thought, before you believed there was a problem?"

With an effort, I brought my attention back to the voices beside me. Every voice formed a harmony with every other. Loud and soft, high and low, male and female, the voices molded into a single beautiful prayer. The meaning of the words floated through the sound. *I have no relationship to thought. There is No problem. There never was a problem.* The question disappeared. There was no question.

We chanted for an hour. At lunchtime, we sat at the rows of benches in the dining area. The high roof covered us just enough to keep off the worst of the thunderstorms. The cook threw sticks at the monkeys tearing along the open-air kitchen walls. I watched the senior student Stephanie out of the corner of my eye, carrying her lunch tray between the benches of students. She sat beside me and with exquisite care poured milk into her tea. Reading her mind, I felt her awe of me and her love and her suspicion because I was sometimes a wild card. I wondered whether Andrew had asked her to keep an eye on me, but I dismissed this thought as paranoia. I noticed my lack of humility. I felt tearful because I wanted to be vulnerable with everyone here, but without language I had no distraction from my loneliness.

I assumed that being in silence also meant making no eye

contact. I longed to raise my eyes to find out what certain people thought about me, to check for affirmation and to give the same. The thoughts that ran in my head were large and very clear because all action and reaction were denied. The wheels of desire and aversion turned freely, uselessly, in my brain, disconnected from action. The games of expectation and praise, encouragement and criticism were on hold—except with Andrew.

We met with him each day. I wanted to thank him, to share with him what I was seeing.

"Anyone got anything to say?"

I raised my hand.

"No, not you, Marlowe."

I felt stung and dazed, unable to find a meaning in his rejection. I knew that Andrew had extraordinary, perhaps omniscient, powers of insight. I was sure that if change came from the deepest part of me, Andrew would know it and make it welcome.

Day 4

The cold morning air made a beautiful complement to the stillness.

Breakfast was my favorite meal of the day: idli and sambal. I relished the tang of spicy curry on each bite of bland semolina patty. I sought out the sweet raisins in the sauce and dipped them in the sour yogurt. I was intimately aware of taste, texture. How could every search amount just to this? I wondered. *So this is truth, nothing more? Nothing that one could ever do could ever make any difference.*

I was certain that freedom meant so much, and that I played such an important part, but now I saw that I didn't mean anything and that it didn't even care whether I existed. The universe was unaffected by my ignorance or my understanding. *So God does not exist. But there is nothing lacking.*

Andrew once again ignored my upstretched arm. His lack of

interest hurt, too; but it inspired me to trust that he had given me everything I needed. I reminded myself a hundred times a day to draw no conclusion.

Day 5

At lunchtime, I walked by the Ganges. I watched the face of a beggar who seemed so quiet. For a second, I envied her simplicity; then I saw her desperation as she caught my eye, her old twisted hands reaching for my pity. I shocked myself for feeling disgust rather than compassion. Children in rags clustered around a tiny saucepan on a small stove. A girl of about ten sat motionless on a piece of sackcloth. She neither moved nor talked, perhaps at peace, perhaps hungry to the point of lethargy. I was shocked by her acceptance. I thought of Becky and Jessica. I knew they were well taken care of in Boston and each day they had the structure of school to support them. Still, I wished they could witness this little girl's silence.

Once again, our Master came he but didn't acknowledge me when I raised my hand. I looked for minute nuances of effect in him as clues about my progress. I focused on no face but Andrew's; met no eyes but his.

Day 6

I was becoming aware of Jody's every slightest movement. If she was cold at night, I knew by the way she held the blanket; if she was afraid, I knew by her breathing. I brought her food and boiled water when she got sick. The sweet sensitivity of silence brought us close. I felt nothing was missing between us.

On my way to the loft I noticed a group of women walking silently towards the Ganges: the "No Women." I saw Ziggy, who had cared for my children when we lived together in Mill Valley. I feared taint.

Day 7

At lunchtime I walked down to the Ganges and lay on a warm rock. I lay spread-eagled, face down on the granite, feet trailing into the sacred water. I felt that my first obligation was to this rock, my second to Andrew: tiny seeds of independence from Andrew lay dormant within me. Then, standing with my feet in the river, I dipped my hand into the sacred Ganges and released into it everything that stood in the way of freedom. I let the water flowing through my fingers take my children away. I promised that I would never again try to control them or mold them to be the way I wanted. With another handful, I relinquished ownership of my career, which made me feel so powerful. My longing for a relationship loosened its grip and flowed of its own accord downstream. Then the hardest release of all for me: money. There was a lump in my chest and hesitation, and then I let go of my need for more money to ward off my constant fear of not having enough to sustain my life with my children in this Community.

We met with dear Master again. I loved him so much, all my cells full to bursting, all my cells exploding with energy; I wanted nothing, needed nothing, sought nothing beyond this second here with Andrew. I was so excited and unable to control my excitement. My hand shot up. He looked the other way. I saw that I was too eager, arrogant; maybe if I was more subdued, he would talk to me.

Day 8

My senses were amplified tenfold. I lay on my pallet escaping the midday heat and recognized surrender in Jody's concentration as she sat on the side of her bed, her thigh turned to bring her foot high, filing her toenails.

In the afternoon, as usual, we met and waited for my beloved Master. I waited in eager anticipation, but he didn't come today.

At night, I lay on my pallet and began another night of

translucent sleep, not awake, nor unconscious. I did not seek sleep nor did I avoid it. Continuing meditation throughout the night left me wide-awake and burning with energy.

My teacher's words lay in my heart like jewels of truth: "The fire of your heart must burn brightly. That fire will give you all the energy, intention, and strength of character to bear with, understand, and ultimately see through your own mind. That fire will be your meditation and in that fire your ignorance, which is all your wrong ideas, will burn."

Burn. I was burning.

Day 9

There was coffee: fantastic, rich, hot coffee. At meditation, my longtime companions, packed so close together in the loft, receded as if they were a long way off, as if I were viewing the scene from thousands of miles away. I saw these sincere, reverent people, trying so hard to understand. They were earnestly focused, but on the wrong goddamn thing! *How ridiculous!* I thought. *Freedom is so simple!* I saw my Master skillfully leading people towards the light, towards seeing, away from mere cognitive knowing. He encouraged their glimpses; he affirmed their tastes of honeydew surrender—but not mine.

Our chanting ended. I wanted to laugh at the farce before my eyes. Running through the throng of students with their somber, downward-looking faces, I wanted to yell, "Stop! You are already free. You need look no more!" I tore down the dusty path, lined with stunted roses, past the women peddling postcards and the crowd around the man with the dancing cobra. I trusted that I was becoming my own guide; and Andrew, my internal guru, was leading me to understanding. I ran across the boulders to the water's edge, and then I laughed and laughed and laughed because it was all ridiculous.

Day 10

After lunch, I picked my way through the human excrement on the steps beside the Ganges and joined the beggars on the overhang of concrete beneath the road. I saw the nest of the holy man and longed to surrender, like him, to the pavement. I could lie down here beside him and never get up. What motive could there be to do anything else?

There is no more to arrive at, I thought. *Nothing matters or could ever have mattered. There is nothing to do, no becoming, no possibility of gain, no conception of more, or less, no conception of knowing, only "seeing." The curse of all time, the fall from grace is wanting to "have," wanting to "know," wanting to "be."*

So simple. But floating free beyond time, I knew I could never say, "I am free!" *I can only reach forever towards the people around me.*

Day 11

The chants carried me until thought vanished and all I could feel was love, like a cloud of light, sparing me from pain. For a while I was afraid of death. I asked myself why. The answer came, *It's only fear of not being you anymore,* and silently I laughed.

I was travelling inwards towards something essential and incontrovertible beyond time and space. I became less and less interested in anything physical around me. I had let go of perception, let go of the foreign sounds around me, let go of the feel of the ground under my legs, let go of the smell of the damp rugs under me, as if I were dying. Sensory deprivation had left me in touch with God but not with my body. I surrendered to death, if it should care to take me.

Day 12

For an hour before we went to bed we chanted, "Be like a strong tree that cannot be moved." I believed that my Master had given us these words to help us survive the night sane.

I woke up in the night terrified by the challenge to see myself more clearly. *See my understanding! I am special! I know better than my Master. I don't need him!*

In defiance of this voice, I yelled out in my mind, *Okay, ignorance. You want to fight? Let's have whatever you've got. I am ready!*

I am cruel, it said.

Let that be as it is, I replied.

I don't care about any living thing, it said...

Let that be as it is, I replied.

I care only about my own advantage. I revere no one and nothing. I manipulate and control. I hate myself and everyone, it said.

Let that be as it is, I replied. I thought, *Maybe there is no end to what I have to see.* I saw that I was Hitler; I was Gandhi; with the same instincts and the same mind; I was capable of the same actions.

Okay, I said to God, *I am beginning to see what I am. Please stop now. Have I seen enough now? Surely this is enough.*

But God seemed to say, *No, keep on going. See what else there is. Maybe there is more.*

In Satsang I raised my hand, but there was no sign that Andrew had seen me. I interpreted his message to mean that I did not need him. I took his silence as permission to find out for myself whatever more there was.

Day 15

"How are you?" Jody asked me on our note pad.

"The diarrhea is worse and the meditation keeps getting more and more incredible," I replied.

As I lay for two days motionless on my pallet, nothing interfered with the flow of meditation. I waited for the sickness to go away, drinking the boiled water Jody brought each time she returned from meditation. On the third day, I ate some of the semolina patties she had saved from breakfast.

Day 17

I made it to the loft for afternoon meditation just in time to see my Master.

"Who has anything to tell me today?" he asked.

In the back of the room, I raised my hand tentatively. Andrew looked at me and said gently, "Not yet."

Had I imagined the gentleness?

I thanked Andrew internally for the image of the strong tree he had mentioned to us once. It gave me courage in my silence when my thoughts were out of control, when I felt I could not stand any more of the Hell of my own mind. Then my mind became totally quiet, and that too was unbearable. I thought, *Maybe I must bear eternal tranquility, unbearable serenity. But... no more intensity or turmoil? Perhaps that would be the worst Hell of all.*

I let myself be steadied by Jody's steady, sure in-breath beside me. I listened for her steady, full out-breath and was calmed.

Day 18

I was wakened in the middle of the night by paralyzing terror. I felt pressured to choose between clinical madness and giving up my life to serve people! *"Go crazy or give to humanity, choose **now**,"* I was told.

"But I am afraid," I said. *"Why do I have to give everything?"*

"Because you have received too much. You have to give for your daughters, for Elaine, for all the women."

"OK, I'll do it. I'll give."

It felt shockingly simple. It fell on my shoulders to understand the cause of human suffering and be unable to stand by. It was the burden of knowing that people only need to turn their heads to change the world.

Day 19

Dearest Beloved Master,
I thank You for being an absolute teacher.

I thank You for holding my attention in emptiness.

I thank You for the companions whose strength give me courage every day.

I thank You for not letting me talk or write.

I thank You for the perfection of your instructions, which save my life a hundred times a day.

I thank You for not letting me stop short.

I thank You for holding me in bliss and demanding from me still.

MARLOWE

Day 20

At breakfast, monkeys leapt from the trees, ran along the compound wall, and tried to make it to the kitchens, but the cooks clattered their pans and dodged their snapping teeth. That was the only action all day.

We met again with our Beloved Master. For the first time, I did not raise my hand. I had nothing to say.

I was deeply relaxed as I walked through the gate and took in the sight of hundreds of happy students, who had been on their separate retreats for the last weeks. I joined the other formal students from Boston. They asked whether I would attend the celebrations at the lay students' house.

I replied, "I didn't know about it. Where is it?"

"Typical!" Shirley said. "How come we know about it and you don't have a clue?" She and Justice exchanged glances.

Taken aback, I was not ready when Justice added, "When you became a formal student, we gave you plenty of time to acclimatize."

Shirley continued, "No one put any pressure on you. But we are going to expect more of you now."

I was dismayed to recognize in my mind the same old fears of rejection, the same tongue-tied response established in the playground when I was seven. In the back seat of our rickshaw our hips pressed tightly together with each pothole. I doubted I was supposed to enjoy this first physical touch in three weeks. My position close to the bottom in the pecking order seemed to be set in stone.

On return to Boston, I walked a knife edge between trusting my intuition and struggling once again to appear confident in the face of deteriorating faith in my ability to connect. My journals from that time are packed with descriptions of morbid attempts to take on my faults: my superiority, victim mentality, resistance to renunciation, self-absorption, lack of surrender to the other women, and selfishness. While I have no doubt that I needed to see these things in myself, the effect of institution-alized negative feedback in meetings, in my house, and at Foxhollow appeared to be counterproductive. The rift between my internal experience and my ability to express it deepened.

Chapter 10

The Lake

Andrew believed that women's conditioning contained something particularly deep-rooted and destructive. He challenged the commonly held belief that women have the inside track on spirituality. In fact, he said that women have a harder time than men facing their own conditioning and being intimate with others. He had singled us out for radical treatment, so we were desperate to win his approval and prove our commitment.

Most of us long-term women students who lived in Massachusetts were sitting naked in the sauna in the basement of Foxhollow, seeking a response to the latest of many crises. This time it was Ashley, one of Andrew's students, who had caused him outrage and offense by her request to reduce her meditation practice. I hadn't seen it happen, but I was here now at the meeting.

Shirley, our self-appointed leader, sat squarely on the edge of the wooden pallet, and said with authority, "Our Master offers you the gift of 'more' and you kick him in the teeth!"

Ashley's thin shoulders caved in, constricting her heart. Her breath barely audible, she whispered, "I am sorry. I've let all of you down."

I admired Shirley. I wondered why I felt self-conscious about a roll or two around my midriff while she apparently did not mind her six or seven fulsome folds. She was saying, "I don't understand what made you respond like that. How could you do it?"

Ashley's face was drawn. Sweat ran down her cheeks. "I was just so tired; I could see no way of doing any more."

"But the way you said it was aggressive," Shirley pointed out. "And it was humiliating for all of us when Andrew pinned your pathetically apologetic letter on the wall for everyone to laugh at."

I had felt close to Ashley when she was my roommate, but in the climate of the Community, personal attachments were a liability. I could see no way of articulating my discomfort about what was going on without looking as if I sympathized with Ashley, so I said nothing in what had become routine betrayal. I shifted on the hard bench, in search of a less awkward way to arrange my limbs. I noticed Erica's grace, which belied the strength acquired through years of practice. I uncrossed my legs and clutched the slats with my hands, then tried spreading them casually across the backrest behind me. Doing so, I accidentally touched the warm slippery back of Missy, to my right. Before recoiling, I registered that it had been months since I had touched anyone except my children.

Ashley was close to tears. She looked so small. Her curly hair had flattened to her head with sweat, and she had flinched into the corner farthest from Shirley. "Perhaps I'm missing something," she said, "but the pain in my back after three hours of sitting is too much. I don't think I can do it."

Shirley, sweat streaming down her shaven head, said, "I can't believe your lack of gratitude."

"I'm sorry," Ashley repeated.

I considered putting my arms around her and saying, "It's okay, breathe with me. We can get through this." But the other voice in my head said, "Better to keep your distance. She's going down. How could that alliance serve you?"

Betsy chimed in, "Don't keep saying 'sorry.' No one believes you."

"Why didn't you talk to one of us about it?" Shirley asked.

Missy, who had been quiet until now, said gently, "I know how you feel, Ashley. It always feels like it's too much. But every one of us, you included, has found that when we make the space for it, there is always a way to do more." She then observed, almost to herself, "I am not sure we are thinking about this the right way. This time it was Ashley, but can any one of us say we've been totally giving to our Master?" She added, "Any of us could have responded this same way. So perhaps we have to look at it as our shortcoming, not just Ashley's."

Several people agreed. I sighed with relief at Missy's clarity and kindness, and wished I could find such words myself. For a moment, there was a sense of safety in the sauna.

Erica said, "We've all had those thoughts, but the thoughts don't matter, it's the actions that count."

Someone else suggested, "Why don't we all do something to acknowledge our woman's weakness?"

Ashley suggested, "What about flowers and a card?"

Erica replied, "We've done that so many times before."

"We need a response to our Master that would really stretch us all," I added.

"Yes," said Shirley. "Something that will show him that, in spite of our resistance, we are going to change, we are ready to take on the ego and fight for freedom." We clung to the clichés of revolution for safety...

"What about an extra-long practice? A double practice?" suggested Ashley, a touch of pink returning to her freckled face.

"That would be appropriate," said Missy.

I said, "How about prostrations?" It was something I could succeed at. I felt so relieved to be contributing to the process that I forgot for a moment about where to put my body.

"Prostrations in the lake?" Betsy suggested.

"You mean full immersion?" asked Missy.

"Yes!" Betsy started from her seat as if to stand up.

"It's nearly November, and this is the Berkshires! No one has been in the lake for over a month. It's too cold now," said Missy.

"I will do it, if everyone is behind it," Ashley said.

No one said anything. No one disagreed. The group collectively offered their Guru this gesture of atonement for women's conditioning. In a day or two I heard, third-hand, that Andrew had accepted our offer.

This was the day we would meet our commitment. Sober, but in good spirits, 25 women wearing bathing suits or tracksuits entered the lake and stood waist-deep in the water. In ragged chorus we cried out:

"Face everything and avoid nothing!"

The first downward plunge was so cold that my whole body gasped with shock. As I plunged, the noise of gurgling, rushing water disoriented me and drowned the other voices.

Each time we raised our arms out of the water reaching towards the sky, we chanted: "Face everything!"

Each time we threw ourselves beneath the water in prostration to God we chanted: "And avoid nothing!"

At first I dreaded going under the water, and I dreaded even more coming out into the biting wind. I was distraught with the pain of cold and the fear of worsening pain in the coming hour. *This mad scheme wasn't my idea,* I thought. *Why did I let it happen? It wasn't even my mistake! Isn't there another way than this? This is madness. Even if we survive, what is the point?*

"Face everything and avoid nothing!"

I found that being under the water was a relief, and hitting the air was more chilling than going under. I gave up rushing to make the plunge go faster. Gradually we began to rise out of the water in unison. As we did, we cried out together and plunged again and rose out together.

"Face everything and avoid nothing!"

Resolution took hold inside me. *I have stamina. When it comes to physical endurance I'm tougher than most. I know the power of my own intention.*

"Face everything and avoid nothing!"

The relentless rhythm continued. Convulsive shaking took my jaw, my arms, my legs. My skull seemed to shrink, as if my head were drying up inside. I told myself, *Give it all I've got. I'll hang in here as long as I can.*

I had on only a pair of shorts; my legs went numb. *Fear is the problem*, I told myself. *I have to let go of it or it will control me. This is my chance to overcome fear.*

I thought about getting out, but no one else got out. My whole body felt numb. My head felt numb. I was afraid I would break my teeth or freeze my brain. *Surely this is more than enough to satisfy the most grueling master*, I thought. *Did Andrew really know we were going to do this? How could he let us? Doesn't he care if we die?* But my heart replied, *Don't be unfair. He didn't ask us to do this; we offered it to him.*

On the bank there was a person watching, but no cars to convey us to the house.

After 30 minutes, first one, then two of us, left the water. Four more of us collapsed and were carried out. Some staggered back to the houses; some were carried.

"Face everything and avoid nothing!" the rest of us chanted, plunging under yet again.

I can't go on, I said to myself. *Seven of us have already left; I'll be in the middle of the pack if I get out now.*

"Face everything and avoid nothing!"

But I've been on the edge of this group all along, I considered. *I'm not really part of what's going on here. But no! I have to prove that I can live this life. I need to gain confidence in this group, or I will be thrown out. This is my chance to break the pattern.*

"Face everything and avoid nothing!"

We'd been in the water 45 minutes. I noticed that I had drifted to one side of the group. I longed to be in the middle. Part of me grieved. *How my heart aches because they have never accepted me! I have never found a heart response from these women who are supposed to be my sisters in love. My heart is bursting to know them, to share with them, but I can't even find the courage to plunge into the water in the midst of them! If I could plunge a few more times, perhaps I would earn their respect. Then they would welcome me.* And another part of me thought, *Fool! Remember the teachings! You are isolated of your own volition. You are not spurned; you just believe you are different!*

"Face everything and avoid nothing!"

But these women are closer to God than I am, I chided myself. *Of course their resolution is greater than mine. Given where they are and where I am, naturally I come out under par, in the water or out of it. It is not my place to thrive or triumph.*

And then I felt the cold inside my bones, and there was no sustaining more. I heard them chorus in bold union behind me, one body of prayer, as I staggered for the shore, feeling myself part of a familiar pattern.

I believe but do not remember that someone carried me to one of the women's houses. I do remember the hot bath that felt ice cold. I remember Kristin, too frail to go in the lake, bringing hot tea to the three of us in this bath. She held a cup for Ashley, who appeared to be asleep propped against the faucets. Then she lifted the cup to my lips because my hands were shaking so much that I could not hold it without scalding myself.

"I can't stop shaking, Kristin," I said.

"It's OK, it stops in a while," Kristin replied.

"But my head is numb. Could I have a remedy for shock?" *What are the long-term effects of exposure?* I wondered.

Like a rock she replied, "Hold steady." I looked into her eyes and saw no fear and believed her.

Kristin stayed for a while, then ran in and out of the bathroom during the next hour. In a while, I realized she was running in and out of many other bathrooms too, helping many women.

As my body started to regain sensation it began to hurt. I was afraid that I had damaged myself. I thought I might die. I was afraid we had gone too far this time. Kristin returned, saw my panic, and sternly said, "If you panic, you affect the others."

I was half-delirious. My other companion, Missy, was silent, but now and then she propped Ashley upright by the shoulders when she slumped over. I began to laugh a crazy laugh at the discordance between the real world—the little village of Lenox down the road—and this situation—so beyond the norm that it made no sense. *How did I get here? I must be crazy. Does anyone know what's going on?*

Ashley was still slumped comatose against the wall. I thought she might be drifting in and out of consciousness. Missy and I prodded her to see if she could open her eyes.

"I think we should get her a doctor," I said, beginning to panic again. "This is not OK, she is not OK. She needs a doctor. Get a doctor!"

But Kristin had stronger nerves and overruled me. "She is OK, it's just the mind. You need to trust."

"I'm scared," I said. "I don't know what is going to happen."

"Everyone is fine," Kristin was steady. "You can choose to be strong."

I clung to her as the only available anchor. *She is right,* I thought.

Ashley was sleeping, the faucet digging into her back.

When I could stand, I joined 15 women in one of the bedrooms. I felt relieved that the ordeal was over and triumphant to have shared it with them. I wondered how many of us had made it through the whole hour, but I didn't want to ask. We leaned against the wall and sat on the three beds and the floor, wrapped in blankets, and began to question how we had reacted under pressure.

Betsy, sharp as always, asked Erica, "Why were you so solicitous to those who started to panic in the water?" I guessed she had made it, though I knew she suffered terribly from the cold.

"I thought I was helping," Erica replied. She was sitting on the floor, leaning against a bed covered with a cream-colored bedspread.

"Perhaps you could have encouraged them to stay in for the full hour, instead of helping them get out?" Betsy continued.

Justice asked, "Was it to support their strength or their

weakness?" Receiving no answer, she continued, "Was it to give you the freedom to cave in yourself, five minutes later?"

Missy rubbed her wet hair with a towel, "I think it is the same mechanism that we have seen in ourselves as women before. It is core to our condition that we want each other weak to gain credence for ourselves."

"What is the difference between the women who stayed in the whole hour and those who did not?" Shirley asked.

"What is there to learn about the power of intention?" Justice looked thoughtful now, her dark eyes turned upwards for a second.

Someone looked at me, "Marlowe, why did you feel you needed to get out before the hour was up?"

I sat now in the middle of the bed. I wanted to lie down, "I think I assumed that it was only a matter of *when* I gave up."

Justice asked, "What if you question whether yours was a valiant effort or cowardice?"

Betsy said, "Is it possible that we have more choice than we think we do, even about becoming delirious or unconscious?"

A woman whose name I did not know, with a shawl over her wet hair, asked me, "Why did you think it was OK to panic once you got into the hot bath?" *How*, I wondered, *did she get that information?*

I replied, "Perhaps I chose to let go because I thought it was over."

"It's never over; our actions still have an effect always," Betsy said.

Someone else asked me, "Do you think you could have chosen to behave differently even though you experienced sensation that was unfamiliar and emotions that were alarming?"

"Maybe. I don't know." My world turned on its head. *I thought I was saving my own life. Did I actually have a choice?*

There were only two groups now: those who had succeeded —

the predators—and those who had failed—the prey. Little by little, the predators teased out from the prey our common pattern of response to discomfort, which led to our decision to leave the water early. We had similar perceptions of ourselves as inherently inadequate. We all recognized the part choice played in the decision of every woman who had failed. In the mirror of their eyes I saw now not triumph, not even credit for effort, but stark failure. I came to see the difference between setting out knowing that I must succeed and setting out permitting myself to determine when I had had enough. Because I had taken the second view, I was doomed to failure.

Three days later, I heard about the message to us from Andrew. He wanted to know how it was possible that any one of us had not been successful. In response, those of us who failed knew that we had to return to the lake.

When the day arrived, I woke early in the morning, already in deep meditation. In my sleep and in my heart I had chanted, "Face everything and avoid nothing" for many hours. It was as if the chant were chanting me. I came to consciousness but made no decision to succeed because success had already been estab-lished. Nothing would stop me: no thought, nobody's opinion of me, no doubt of my own worthiness. No cold, no icy wind. I would die in the attempt if necessary. It wasn't that I was deter-mined. It was that there was no other possible outcome.

We walked down the stony trail towards the lake, carrying towels over our arms as if going to the beach. I told Erica of the time I ran a half marathon in 96 minutes; she told me of the time she walked 35 miles. Yet both of us knew that we would now need a different kind of resource. Aware that Ashley had fallen behind in silence, we hung back and lied to her that the weather was not as cold as last time.

That day we had no one to watch over us, no one to carry us home if we should fail or fall, no one to tell us when the hour was up. We set the alarm clock and stood it on a rock beside the choppy water, unaware that we would not hear it. We picked our way across the prickle of stones that lay between us and the bitter cold. Our feet sank into the ooze of mud as we moved out into the lake and we began.

"Face everything and avoid nothing!"

At first my teeth chattered, but then banging against each other. I wondered if they would crack. I revisited my first attempt, through the pain, familiar now, until the numbness travelled through my limbs. Plunging continuously head under, again, and again, and again. Back to the sensation of my skin tight against my skull and wondering at what point my brain would freeze. This time I knew that I would travel through the shock of cold beyond which the body was not supposed to go, and keep going through fear of death and ghastly doubt to whatever lay beyond.

I forgot about my body and watched Ashley and Erica give their hearts in search of humility. I felt intimately bonded with them. I set the intention of my breath to pour warmth and strength into their limbs. This joint physical challenge had shattered my sense of separation from them and built a warrior's resolution...

"Face everything and avoid nothing!"

All feeling left me; I felt no more pain. On the banks, the lovely, ragged alders turned their gaze on me, and I smiled with them. The horizon drew my focus. The faraway hills held me steady each time I lifted my head out of the water.

"Face everything and avoid nothing!"

The women were gone. The shore was gone. The clock was gone. All reason for being here was gone. I wanted nothing. I had no desire to leave that lake... Our chanting flowed.

"Face everything and avoid nothing!"

I lifted my hands in thanks to God and plunged through the water to my knees in wonder. I raised my hands in praise and bowed down in obedience. Chant and flow, chant and flow, finding truth in spite of, or even because of, the extreme cold.

I noticed the other women falter and struggle towards the shore. In a twisted expression of Andrew's fifth tenet, care for the whole, I shouted, "NO! We must not stop. This is all there is. Come back! Take my hands; squeeze tighter. Together we will not stagger!"

As a single unit, we raised into the air and plunged deep down into the swirling water. The rhythm continued.

"Face everything…"

Strength grew in our limbs. Our voices filled and our muscles freshened. We cried out across the lake.

"… avoid nothing!"

The roar of water drowned the alarm clock's bell. Far past the hour, we dimly recognized Kristin on the riverbank, who had been sent to look for us.

Afterwards, in the hot bath, I renounced the hysteria which had gripped me last time in the aftermath of physical shock. I held steady against the flood of emotions which a week ago had seemed so real. We three looked one another in the eye and knew we were doing what we needed to do. I disregarded the thought that I was not worthy of triumph over my own mind, and I watched my rising panic move off to one side. Even when numbness turned to pain and I wanted to sleep or dissociate, I did not decide that it was more than I could bear. *Erica and Ashley are here*, I reminded myself. *They need me to be with them. They do not need my fear.* We poured ginger tea for each other and wondered what we would eat for dinner when we stopped shaking long enough to hold a fork.

Chapter 11

Sheetrock and Steel

Franz Schubert said of the songs he wrote, "When I wished to sing of love, it turned to sorrow. And when I wished to sing of sorrow, it was transformed for me into love." (1839)

A dozen formal students, including me, lived in three houses in Boston. My children and I were placed with another single parent and her teenage boy. Our children were 14, 16 and 17. Each weekend, she and I left our children alone and drove three hours to Foxhollow. From Friday to Sunday we would become part of the larger Community, offering service (cooking, gardening, building) and attending meetings.

At first, becoming a formal student was wonderfully exhilarating. I felt honored to be given this rank after having been a lay student for so many years. The prostrations, meditation, push-ups, and immersion in the lake had helped build my inner strength and courage. However, it did not seem to carry over into the emotional courage I needed to be an active member of the group in Boston. I found it hard to fit in, and the intense scrutiny, the norm for formal students, was not helping. I am not sure to what extent Andrew and his students were trying to be helpful in exposing arrogance that I could not detect in myself, and to what extent they tried to pull me down, like a pack attacking the weakest member. I am sure that my drive for purity became overlaid by a drive to satisfy my peers and avoid Andrew's anger. My confidence waned and my capacity to trust my own judgment was eroding. Most significantly, like Heidi, the woman who left the formal Community shortly after I entered, I was growing confused about what I was supposed to do and how I was supposed to change.

I was unable to see the impact of my monastic life on my teenagers. Though I had once worried that my children would not be included among the other Community children, now they spent unsupervised weekends in a pack and I worried about what they would get up to. There were several Community houses with children in them and some of them could drive. They moved to some extent between the houses. I wanted to believe that the children would support each other and collectively care for each other. Sometimes I challenged the wisdom of leaving them alone, but the response was always that my priority should be on living the teachings.

Jessica was growing into a beautiful young woman. I knew that, before long, she would find it easy to make deeper connections with the boys her age and I also began to suspect that she might be experimenting with drugs. I heard that she sometimes drank until she passed out; even the other teenagers regarded her as lacking self-control. When I tried to bring it up with her, she answered in short responses that hid more than they revealed—the type of responses many parents of teens receive.

Becky remained unhappy at school and remedial support did not seem to improve her grades. Community teenagers gathered often for unsupervised drinking parties and Becky attended, but sat in silence throughout. She had taken the compulsory school abstinence program to heart and, for the time being, followed through on her commitment to forego all alcohol and drugs. She must have sat helplessly watching her sister get drunk.

Meanwhile, the messages I received from senior members of the Community indicated that I should show greater commitment to the Community and be careful not to fall behind the other students. Stretched thin and exhausted, I berated myself for not giving more. Finally, I met privately with Stephanie, the senior leader of the Boston group. Sitting cross-legged on a cushion in her office, I told her, "I am committed to living Andrew's teachings, and love this life, but I am overwhelmed. I work 40 hours a week in a demanding job; I commute 50 minutes each way; meditation and prostrations take three hours a day; I help cater the meals for 18 formal students each day; and go to meetings at least three times a week; and then on the weekends I travel with everyone else to Foxhollow for the weekend. I have almost no time for my children."

I paused, assuming that together we would brainstorm a solution. Outside, I heard the carpet being vacuumed by a lay student and the swishing of traffic on rain-soaked Mass Ave. The siren of a police car soared into earshot.

Stephanie said nothing. I searched for understanding in her gray eyes and found none. She sat precisely, her hands folded neatly in her lap.

"I don't think I can go on like this," I continued. I dropped my eyes, contemplating the humiliation of stepping down.

"We all feel the same," she said. "We all feel like it's too much all the time." When I looked up, I saw her gazing out the window, not at me. Stephanie had a child too. I wonder now whether she couldn't face me because she was experiencing the same emotions. Was she also feeling pushed over the edge?

"I want to pull my weight," I went on, recapturing her attention. "But I don't understand how there are enough hours in the day to do everything that is important. Can you help me?"

"Are you doing it?" she asked, her voice neutral, which in the circumstances felt cold.

"Kind of," I said. "But I am selling every part of my life short."

This was as close as I got to open defiance. At university, I had been one of six students leading 2000 others in rebellion against authoritarian professors, but in front of Stephanie I was unable to hold my ground.

"What happens if you drop the idea of what is possible?" she asked.

I replied, "I understand that ideas of limitation can be an

illusion. I have seen that I can go beyond expectation when I let go. It is true that I limit myself all the time. But..." I was cornered. I said nothing more. I stood up and left the office.

A few days later, I received a message to call the office at Foxhollow. When I did so, the person answering the phone read me a message from Andrew. It said, **"Marlowe, you are blowing it!"**

"Thank you," I said to the messenger. "Is there anything else?"

"No, that's it," he said. "Do you want me to read it again?"

"No, that's okay, I think I got it." I hung up.

Does Andrew know I'm cutting my practice? I wondered. *Is someone spying on me? Was this Andrew's answer to my appeal to Stephanie?* I had heard rumors that the walls of a secret part of the basement at Foxhollow were covered with life-size cartoons of women's conditioning, showing them as aggressive and competitive. Women sometimes were sent there for hours to reflect on their predatory nature. Later I learned that one woman in this basement had buckets of paint dumped on her head as a punishment for displeasing Andrew. Women and men were sometimes renamed with stark reminders of their weaknesses, among them were Mad Dog, Mephisto, Tamasa, Dizzy and Raging Bull. I wondered what mine might be. Many of Andrew's tools seemed designed to shock students out of complacency and jumpstart them in a new direction. The five-word phone message catapulted me into a spiral of confusion. It had been intended to accelerate my movement; instead it catapulted me into despair.

Andrew kept us so busy that we had little sleep. I thought he wanted us to give up control of our lives and live in a state of free-fall. I did love the moments of surrender, when it seemed that I could move beyond normal boundaries, as I had discovered in the lake. Yet now, as the women often told me, instead of surrendering to Andrew I grasped desperately for moments of rest. Pathetic they said. Selfish.

At about this time, though I did not know it, dozens of

instances of abuse more intense than sleep deprivation were taking place in the name of freedom; later I heard that students' car keys and passports were taken to prevent them from leaving. They told me about slapping and beatings among the students closer to Andrew. If I had known about these things, I doubt if it would have caused me to leave. It became automatic for me to suspend judgment when I registered the pain of those who were being bullied and abused. I had had a decade of practice at giving up my own agency. I abandoned my conscience in incremental steps.

I cannot find in my memory any trace of holding Andrew accountable for what was wrong. I believed he had a compassionate agenda and that any errors in judgment occurred because he lacked information about our daily lives. I had not acknowledged that he was fallible. I had not seen that, because he was both isolated and revered, he was deprived of the give-and-take and subtle interaction which enable people to adapt their actions according to the effect they have on others. He could not look into someone else's eyes to learn how he was doing, because when he looked into someone else's eyes, he saw only fawning admiration.

I believed that I could not judge Andrew's inconsistent actions because any opposition I felt to his authority evidenced my lack of understanding and commitment. Yet I wonder that I allowed one glaring contradiction. Andrew's agenda was to help us become independent thinkers; in fact, he published a magazine with the avowed agenda of challenging all assumptions. Yet, as his students we spent many hours discussing independence, without mentioning our growing dependency on him. Independent thought was becoming harder. I had not yet seen that the human mind is capable of absorbing extraordinary contradictions.

Now, unsupported by Stephanie, I had to find my own solutions. I started cutting my daily practice. First, just a minute or two from the three-hour morning practice, but enough to feed an inner weakening. I felt unclean when I wondered for the first time whether my roommates noticed. Gradually, I cut more and more time from the hours I had promised.

I knew I had either to stop being a formal student of Andrew's or to find a way to earn the same money I was currently earning for half the working hours. Now employed as a full-time autism specialist, I offered workshops and visited clients' homes and was hired out to consult with school districts. One of my company's clients, a local school district, asked me to work for them privately at three times my present rate of pay. I asked my employers whether they might allow me to build up a consultation practice and renegotiate my terms of work. Naïvely, I told them that I had an offer from one of their clients.

They refused.

The next day, my boss fired me. She explained, "You have broken your contract with us. You cannot talk to our clients about working with them privately."

I found a box and threw into it puppets, fire trucks, crowns and swords. I placed unfinished paperwork in the file. I took down the photographs of smiling children from above my desk and placed them in a folder. My boss helped me carry the boxes out to my car.

My work life had always balanced my life in the Community, but now the two collided. I had been fired. I had no idea whether I could build up a private practice. Simultaneously, I was not doing well in the Community either. Desperate to regain my moorings and make good in the eyes of my peers, my first action was not to take my children for a vacation, not to look for work, but to send a request to Andrew to go to his three-week retreat in France. All these years I had defied Community norms in order to maintain connections with Jürgen and family in England but now for the first year ever, I would break my promise to my brother and not visit England. I had invested too much for too long in the spiritual search for freedom to quit.

Stephanie reported back to me that Andrew had decided that "given my recent behavior," I would not be allowed to go to France, but should instead help build the new center in Boston. I would live on my savings and volunteer as construction manager. I would research supplies, purchase building materials, supervise and organize a team of 60 volunteers, and make a video of the project. Most of all, I would have a chance to please Andrew and give something back to the Community.

On a hot Boston summer day, with humidity sticking clothes to skin, I walked into the drab, industrial rectangular building for my first meeting with the full-time crew. I heard the screech of a saw slicing through metal. Someone shouted "One, two, three, **shooting**!" It was Ed, on top of the scaffolding, aiming rivets into a steel beam. This was our one-second warning to block our ears from the deafening screech, but our fingers seldom made it in time. Ed's black hair and black tee shirt drew attention to his intense energy. He had been sheetrocking and mudding since he was 16, which in this context gave him status. Tools weighted his belt.

Glen, the leader of the project, asked me to join a planning meeting in the next room. The architect, a builder and a couple of other men were already clustered around the plans for the meditation center, which lay on a sheetrock table supported by two sawhorses. My new role made me nervous. Two of the men, having taken vows of celibacy, had shaved heads. They shifted from foot to foot and laughed nervously at the huge project ahead.

Glen ran his finger across the plans, his voice revealing an accent I recognized as coming from the suburbs of London. He looked like a 6'2" rugby player, but was more reserved than the other men, yet when he made a suggestion the others usually accepted it. His natural leadership had blossomed recently in response to his status as a formal student. Intuitively, I knew he could oversee this complex project, holding steady even when things got tough.

Our voices got lost in the sound of drilling. I spotted the architect, his bald head bowed, his mouth thin and straight. He adjusted the glasses on his nose, pored over the cardboard model on the table, marked it with a pencil, and stood back to look again. He described his vision for the meditation hall: "You will look up through the opening in this circular ceiling with the sense of limitless space above, lit up by dozens of small lights like stars." He confided to me that he worried about executing these complex plans.

I told him, "If you get your vision across to the whole team as you just have to me, you never know what will happen." From that moment on, we were friends.

Ed was still shouting, "One, two, three, **shooting**!" He held his level up to the beam and nodded in satisfaction.

At the end of the day, after most of the workers had left, Glen remained on a ladder in the middle of huge piles of building materials. His eyes followed a thin red pencil-mark which traced a 30-foot diameter circle. This was to be the circular meditation hall. He sighed; not much ruffled Glen. "This is a big job," he said. "There are only three trained workers and they are doing it for free at the end of a day's work."

"But look at the motivation and the spirit," I said. "We all know what happens if we stand behind a clear intention. And we have 60 volunteers who will stand behind that intention. The very endeavor will change us all." My own determination surprised me.

Glen puffed out his cheeks and breathed out a sigh of relief. He spotted a loose beam and jumped down from his ladder to fix it.

We had embarked on building a center magnificent enough to hold the perfection of our master's words. Every aspect of it would reflect his clarity and purity. This vision would bring us together and hold our focus for four months.

A few days later, I caught sight of myself while glancing through that day's film. There were the beginnings of deep lines around my mouth and jaw. I felt disappointment that, even after so much yoga, my shoulders were still rounded. What a shame, I thought, that posture gives away inner defeat.

Little by little, the memory of my recent failures receded. I started to relax, enjoying being in the middle of a busy project.

After a week, the metal beams were erected at their full 12-foot height, filling the space like a huge, silvery skeleton of some extinct dinosaur. The curve of the meditation hall dominated the former warehouse. Over the next two weeks, sheetrock began to cloak the steel and flesh out the walls to reveal their final bulk.

In my makeshift office, in what would one day be Stephanie's meeting room, I sat comfortably cross-legged on the floor, surrounded by phone books, brochures for building materials, and folders full of notes. I phoned to thank Missy for the dinners she had been cooking. I scribbled a note to myself on a piece of sheetrock to buy quarter-inch nuts with washers, and a three-sixteenth drill bit. I felt for the first time since becoming a formal student that this team respected me for my intelligence, my ability and my organization. They knew I could hold hundreds of details in my head. Why did I, who had no background in construction, feel so comfortable as part of this team?

In a pane of glass propped against the wall, I spotted my reflection and smiled. This was no longer the sight of a person who was struggling. I was deeply at home. *What is it that has shifted in me?* I wondered.

Two months into the project, we had established a comfortable rhythm, even though building this huge center felt like creating a drama bigger than all of us. Fifty or sixty volunteers supplemented the regular crew of skilled workers and the excitement among all of us was palpable.

Peter, a very shy man, had earlier today demanded, "Film

me!" Then, looking boldly into the camera, he said, "This is the most incredible time of my life!" An Australian social worker scanned the ceiling looking for insulation hangers still left behind. Like many people, she had been on site after work five nights a week. She often didn't leave till 11:00pm. Once home, she would likely complete her daily meditation practice. A librarian arrived, took off her navy blue suit and pumps and put on a pair of overalls. She reorganized the tools in the storeroom until everything was in its place. Then she hoisted trash bags filled with broken sheetrock and wads of insulation into the back of the truck and drove to the dump. Encased in protective gear and mask, a young Dutch man was spray painting the ceiling. He seemed happier than he had been in all the years he had lived in the Community. Peering through his mask at me, he said, "Andrew is going to be so happy when he sees this!" Three teenagers carried a truckload of sheetrock into the passageway, two sheets at time.

I thrived in amidst this chaotic order. It seemed a natural fit for me to support 50 volunteers and coordinate their activities, training and food.

Glen wiped the mist from inside his goggles. He leaned into the bench with his left hip to keep a metal bar steady, and with complete focus he used his right hand to guide the saw along a black pencil mark. The saw screamed into the metal plank.

"Shall we pause for smoothies, Glen?" I asked when the saw hesitated. Three women had spent the last hour making mango smoothies for 50 people.

We all took a break to sit on the concrete out in the warm Boston sun, feeling comfortable and relaxed. A short, stocky physical therapist smiled broadly into the camera and expressed my thoughts: "Everyone is alive, laughing and focused on creating together. This is an extraordinary phenomenon." Usually he barely moved his mouth when he spoke, but now every muscle in his body illustrated his point, "Nobody wants to leave the site. No one even needs to sleep. What's happening to the people here? They are exhausted; and yet every day, they work harder and become happier. They don't even get paid!" His eyes sparkled. "Now, I really must get back up this ladder," he laughed, and I laughed too.

I found the building project so healing that I wrote to Andrew, as always crediting him for my growth, my happiness, and my strength. I knew he read all the letters he received. I had no doubt that I was now living the teachings.

Dear Andrew,

On a derelict wasteland, a handful of friends who meet in the teachings transform a utilitarian concrete box into a vision of the unborn. How is it possible that, even as the steel and fumes tear our muscles and sap our strength, our hearts are filled? Putting my attention on this building has made it possible for me to stop trying to be with people, stop trying to get it right, stop trying to prove that I am enlightened. What matters most now is that the way we work together should be as perfect as possible. At its best it is so beautiful that everyone who picks up a paintbrush is swept up by the sustaining energy of being together in this creation.

As you have told me many times, experiences of love and ecstasy come easily to me, but living what I have seen has often eluded me. You have said, "When are you going to stop having revelations and start living what you have understood?" On this building site, the dichotomy between revelation and action does not exist. The connection between bliss and the manifestation of love clearly lies in figuring out where to buy a one-inch steel stud, or which person would be best at cutting vinyl strips.

The formal women say now that that they no longer feel separate from me. This kinship I know to be the most precious element in my life, though every day I fall short of nurturing it fully.

Obedience to you and this sacred service is saving my life. I have discovered that the construction site is a small beginning to under-

standing the context around you. For this gift I am most grateful.
Thank you, with all my love,
Marlowe

I had barely left the site for three and a half months. Those of us who could work mornings would arrive by 8am having already done two and a half hours of practice, the perfect preparation for each day. My journal entries from the time appear to be an honest reckoning with my desire to think that I had nothing more to learn. Each day I tracked the thoughts about my superior understanding and set my intention to stay awake. For those three daily hours of meditation and prostrations, I would question my motivation for wanting to be a leader. Unlike the early days when I saw myself as a witch, I could now look at myself without flinching. I would stand up from practice excited at the prospect of the new day. I felt alert all day until I fell into bed for a brief five hours sleep.

I was at this time excused from group meetings—the constant assault on my self-esteem in the name of helping me see my ego was on hiatus. I still saw little of my children. But they relished their freedom that summer in Cambridge. When I did have time for the kids, we were relaxed and happy, mirroring one another. Was it true then that when I lived the teachings the children flourished?

The architect's vision of the circular meditation hall was becoming a reality. A drop ceiling ringed the circular meditation hall opening up to a domed ceiling sparkling with lights like stars in the night sky.

One day, I watched a woman total the sales of biscotti and pretzels so she could restock the snack bar. Her sweat-streaked hair was tied loosely back; her paint-spattered face shone with satisfaction. Her sharp features had once kept me at bay, but they now had a softened look. I felt she was not so distant. Tallying up everyone's snack bill, she said, "This is the only Community I've ever lived in where you can have an honor system and not have to build in an allowance for cheating. The standard is so high!"

She and I had known each other for 12 or 14 years and our roles were now reversed: I was a formal student and she was a lay student. She looked at me curiously for a second. "If you don't mind my asking," she said, "I hear you are leading this construction job beautifully, inspiring everyone to attend to every detail. What has changed?"

I said, "It's like I'm no longer looking over my shoulder to see if I am good enough."

We looked up in wonder at the half-finished ceiling of the circular hall. Mundane tasks had become transcendent exercises. We looked back at each other. Our eyes met in recognition that we lived in a context in which we could, at moments, soar, showing unknown potential.

At lunchtime, a No Woman brought big trays of lasagna for the crew. This woman had supported me when I returned from my travels across the desert and had given us strength in the bathrooms when we came out of the lake. For years, she had been a formal student. Now, having fallen from grace, she would have accepted Andrew's offer of exclusion and intense practice in order to have a chance of returning to the Community. She was neither engaged in the Community nor psychologically able to leave. Accepting Andrew's value system, she saw herself as poorly as Andrew saw her yet believed the situation was a gift.

Women like this were outcasts. Like ghosts, you knew they were there but you seldom saw them. One woman who ran away was intercepted at a train station and brought back, but most stayed because they had turned over their decision-making to someone else. Sometimes they were not allowed to do service, even cleaning. Often they made financial "donations" in order to be allowed to stay. One No Woman who begged to be allowed back was banished for weeks to a hotel room, alternately left alone and intimidated by students. At her weakest, she could not resist the "hint" that she could show her dedication by giving Andrew her one million dollar inheritance. I never asked myself whether it was wrong to treat people this way.

Today, because we had run short of volunteers, normal restrictions were lifted, allowing this No Woman to make food for the volunteers. I had asked her to hand off the food at the back door so as to minimize her interaction with us. Instead, she brazenly brought the food into the kitchen and started serving the workers and tidying up. Like a slave she tried to avoid my eyes. I recoiled from her ingratiating presence. But as a formal student, it was up to me to respond to the situation.

I drew her on one side and asked to speak with her. She froze, dropping the ladle onto the table. I said to her, not harshly, but firmly, "This is really embarrassing, but we only asked you to bring the food. It's kind of inappropriate for you to be in here with everyone."

"I am so sorry," she said. She began to add, "I didn't mean—" and then she left.

I said nothing. It was becoming natural to me to hold others to a standard. But it was easy to blur the line between helping others to grow and pushing them over when they were vulnerable.

At the end of the day, Catalina, still wearing a leather apron full of tools, swept up the debris from our labor. She was one of our few trained people. She stretched under the workbench to get the curls of wood shavings from under the saw, then moved to gather fragments of metal stud into a pile.

Catalina's hair was just beginning to grow after years of celibacy. She had just been demoted from being a formal student, so her vow was automatically lifted. I wondered what insult to Andrew was the cause of her changed status. She looked tired. Although 15-hour days were common in construction, I wondered how much practice she was doing after work. She didn't look happy. At one time she had talked with Andrew with confidence and grace. It was painful to see her at such a terribly low ebb.

I helped her drag a particularly heavy sack of debris into the sunlight of the yard. As we leaned for a second against the broken chain link fencing, I asked about the area that needed to be mudded.

"I don't know how many square feet it is," she said. "But it's a hell of a lot. Sixty buckets of mud and a hundred feet of arch bead."

Then she said, "You are the heart of this project, Marlowe. That is what everyone says."

I returned to my office and sat down on a piece of sheetrock lying on a bucket. I phoned volunteers and arranged for paint samples for the kitchen ceiling, a team to sand door frames, and a truck to collect the final delivery of sheetrock. It had been a really long day. Glen came in and told me that Andrew would soon visit the site and meet with the formal students who had been involved in the construction. He was not sure of the date. He asked me if we had enough volunteers for the morning, and I said yes. "When volunteers sign up, it's always an underestimate. There has never been a day when we had fewer than we expected."

Three weeks later, Catalina "accidentally" leaned against one of the construction workers while they were relaxing against a truck. She was only a lay student, so it was not appropriate to push her too far; but, I reasoned, her flirtatious behavior, so soon after being celibate, was an embarrassment.

I found a moment to speak with her alone. "Catalina, I wanted to mention that sometimes it seems like you are sending pretty explicit messages to some of the guys on site." I mentioned some examples. "It made me wonder: two weeks ago you were celibate, right?"

She had spent years without human touch. Now demoted, she was also spurned by the entire formal Community. Only the workmen treated her like a normal person. Yet I felt justified in perpetuating the Community taboo on flirtation. A year earlier, I had seen that this Community didn't understood the transformative power of sexuality; yet, now that I was in a position of authority, I effortlessly rearranged my thinking according to party lines to admonish Catalina.

Flustered, she turned away and became distracted. "There might be something in what you say, but right now I have to find my tools. People just keep borrowing them. I'm not going to make a fuss, but I would really like my tools back."

The next day, she didn't show up. Without a word to anyone, in the dead of night, she had gone. I was hurt. I wondered if I had pushed her too far. I knew now why she had wanted her tools back so urgently. I had no doubt that wherever she went, her life would be paltry compared to ours. I remembered Andrew's words: "Anyone who leaves will be haunted for the rest of their lives." I made no attempt to contact her. If I had, it would have been with the sole intention of talking her into returning. According to unspoken Community rules, my compassion was limited to the revolving cast of characters committed to Andrew Cohen. Once someone left, they ceased to exist as real people.

At the end of the day, I filmed our progress and spent a couple of hours editing the video, wondering whether Andrew would ever see it. It was more like a work of art than a building; and the work of art was secondary to sharing the creative process of working together. In our relative isolation, beyond Andrew's scrutiny, we had found healing and clarity of intention. I asked myself, *Are we making a place of prayer for our teacher, or is this effort the prayer itself?*

A week later, the plastering was completed, transforming the jagged outline into a sculpture of elegance. Each curve was engineered to dovetail seamlessly into another. Images of space and light emerged with a shift of lighting. Shadows brought to light a new aspect of the architect's design, but my eye was always drawn back to the meditation hall. The curved walls led me irresistibly inwards, towards the center.

By throwing myself into this project, I had begun to understand Andrew's fifth tenet, "For the sake of the whole." I now saw the first four tenets as a road map for living the fifth. And if tomorrow I faltered in giving to the whole, then I could fall back on the other tenets to get me back on track. I rediscovered this truth every moment. This, I understood, was the revolution that Andrew described. Meanwhile, things were falling into place for me professionally, too. I had begun establishing myself as an educational consultant: reducing my hours, doubling my income, and making Community life more feasible.

Andrew would be coming on Saturday, and we were under pressure to finish before he came. He had not seen the project during construction. I could not wait to show him the result of our work.

Outside, a team was sanding door frames. Inside, the walls and ceiling were now covered in insulation padding. Someone lay on his back beneath the rafters, welding lights to the joists above, which made bursts of sound and light rip through the center of the hall. There were ten painters priming walls. The teams changed throughout the day; I tracked how many coats of paint were on each wall. The librarian was scraping the floor, which was now a mess of plaster, paint, and glue. One of the Israeli women arranged 30 individual lunches of Middle Eastern food.

I heard the sound of sanding on many walls, like the steady sound of waves. Three women were priming.

Jessica dropped by sometimes, and I instructed her, too.

"That's great, Jessica. Can you see how there's a little bit of shadow?"

Jessica smiled as she caught the precision that I was looking for. There was no resistance to feedback in her now. Her hair was tied up in a little tuft, out of the way of the paint. Little wisps hung down. Her lightly muscled arms and long, graceful legs belied her strength. Although she had once been timid, she was growing into a beautiful young woman with signs of inner strength. I was proud of her for finding her place on this team. She noticed me watching her, put down her roller, and wrapped her arms around me. I hoped that she, like other students' children, would one day decide to have Andrew as her teacher.

I tried to disregard my foreboding that when the project ended something might be lost. It's only a thought, I said to myself. *I should not project thoughts of insecurity outwards, manifesting old rules that swallow me alive.*

I reviewed my film at the end of the day. I noted with satisfaction my quiet, focused movements as I talked to the delivery guys. I picked a clip of a fleeting triumphant smile towards the camera as I unloaded a sack of plaster from the truck. Then I saw a clip of Glen. He had changed too. There was a calm and clear look about him as if beneath the surface, everything had smoothed out. It had been a very good partnership.

After four months, the project was nearly at an end. The baseboards were in place. Ed had finished most of the lighting. The plum-colored kitchen cabinets were fitted. The doors were painted and hung. The dishwasher was installed. The undercarpet in the meditation hall was followed by luxurious plush red pile.

It was time for a group photo. Forty people crowded into the circular hall and climbed all over the scaffolding, which sagged and wobbled under the weight. Across the crowd of people, Glen caught my eye and nodded an answer to my unspoken question about whether the scaffolding would take the strain. We took pictures full of laughter and celebration. "We could build a new center in London," one of us said. "Or Amsterdam, or Israel, or India." But this life was not about personal friendships. I knew my personal feelings were irrelevant. The process of coming together was the miracle and the individuals simply carried the baton for a moment.

Andrew came at 9:00 on Saturday morning. I was not invited. At 9:30, the last painting crew would arrive. I parked outside the center to get the equipment ready for them. From my car window, I saw Andrew's unmistakable head of thick black hair. He was talking with Glen, Shirley and a few others, facing away from me, standing stiffly as if slightly self-conscious. I had to walk past them all to get to the door. I didn't know whether to sneak in and pretend I hadn't seen them, or stop and greet Andrew even though I hadn't been invited. And I didn't know whether I had been excluded because I had done something wrong.

As I walked the no-man's land towards the group, I dreaded the moment that one of them spotted me. Glen smiled at me. I glanced acknowledgement to Andrew, then looked away and said, "I am sorry to disturb you, Andrew; I have to get in to prepare the work for the teams." He didn't say anything, but he looked uncomfortable. I wondered if it was his discomfort or mine. I made my way through the interminable silence to the door and disappeared inside with relief.

Afterwards, Shirley said to me with her familiar tone, "You didn't have to act so weird when Andrew was there. Couldn't you have just been normal and unaffected?"

My roommate Erica was mystified by my not being invited. She said, "I know you are hurt, Marlowe, but everybody here has acknowledged the change in you and has told you many times how wonderful that is."

I blurted out my feelings with more honesty than I had done for years. "One word of acknowledgement from him would have changed my world. It's so unfair."

"I know," she said kindly. I could feel her compassion, but even though only the two of us were present, she would not break the taboo on criticism of Andrew. In addition, we knew that, even though we were very close today, our circumstances might change and one of us might quote the other. In other words, our friendship might become fuel for our own upward mobility at any moment.

Erica said, "I heard that Andrew said, 'Marlowe just did what I asked her to do.'"

"Oh," I responded. "It felt like so much more than that."

I was silent for a moment, searching desperately for the message in Andrew's actions. Finally I said, "Each day that I have spent on site has been a gift, each day an affirmation of joy. How could I be so petty as to think that he should thank me when I have received so much? To me it feels thrilling and new to give so much, but perhaps to him this is normal. Perhaps I could live like this all the time without making anything grandiose out of it. What do you think?"

"It makes sense," she said. "There is nothing special about Marlowe being a leader, organizing, responding, being alive. That is just the real state of affairs."

I went on, "And Andrew sees that already I am starting to take a position in being the one who can give something special. He knows that if he had acknowledged the change in me, then my sense of self-importance would have become bloated, so he dare not do it. There is such a teaching in everything that he does. He cares so much about us."

Although we rationalized why Andrew had ignored my work, I think we knew that we were rationalizing.

This might have been the moment when I had an inkling that my private response to the situation trumped what the Community thought. A part of me had grown strong during this building project and would not leave me even if things got tough.

We returned to the daily formal student dinners. When I first became a formal student, Jessica and Becky had joined us, but their refusal to engage even in simple conversation meant that everyone was relieved when it was decided that they should stay home and fend for themselves with TVP (textured vegetable protein) and jarred pasta sauce, doing homework and playing video games.

I sat at the end of the table. I wanted the butter for my potato; it was just out of reach. I waited for a pause in the conversation. I heard, as if through a long tunnel, a conversation between Stephanie and Shirley about Bosnia. There was no pause in the conversation. *Look*, I told myself, *there is no way that you are so wimpy that you are incapable of asking someone to pass the butter*. But on the other hand I wondered which was worse: to have another whole dinner go by without my saying anything, or to have another dinner go by and my one utterance be "Pass the butter, please?" *I could say, "Stephanie, would you mind passing the butter?" No; that's too English. Or what about, simply, "Can I have the butter please?"* Appealing for help, I looked at Glen, who for four months had seen another me. I saw the puzzled expression in his eyes. I did not look at him again. I had no explanation either.

I would not for years know that I felt angry with Andrew and was turning the anger in on myself, nor that I felt mortified that my children had for so many evenings seen me unable to stand tall in the room of formal students. The roller coaster of life in the Community had taken me down. However, according to the second tenet of Andrew Cohen's teachings, The Law of Volitionality, *I am 100% responsible for everything that happens to me, and for everything that will ever happen to me.* Consequently, behaving like the victim was the worst crime of all.

Chapter 12

The Discussion Group Weekend

Question: "I worry about dependency."

Andrew Cohen: "The path of truth is not a path of independence. The path of truth is a path of total, absolute dependence on the truth. If one meets a real teacher, it's very difficult to have only a casual involvement. Ultimately it ends up being either complete involvement or no involvement at all. That is because the nature of what is being shared is Absolute. That is why it demands every-thing. What is demanded is your individuality. It is a wrestling match between teacher and student. That is what spiritual struggle is all about."

Question: "There is something about giving up my individuality that is terrifying."

Andrew Cohen: "It is to receive help in facing that fear that you go to a teacher. Don't be so concerned about dependence or indepen-dence; just be concerned with being Free. You can't protect your independence and realize freedom at the same time."

Andrew Cohen, *Enlightenment is a Secret*, 1995, p. 114

My weekdays started at 4:00am with three hours of spiritual practice. I had had to stop my beloved practice of 500 prostra-tions because of knee damage and had replaced it with 500 full push-ups instead. I was thrilled by the rhythmic, arduous challenge accompanied by chanting. Recently, though, Andrew had told me to replace push-ups with a mere bow of the head. I explained that push-ups strengthened me in mind and body, but he was adamant. Practice was followed by an hour's commute to my full-time job as a consultant. Like all formal students, I slept four to five hours a night. We got used to this to some extent, but I had a perpetual feeling of dread that one of my tasks would rob me of an additional half hour. I still thought that my life in the Community would benefit my children and me, but thoughts are more malleable than we know. I was in so deep that the only way out seemed to be forward.

This weekend, my housemates and I were expected to go to our Master's center at Foxhollow. Also this weekend, Jessica would take her SAT exam, and she had asked me to drive her. I knew it would be a stressful day for her and I was clear this time that she was my priority. I explained to Shirley and Justice that I would stay home from Foxhollow and drive her. Shirley smiled and said, "Maybe you are right, let's look at it." Justice, however, challenged me, asking, "Is that for your sake or hers?" I admitted that it was likely for both of our sakes, but primarily hers. Shirley wondered whether I might be holding onto some old notion about being the perfect mother.

Suddenly, the issue didn't seem so clear to me. I struggled to separate out my tendency to try to be the "perfect mother" from my genuine concern for my daughter. Behind their words, which felt so wrong, lay the knowledge that defiance of the women in my group would be reported to Andrew and added to the evidence of my lack of seriousness. This, I knew, could have consequences.

Justice furrowed her brows. "This is the discussion group weekend. It's powerful for all the formal students to come together in such a big way."

"I know," I said.

She pushed her advantage. "You have been struggling lately. You ought to question whether you really want to be with everyone in Foxhollow. Maybe you are avoiding something."

I was quiet.

"Besides," she said, "it is a good opportunity for the children to support each other."

A few years earlier I would have disagreed, but now I thanked them for their clarity. I neatly packed away the thought that Jessica seldom asked for anything and agreed to go to Foxhollow. I tried to line up my gut response with my new beliefs. I waited for my longing to go away, then called Jessica.

"I'm sorry," I told her. "The discussion groups are really important; they only happen twice a year. Do you have a timetable for the bus?"

"It's okay, Mom," she said without surprise, as if she didn't care. With an inkling of guilt, I remembered the day a year earlier that I had followed guidelines from Andrew, to make sure my children knew that they were not the most important thing in my life. I pushed away the thought that my choices over many years had hardened her.

Three weekends earlier, Andrew had met privately with the Community children in Foxhollow for the first time. Becky had refused to go despite my encouragement. Jessica had attended. She later told me what had happened. Andrew told the children about the failings of their parents, continuing a process of splitting child from parent just as he had split married couples. (The most intense example of this splitting was when he forced a father to tell his young teenager about her mother's decades' old extramarital affair.) With scorn, he told Jessica that I had barely been a part of the Community until the last year or so. He then divided the children into two groups: those who committed to his teachings and those who did not. Out of a sense of expectation and because she was generally a good girl, Jessica tentatively committed.

Andrew's teachings spoke to my heart and moved me deeply. The art of the discussion group, however, always eluded me. The stakes were high, the pressure to "come through" intense. Through them the eloquent and articulate achieved favored status. I was neither. Over the course of the weekend, we rotated through seven or so groups each consisting of eight students led by a senior student. Without preparation, we would read and discuss a short text written by Andrew. The expectation was to be real and in the moment with each other while expressing our passion for the writing. These groups were important as a measure of our growth.

The first group began by discussing a text about dependence. I chose to speak first. No one responded. Ten minutes later, another student expressed thoughts very similar to mine. He was hailed as moving the discussion in a fruitful new direction. I felt confused. I decided that I might have said words of wisdom, but not in a way that engaged with the other students. I was not off to a good start.

In the next group, someone read aloud from Andrew's writing: "You will realize that how you think makes no difference, and you will see how nothing you ever think could make any difference..."

Desperate to speak, I gathered my courage and said, "If I believed the contents of my mind right now, I would be paralyzed and unable to say anything. I will not do that. I can, right now, make the decision to go beyond the limitations of my mind and not be intimidated by fear. This is volitional. I actually have a choice."

The architect I knew from the meditation center was in that group. He smiled warmly at me. Ever since our work together, I had felt his affection. I clung to his subtle encouragement.

"That's a good example," the group leader said, and I felt buoyed up.

I made my way across the newly landscaped gardens to the next meeting. I remembered two weeks earlier, when I had been pruning shrubs in a new flowerbed outside Andrew's house, Stephanie had walked past and hissed at me, "What are you thinking? You are right in view of Andrew's window! Do you think he wants to look out of his window and see you? How insensitive! Totally disrespectful." I knew what she meant. Andrew should not have to be reminded of a student who was stubbornly refusing to be free.

Shirley walked with me and said, "I think you are showing great courage. In the last meeting you kept on struggling, but you made it. Just try not to personalize everything." I clung to this rare encouragement from Shirley, hoping it would dispel my suffocating anxiety.

The text at the next group triggered my memories of hiking in the Utah desert when I had discovered that my lust for experience kept me from directly engaging with people. I had learned that, when I let go of desire, I saw the world in startling clarity—that what distorted my vision was my ceaseless struggle for more. I had tasted freedom. With an effort, I brought myself back to the group. In the desert, I had understood Andrew's teachings; and now, in this discussion group, I needed to articulate what I had learned. I tried to relate it without sounding too personal. I said, "I think that when we realize we are no more than the sum of our desires, it becomes clear that we are slaves who listen to the mind."

"That's true," the leader replied. "But it sounds kind of intellectual."

I had missed the point. I was speaking from memory and personal experience when the point of the groups was to respond spontaneously and impersonally in the moment. My references to my experiences separated me from people. *How can it be*, I wondered, *that even my experiences of love and connection are not a gift to anyone, not even me?*

The leader's slight rebuff sent me spinning into fear, which was triggered easily in me. Shutting down would get me into trouble. The skin across my forehead shrank and my eyes strained in their sockets. The words spoken seemed to float just beyond my comprehension.

Someone read, "… lost in and hopelessly distracted by thought…"

I recognized myself, and for the rest of the meeting I said nothing.

Once we were back outside, Shirley returned. "I should never have said you have courage!" she began. "Kurt says the way you are behaving is despicable. As a formal student, how can you not be rooted in the teachings already? You shouldn't have to go through doubt like this!" Kurt had been the head of Andrew's security team for years. He was a martial arts master, and doubt seemed to be outside his experience.

I had no reply.

At coffee time, the senior student Damien took me aside. He was at the top of the hierarchy. When he first became a formal student, he had greatly encouraged the students in the Lay Community. He had had a generous smile back then. Now he was feared.

"What's going on?" he asked me. His bearing told me that there was no room for evasion; his piercing gray eyes had a way of seeing through me. Yet, I trusted his support almost as much as I did Andrew's.

"I am sorry," I said. "I can't believe I have been behaving so badly—so selfishly. I'm not giving anything to the groups."

"I see you understand your own condition," he said. "You have to take a stand with it. Andrew has given you everything, but you are making no attempt to apply the tenets of his teachings in your life. You are so arrogant that you think you alone don't have to take the practice seriously. You are stuck in your ego and just think it is all about you. This life is about giving to something much bigger than you. The whole point is to be no one."

"You're right," I said, with desperate cunning. "I have been relating every experience back to myself. In that last discussion group," I said, trying to talk the talk, "everyone was so simple and real with each other. I have been so uncaring to everyone."

Damien encouraged me to do better. "This practice is only about being together in a simple way," he said.

"Thank you," I said. "This is volitional, and I can change."

I made my way across the wet spring grass to the next group meeting. I took off my shoes and placed them down carefully, so no grass would get on the carpet. I was relieved to see only six chairs in the room; I sometimes did better in smaller groups. Unfortunately, I had no ally in this session. Three women entered laughing and sat on the other side of the room. I felt dread. Previous experiences of humiliation were imprinted in my memory. My face stiffened. I tried to make the muscles of my jaw relax.

If I couldn't succeed in these groups, I would have to stop being a formal student. Then I would have to leave my house; I remembered when I was made homeless overnight. Perhaps I would be banished or isolated. Perhaps I would be sent to the basement where, I had heard, there were life-size images of Marilyn Monroe, cartoons of Andrew being attacked by women, and something about blood. I knew Andrew would do whatever it took to get me to change my behavior, if he did not altogether give up on me. Perhaps, when he heard how little I cared about the discussion groups, he would give me a new shameful name, put me into silence, or instruct me to live alone. Perhaps I was not even important enough to have a name.

Worst of all was the thought that I might have to leave. Leaving represented failure in the Community value system, and I did not have much of any other value system left. Being Andrew's student was central to who I was; being seen and valued within the Community was akin to being alive. Even the most grueling struggle to keep afloat within the Community seemed of greater value than leaving it.

My back seemed not designed to fit the chairs, with their lightly padded seats and upright wooden backs. The young maple outside the window waved its branches hopefully in the wind. Other students came in; chatter faded; eyes closed. The discussion began. I made one more unconvincing attempt to articulate passion for the teachings, but the text, which once would have inspired me, was incomprehensible. Damage control was my goal now. I crossed my legs and tightened my jaw. I moved with deliberation, trying to show no fear or anger, trying to show so little definition that no one could get me. *If I can disappear, I might be okay.*

Kurt was one of the participants. He sat comfortably on the wooden chair, his back like a strong tree, his crew cut emphasizing his steady gaze. A few years ago, I fainted multiple times in Satsang. He had diagnosed this as resistance to change.

Damien entered and sat in the leader's chair. He looked directly at me. Tears of isolation were locked somewhere inside me by years of questioning every impulse for validity. I was a shell-shocked husk, trying to force inspiration to the surface. I couldn't feel anything at all.

I said nothing, which was not a good idea.

Afterwards, as Damien and I stood together overlooking the valley down to the lake, he said, "You are completely mad. You understand your own condition but do not change. You are behaving like an egomaniac." His eyes turned towards me with the hardness of steel. "How can you behave like this?" he hissed. "A year ago you had such fire! I was told you were a hero that time in the lake. Now you have created so much negative karma! I have no choice but to take you out of the discussion groups."

I said nothing.

I returned to the house where I was staying in Foxhollow and lay on the bed with my eyes closed. I became a tiger pacing back and forth in a deeply dug pit of earth. The sides were smooth and high. People peered into the pit and I roared back in anger, swatting at their legs in a vain effort to catch them and drag them down.

This is me! I thought. *This is what Andrew is showing me.*

And then I saw something else: a person lightly walking in the sunlight above the pit, free of all burdens.

The tiger and this person had no connection with each other, as if I were splitting myself in two.

"How was your weekend, Mom?" Becky asked when I got home.

"It was great! It's so wonderful talking about the teachings in depth with everyone." *How would she understand it if I told her the truth?* I wondered. *How would she understand my lies if I did not?*

"That's great, Mom." Becky was learning to use superlatives without any effect. She used to be exuberant and expressive.

"What did you do this weekend?" I asked her.

"Not much." I knew she would not invite friends to our house because she did not want anyone to know how she lived. We had never spoken about it, but we both understood that outsiders and family would find much about our lives suspicious or even dangerous. Becky found the ultra-rich culture of the children of her school alien to her. She tried basketball one semester and tennis another, but ball skills were not her strength. The friends she chose were eccentric and therefore perhaps less judgmental than others. I was dependent on the goodwill of their parents for her transport to school and much of her social life. She used to take delight in hugs and cuddles. Now I could not remember when I had last touched her, or when she had last sought it.

Erica, seeing sadness in all three of us, suggested we take a day to have a nice time together. So my daughters and I drove in silence to the Aquarium. We looked for a short time at the fish, but none of us had anything to say. My mind was consumed with what I should be doing to put things right with the other students. We returned home.

"Are you back already?" Erica said in surprise.

I realized I had failed to follow even her instruction.

The following week, I sent a letter and flowers to the 50 formal students at Foxhollow.

Dear Brothers and Sisters,
I am sorry to all of you for pulling down the discussion groups last

weekend. The picture of your loving, open faces haunts me, everyone reaching out to me, and the fact that I rejected every one of your outstretched hands. In my insanity, I completely identified with my dark side and abandoned my conscience. In the context of this sacred struggle to come together, my conscious separation of myself is an act of destruction towards you all. In this delicate fight to maintain an impersonal view, it was sabotage and betrayal to insist on being intensely personal and self-obsessed.

In my diary I wrote:

I am a dark force, a cancer in this sacred Community. All along, I've undermined this movement towards the impersonal. I've understood everything and lived none of it. Bottom line: Do I want to be someone or to be free? What am I going for? I'm going for freedom; I'm going to follow through, whatever it takes, to drop this vicious pride that punishes all around me. And Stephanie is my role model.

Chapter 13

The Silver Thread

Honesty without kindness makes us grim and mean...
Pema Chödrön (1997)

I was consulting to a special education class in which the teacher needed guidance on handling a classroom of six children with autism. It was a misconceived concept to put them all in one room. One was reading *Gone with the Wind*; another was still in diapers and could only say two words—"candy" and "no"—and a third pupil threw herself on the floor biting her hands several times a day.

I was sitting in the teachers' room at the head of the table facing the window. There were some tired flowers on the table. I was eating salad and tempeh out of a Tupperware container.

The drama teacher was saying, "I was thinking of making the tale of Babushka into a play and having as many as possible of the third graders involved."

A middle-aged teacher was talking about her friend's husband: "You are so lucky. He takes you out for dinner and brings you presents even when it is not your birthday!"

I saw contentment on her friend's face. *These women have no idea,* I thought, *what it is to live an independent life and to go beyond the slavery of small town conditioning. They don't even know there is an alternative.*

"Marlowe, it's for you. Someone called Stephanie," said a colleague holding the phone.

I looked at the tired flowers on the table, one of those readymade combinations standing in cheap molded glass that you find in gas stations. I thought, *I don't understand why inexpensive flowers are so ugly and baby's breath is nearly always a mistake.*

I took the phone. "Hi Stephanie. This is Marlowe."

"Would you mind stopping by my office this afternoon?" she said.

"Yes; sure," I said, trying to sound nonchalant. "Any particular time?"

"No, no finish your work," she said.

I should have stayed to the end of the school day. I left immediately.

I walked into the center. Feelings of wholeness were now a distant memory. When we were building the center, this had been my office. The design team had spent hours deliberating over the stark, unyielding teal blue on one wall. Staring at it, I waited bleakly.

Stephanie did not gesture for me to sit down.

Maybe she will give me a more rigorous challenge, I thought. *Perhaps a request for money? Maybe celibacy.*

"I am sorry," she said, as if someone had died.

Either I was going to be thrown out of the Community altogether or I was to be a lay student.

"I had really hoped you would make it." She was struggling with the words. "It's probably not really a surprise to you. We are making you a lay student."

I felt unprotected from this stark failure, even though a part of me knew it was coming. I was ashamed. Thoughts flashed through my mind: I had tried to meet the standards of an absolute teacher of enlightenment, I had given my all and I had failed. I had wanted to contribute to a momentum that would change the world for the better, and I had failed. My commitment was proven inadequate.

For comfort, I tried to think logically about the situation. As a lay student I would remain in the Community, surrounded by others with a commitment to this sacred life. I didn't mind having to move house yet again. But most painful was the grueling public and personal recognition of my resistance to growth and change. I lost status, respect, and responsibility.

I went home and found Erica in tears in the attic bedroom we shared. I had been so immersed in my own struggle that I was surprised to find she was suffering, too. She had been given an ultimatum: she could leave the Community or go on an indefinite retreat to Foxhollow. This would be a severe and grueling challenge. It meant six hours a day of chanting meditation and prostrations in addition to service, cleaning, cooking, and gardening. Also expected was a "donation" of $10,000 to Moksha Foundation, which supported Andrew's teachings. She would have to leave her son, buy a car, leave her job in Boston, and find another part-time job in the Berkshires. Her son who had recently been fired from a part-time job was in his last year of high school and barely passing classes. I offered to help with her son.

Erica had looked radiant after first meeting Andrew 15 years previously. Andrew had held her up as an example of inspiration to the rest of us. I remembered her sitting at the kindergarten door in Totnes, waiting to take her sons home. Other parents were drawn to her kind and sensitive words and hailed her as a lovely person. I wondered now what had happened to her. I would miss her.

Normally when people changed status, they left that very same day often just with their clothes. This time, the formal students did not need the house we lived in. Erica moved to Foxhollow. One day I was living in the formal co-op with all expenses shared, the next I was left with the house, the rent of $2,500 a month and three teenagers. But the demands on lay students were less and I would have time to sleep and to be with my children.

The girls had long since stopped commenting on the ever-changing shifts imposed on them. They may have grieved over the loss of friendship and intimacy when people moved, but we never talked about it. As a lay student, I felt simultaneously bereft and relieved to not have the intensity and urgency of the women's meetings. However, I had lost the attention and care of Andrew himself—I had lost the hope of imminent transformation.

My only remaining responsibility within the Community was arranging the flowers at the meditation center twice a week. I loved this task. It was not a hard task, not really a high status job, but the results were visible to the whole Community when they came in for Satsang. This fragile silver thread of creation was all that was left of the passion that had inspired me to move from Devon to San Francisco to Boston.

The following week, at the center I had once helped build, I stood back and admired the long stalks of larkspur, cow parsley, ferns, and flocks. It always seemed more luck than skill whether or not a flower arrangement worked. Therefore I always had the fear, *What if I can't do it today?* I rearranged a single stem of larkspur so that it didn't throw off the balance and watched the whole arrangement leap into life. *That's it. Pretty good!* It was as if the arrangement took off in spite of me, at least on a good day. The delicate beauty of this one drew me in. I loved the softness of the contours and the subtlety of the greens.

It was still early afternoon. Carrying the vase, I slipped off my shoes and followed the curved white walls that led towards the great expanse of space within the circular meditation hall. As usual, I felt the stillness, as if here, in this one space, there was no room for complication or indulgence. As my feet sank into the deep red pile carpet, I noticed the orange of the round cushions, already arranged in neat semicircular rows. I glanced up at the celestial lights above and remembered the hours that Alan had spent welding each one to the joists. I knew every piece of steel and wood that lay beneath the surface. I so enjoyed being allowed to make an offering in this place that I loved so well. Being one of the band of volunteers building this place had been the happiest time of life.

Being careful not to spill a drop of water, I placed the elegant cream vase on the finely finished wooden table next to the leader's meditation cushion and stood back for a moment to review the angle. When I was three years old, I could look into the center of a primrose and find peace. I would talk to flowers, although I already knew it was better not to tell anyone.

Shirley came in. From all the way at the back of the hall, she glanced at the flowers and proclaimed loudly, "Too English!"

I looked around.

"Not enough *Shakti!*" she yelled.

I looked again at the larkspur, cow parsley, pink snapdragons, and lavender. *Of course she is right,* I thought. *Not enough cosmic force. This arrangement is too wimpy and delicate, not enough contrast, not dynamic enough.*

Shirley was working out regularly now, and her body showed it. But instead of confidence, her face had a perpetual driven look and her skin was taut. I wondered what had happened to the range of her emotion. Her bald head softened no part of her expression. I remembered Shirley as the academic with long black hair who had arrived at the Community a few years back, at the top of her profession: very sure of herself. And now was this her only status, giving me reflection on my flower arranging? She spoke in strident imitation of her master's voice.

Although Shirley was still a formal student and I was not, we would both be back here tonight to meditate and drink tea.

Looking at the flowers through her eyes, I saw a display of nostalgia, flowers gaining third prize at an English flower show. This was not a suitable focus for meditation on the words of a radical teacher who saw things in black and white. Immediately I said, "You are right; I will do them again."

"Do you have time before meditation?" she asked.

"It's possible. I will do it."

As I drove away, I remembered for a moment another Shirley that I had known a long time ago, when I was seven. I was new to the school. Shirley Everett had freckles and curly hair. She yelled from her favorite spot at the far end of the schoolyard to announce the start of a new game. A group of ten girls circled eagerly around her, waiting to be picked. Shirley poked each of our stomachs in turn and towards the end slowed down her counting, to calculate the conclusion.

"O–U–T spells 'out,' and out you must go!" she said. "Marlowe, you're not in the game."

Narrowly missing a large Mercedes on Massachusetts Avenue, I brought my attention back to the flowers. Deriding myself for maudlin self-pity, I drove to Formaggio's Kitchen, the most upmarket source of flowers in town, and found that they only had more delicate pastel blossoms. I needed something with more *Shakti*. I tried Star Market, which didn't usually have the same quality of flowers, but I thought maybe there would be something more dynamic. I paid out of my own money for the freshest, brightest gladioli I could find and huge Shasta daisies. On returning to the Center, I collected all four of the vases, lifted out the previous flowers, threw them in the trash, and started again.

Sometimes it seemed as though the flowers arranged themselves without my intervention, but not today. The Shasta daisies began to look disheveled. I jabbed in the spiked stems in repeated attempts to ward off disapproval. The red gladioli looked as though I had just stuck them in. *This is just not coming alive, and nor am I,* I thought, *but since my judgment has been off all day maybe I'm wrong about this too.*

This time, I approached Justice. Usually I felt more warmth in her than in Stephanie. I loved the way she turned her dignified, smooth head towards me. Justice was once so warm and bubbly that it had been suggested to her that she stop hugging people and watch out for her ego hiding behind her charming smile. I stood in front of her as if across a moat, having no idea how to access friendship. I looked for the softness in her eyes.

She said sternly, "We know you are capable of better than this. What's going on?"

I was sorry to disappoint her. I felt like an ungainly child near her poise. "I'll do it again," I said.

I threw out all the flowers, drove to three specialty shops, and spent $250 on a tropical theme: sunflowers, birds of paradise, hibiscus, and red hot pokers. I made my way through rush-hour traffic back to Mass Ave, into the Center, and rushed four new arrangements into the hall. I thought, *Surely more Shakti in this?*

The flowers were transformed by my lifeless touch into unintegrated stalks, staring back at me with dismayed faces. Looking into Justice's face, I thought, *What am I? A child looking for affirmation from the grownups? Andrew never wanted us to relate to one another without dignity. He said we would grow bold and independent.*

"I have no idea what you are going to do now," Shirley said, of the vase of expensive stalks. "I don't know what you can do."

She left the room.

I ran through my options. Anger would be seen as the ego acting out; protest would be interpreted as defensiveness; tears could only be indulgence of weakness. Every possible response would only be my ego, so I was trapped. I searched inside for the response that comes from nowhere, the response before thought, which even in the face of terror can set one free, but there wasn't one.

Justice came back in and announced, "I have called Foxhollow. Missy is coming right away. She will do the flower arranging from now on."

Inside me, the fragile silver thread snapped.

Chapter 14

The No Woman

Four large china mugs with matching lids stood side by side on the kitchen counter. Sumi, her black hair hanging over the counter, removed the lids and stirred vigorously to make the tea as strong as possible, before adding the milk. It was Typhoo tea. My mom had sent it to me for Easter from England. At home we never stir the tea but here it is different: we need every extra particle of caffeine. It was 5am and we were taking our first break in meditation practice to drink tea. I relished the feeling of necessary exhaustion as we set about our ritual. The four of us didn't talk and didn't make eye contact until after breakfast.

Out of the corner of my eye, I noticed Missy's light curls, turning gray here and there, framing a look of confusion on her broad, open face. She picked up her cup tentatively, as if not sure she had grasped it in the right place. Her touch was so light that I wondered if the cup would fall. I knew her melancholy. I felt her pain at being cast out of Andrew's inner circle. For years she had been his trusted confidant. I loved Missy and loved living with her. For me this was a happy time. For her it was not enough. I wished that she could be happy here with us, but I understood.

Betsy leaned forward to pick up the fourth cup. She had been training for a marathon before it was suggested that she join this house. She was still in shape, though she had lost the will to train.

The four of us—Sumi, Betsy, Missy and I—returned to sit in our small room at the top of the house. Our chairs were arranged in a square, facing a picture of Andrew and a small-leaved vine. We had chosen a picture of him looking grave. I had a photo in one of my boxes of Andrew in the early days, head thrown back, laughing. It would not have been fitting to use that photo now. Our lives were a somber endeavor to move us towards humility. On the floor was a threadbare turquoise rug. Missy always liked that rug and resisted all our attempts to replace it with a newer one. The faces of the vine leaves arched their heart-shapes towards me with tenderness. The vine was straggly, but I had grown to love the flow of the pink stems over the edge of the pot onto the brown, hand-thrown dish underneath. I still have the plant. It has grown a mass of shiny leaves that overflow onto my husband's bookcase.

Four women and my two teenagers lived together in a house in Cambridge. We did not go to the Center. There were no meetings. We had lost the right to communal meditation; I understood that other students should be spared having to witness our humiliation. We had been stripped of the privilege of doing service. We all had jobs but no social life. Andrew hoped that we would be shocked by the humiliation into rejoining the Community with gusto and humility. He hoped that our intransigence would shift and we would recommit to his movement. We had been given no guidance on whether to practice. How we conducted ourselves was up to us. Sometimes women in this position were called "No Women." We knew we were "No Women."

I did not know it at the time, but living as a "No Woman" would prove to be a turning point for me. I thought that I was working to rejoin the Community; however, I had learned over the years to censor my thoughts. We all learned this. Like pruning a tree, first we lopped off a few twigs here and there, and then a branch of thinking or feeling, and then another branch. We reframed our internal experience so it would fit the Community mindset. Even living without contact with other Community members, we No Women continued to think and feel within the same confines. The spontaneous expression of ourselves was stunted and feeble. You could tell a No Woman from the way she walked.

We had given ourselves a daily practice of two and a half hours of chanting. We breathed and chanted in unison, phrase by phrase, a whole book, every morning.

> *When our relationship to life is based upon waiting,*
> *It's not possible for us to know*
> *What it's like to be truly alive...*

I gave in to the rhythm, letting my spirits soar to where fear and exhaustion could not touch me. I felt the wisdom of Andrew's words as we chanted them for the thousandth time. I am not sure now whether I had truly learned how to meditate on the divine or whether, instead, I was using the ritual and rhythm to anaesthetize myself from underlying thoughts and feelings.

> *Liberation rests on the explosive recognition*
> *That thought is not self,*
> *That thought is only thought...*

Betsy's head began to nod in sleep. Someone kindly picked up the chanting pace in response. Stirred, she rejoined the chant and once again sat wide-awake.

> *We will find that when we experience joy,*
> *There is enormous room inside our hearts for others...*
> *But when we experience fear,*
> *Then there is rarely any concern for anyone other than our own self.*

I lost focus and thought about the heavy traffic on Route 95 that I would face on my commute. Missy's eyes boring into the back of my head brought me back. We were exquisitely alone and minutely connected. Each of us knew the melody exactly, though there were no marks on the page. I felt grateful that Andrew had brought us together and offered us a time of intense, focused attention as an opportunity to change. It felt good that he thought about me enough to have considered what was best for me.

After a few months, the indignity of this situation wore off. We were weary travelers who had learned to care for one another, perhaps because of our long and painful journey. We had become aware of the damage resulting from one another's internal voices of condemnation and critique, and we had become gentle. There was no one here to report to those higher up. We did not accuse each other of "not going for it." We didn't hammer one another to change. And besides, none of us wanted to use the old tools of coercion. When one of us made a mistake, the others offered up reflection, like food, to be received if and when the other was hungry.

I recognized for these few months feelings of peace and companionable ordinariness. And in this companionable ordinariness I began to feel moments of spontaneity. I would sometimes forget to monitor my words before I spoke. I would bound up the stairs in delight like a child and flop on Jessica's bed when she was listening to music in the evening. I would even laugh.

Sumi, from Indonesia, had been young and beautiful when she joined the Community. Ten years of house cleaning, the only work she could find, had taken their toll. She moved heavily, as if it were an effort. She could not afford the chiropractic treatment she needed. Now and then, we explored with her what stood in the way of her mastering the graphic design program which might be her passport to self-respect and survival in this foreign country.

Even though Missy had once been Andrew's most trusted emissary, among the No Women she took no position, and we met as equals. No one was scoring points anymore, and no one kept the score. Missy was deeply hurt by being outcast and by the loss of many friendships. Although she felt crushed, she could not hide her graceful spirit. It was as if she had been dismantled inside, her soul now almost numb. But she continued to be gentle and wise.

When Betsy had first met Andrew, a door to spiritual life had opened wide for her, and we saw in her face vitality, wonder, and openness. Back then, she could meet Andrew's gaze, and, side by side with him, push the edges of dharmic understanding. She could speak up from the back of a meeting of 300 people and ask him to explain himself more clearly. She was also critical. We used to hide our mistakes around Betsy for fear of being lashed by her tongue. But a couple of years before, after my first failure to endure the lake for an hour, it was Betsy's radical and stirring words that had inspired me to succeed.

Over the years, however, Betsy had become fragile and vulnerable. The skin on her face seemed dry. I saw who she might be in 20 years' time. She seemed unreal. I remembered how warm I had felt each time Betsy and I had cooked together years earlier, when we were both doing well. But now, when I looked into her eyes, there was no one there. With a shock, I realized that I understood this experience because I had been there myself. I was seeing my own past and perhaps my own future. I allowed the thought to become conscious that Betsy was—sensibly, perhaps—defending herself with old patterns developed over years of trying to be something she was not. Later, in a Master's course on psychopathology, I would identify this condition, which so many of us entered during downward spirals in this Community, as a loss of sense of self: a condition in which the constructive part of our ego is so diminished that there is little to hold on to. This condition is often the result of trauma.

Within our group of No Women, Betsy began to relax and trust. She began to talk about her disconnected feelings. She traced the threads of disconnection to her troubled relationship with her dictatorial father; it would have been unthinkable to trace these threads to Andrew Cohen as well. I did not make that connection either, at the time. Radiantly she shared with us the lifting of a burden of anger. We celebrated with her each day the new tenderness in her. This tenderness led her to connect with my shy and inaccessible daughter Jessica, who was much in need of warmth. The two of them often chatted while Betsy ironed her office clothes for work and Jessica made toast.

The women, witnessing my parenting, steered me steadily in the direction of gentleness and consistency. One day, I saw Becky's fear of me in her eyes. Gradually, I became aware that over the last years my parenting had become harsh and driven by my own fear. Senior students had intimidated me and, in a parallel process, I had intimidated my children. These women saw that dialogue with my children might not be too late. In our isolation, we were beginning to dismantle the culture of fear.

One Monday, without warning, we were summoned to Foxhollow. We were all nervous, yet tentatively hopeful, because we knew we had progress to report.

I cancelled my consultation at a school on the North Shore and drove the two and a half hours to Foxhollow with my house-mates. In the car, we voiced our more optimistic thoughts:

"I wonder who will meet with us!"

"Not Andrew himself." (We knew we did not merit his direct attention.)

"It could be Damien." (I hoped it wouldn't be Damien.)

"Probably Damien," said Missy.

"I wonder if they just want to check in with us." (This was the most benign possibility.)

"It might be another change." (Missy didn't say what all of us were thinking: maybe they would split us up, elevating some and not others.)

"Another house move?" (I could handle another house move, no problem.)

"Maybe we will be allowed back."

"What's been happening between us is so beautiful; we just

have to stay in touch with that," a thin voice added. (I wondered if our experience would be applauded or invalidated.)

Andrew Cohen was unpredictable and erratic. We all knew that anything could happen.

As we drove between the rows of stately white pines leading to the mansion, I once again pushed away the thought that this was a grand house for a man who taught simplicity. Many times I had prepared myself to enter Foxhollow. Over the last two years, this driveway had evoked in me excitement, passion, confidence, terror, resistance, love, and now a rather fragile hope. Two years ago, I reminded myself, I had walked into this mansion fearless and passionately eager to face everything that stood in the way of seeing myself in the mirror. Now I asked myself, *Was that spirit the call of the unknown in its full glory? Or was I foolish to underestimate the strength and arrogance of my ego? Or both?*

I half-expected that we would be ushered in through the rear entrance, but instead we walked up the steps to the front door. Erica and another woman were arranging bird of paradise flowers with bulrushes in the entranceway. I had met Erica in the farmhouse in southwest England more than a decade previously. We had talked with excitement about embarking on a great adventure together. We had met the same challenge in the lake. We had been housemates and looked after each other's children. I wanted to reach out to her with a smile and talk to her; but instead, aware of the rules surrounding my status, I nodded with minimal recognition. She ignored the overture.

The four of us No Women entered the formal sitting room, took our places cross-legged on the thick pile carpet, and waited in silence. Sitting cross-legged was still painful for my back and knees, but I had learned how to shift my weight from time to time so that the legs didn't go numb. I calculated that if I shifted position now I would have a full 45 minutes before the pain set in, which might take us through the meeting if they came in soon. *After all these years I should be better at sitting cross-legged,* I thought. I studied the satisfying, symmetrical curves on the recently renovated moldings high above. I would have loved being on that project. I felt a tremendous sense of loss that I had not continued working on the building teams.

We waited. My anxiety built. I thought back to a meeting with Andrew ten years ago when I had complained that his being an hour late had affected many people in my life. Andrew, furious, had told me that I was being petty and I had my priorities wrong. Now, as a No Woman, I knew better than to feel angry or even irritated by waiting. We had had many hours of practice at feeling less and less. Having censored our core ability to discriminate feelings, there was no more challenging right and wrong. Control of our thoughts followed easily. I shifted my position again.

After an hour or so, Stephanie and two others entered silently and sat down on cushions facing us. I was glad Andrew and Damien were not there. Their faces were blank. It had been three months since we had seen another student, so they did not know what we had been doing. They asked. We told them that the discipline of the practice that we had given ourselves was powerful and strengthening. One of us told them with cautious excitement about how we were moved and inspired by the changes going on for Betsy. Each of us described how our conversations and practice were creating intimacy between us. Then Stephanie, the most humble and respected of all Andrew's students, told us that we had been given so much for so long that it was shameful we should be satisfied with the miserable lives we had.

Inside, I felt a small voice say softly, *I am not ashamed.*

Stephanie, more vehement now, said we should be desperate, torn apart by being away from the Community, and that we should be ceaselessly striving to get back.

The small voice said, *I am not sure that I want to go back.*

Stephanie said she was shocked that we had become satisfied with having a good time and loving one another.

Inside me, the voice said, *The love that we have shown each other is what matters.*

Shouting at us now, Stephanie asked whether we cared only about ourselves. She said this teaching was not about personal enlightenment. We shouldn't be here, she said, if we were only in it for our own satisfaction. Didn't we want to be warriors in the foremost world revolution? She looked at Missy, who had been her lover and partner when they joined the Community, and said, "You have gone so high, you were capable of so much, how could you walk away from this? You were a warrior once." And then looking at the four of us, she shouted, "You were all warriors once!"

No one replied.

For the first time in months, I felt something resolute inside me. I felt that Stephanie was fundamentally mistaken, that our lives in the No Woman house were not shameful. I was angry that Stephanie should have the power to trash Betsy's growth. I could not reframe my feelings out of convenience, nor to keep out of trouble. Submission was not a possible response. And I could not now believe that Stephanie spoke on behalf of my own true inner self.

This one independent feeling formed a wedge between me and the guru system.

On the two-hour drive back to Cambridge, nobody said much. When we got home, I asked if we could have a meeting. We went upstairs to Missy and Sumi's bedroom and sat on the threadbare turquoise carpet square. Quietly, I said, "I love you; I love living in this house with all of you; and I love living with my children. There is so much tenderness between us; we care for each other and we share our lives. But if this is a place where these things are not valued, then I am in the wrong place."

There was a long pause.

I was expressing doubts about the Community out loud for the first time in 15 years. Even now, I could hear two different responses inside myself. The Community voice said, *These shameful doubts are the work of my ego. If I see that these thoughts are the ravings of my ignorant, selfish mind, then I should not believe them!* And the new voice, neither strong nor strident, said, *I don't agree with Stephanie!* Somewhere inside myself, I identified this as my own voice.

Everyone was strangely silent.

I kept talking, though I could hardly find the breath to do so. I told them that when Stephanie said that we should feel ashamed, I didn't feel ashamed. When she said that we should be torn apart by our miserable lives, I realized that I was not torn apart by being excluded from the Community. I said that the kindness and support that I had known in this house had been hard won over many months. It was not something I would throw away like trash.

"Is there anything else?" Betsy asked.

I found it easier to talk now that I had started. "I will always be grateful to Andrew. He opened the door for me to a spiritual life. He helped me to see what other people see when they look at me, and in his Community I have learned how to live with people."

"Then why are you talking this way?" Missy asked.

Without hesitation I repeated, "This is not the right place for me."

If this conversation had taken place in any other household, someone would have tried to rekindle the passion that had once soared inside me or would have appealed to my conscience to sustain the whole. They might have angrily pointed out that I was weakening others, but this time nobody disagreed. In fact, nobody said anything much.

Jessica, now in her last year of high school, was staying with a friend. I told her over the phone that we were leaving. She said,

"But I was brought up to think that the Community was our home, that it was the only place that was right."

"I know, Jessica. But it isn't the right place for me now."

"Why have you changed your mind?"

I said, "I think what Andrew is teaching has changed. It's pure, but there's no heart in it. You know how hard I can be on you and Becky? Well, I'm just as hard on myself, and in this Community my own harsh judgment is reinforced. I have given this my best shot, but I can't keep going with this intensity. It is just too much."

"I think I understand," said Jessica. "But, Mom, being in the Community is still the best thing that could have ever happened to me."

I told 16-year-old Becky at Christopher's Restaurant. We sat in one of the wood-lined booths. Becky ordered her usual hamburger and fries. When she asked why I was leaving, I said, "It's a very demanding life." I could not yet fully own my insight that I did not believe the Community line. Instead, I reverted to Community-think and blamed myself. "I was too selfish. It's too much. My insecurity is stronger than my desire to give to the whole."

"It is OK for me, Mom," Becky reassured me. "Most of my life has no connection with the Community now anyway, but what about you? It's been your whole life for 15 years—your friends, everything you believe in. Will you be okay?"

"I have always tried to follow my heart," I said. "It's the only guide I have. It has to be right."

I knew that I was now on my own, yet I had assumed my housemates and I would figure out what to do as a group. I imagined my friendship with them continuing in a different form. But the next day, after they had met without me, they told me that I would assume responsibility for the $2,500 house rent and they would look for a small apartment. It did not occur to me to question this decision. I had ostracized myself even from the

No Women.

If I had thought through what their response to me might be, I would have known that they would need to close ranks against me to keep themselves unscathed by my leaving. It certainly never entered my head that they would want to leave too. When I encountered Missy many years later, we figured out that we had both left during the same month, but each of us had forgotten the other's drama. Betsy and Sumi would leave too, within a couple of years.

I was unable to conceive of the extent of separation between us. I imagined helping them find a new house, lugging furniture, and packing up the kitchen. I did not want Betsy to risk her job by taking another day off work. I did not want Sumi to lift heavy boxes with her bad back. But I had broken the contract, and in their minds I could no longer be their companion even when they needed help. In order not to expose them to the embarrassment of being face to face with a traitor, I offered to leave for a week to give them a chance to get organized. It was a painful time.

Becky and I went camping for a week at Brewster Beach. We played mini-golf every day.

One afternoon, as she drove off the tee towards the mouth of the pirate cave, she asked, "Why did we have to come here camping, exactly?" Sensing that the taboo on negativity towards the Community had lifted, she had become angry, protective and persistent.

I replied, "Because I left the Community and the others needed time to find another place."

"Why couldn't we stay with them in the house?"

"Because once someone has decided to leave, then it's like a marriage: it's over. It's best if we don't see each other."

"But why couldn't they leave? Why did it have to be us?"

"Because I was the one who broke the contract. I am sorry," I said. "I didn't mean it to end like this."

I did not share my suffering with her. I believed that she was better off without it. Besides, all three of us had a long habit of keeping things inside.

"Can we have a vacation one day because we want to," Becky asked, "instead of because we have to get out of the house?"

"Yes," I said. "We will have real vacations. We will go to Morocco and we will hike to the bottom of the Grand Canyon. "

"Really, Mom?"

"It's a promise."

And we did. We spent New Year's Eve in Morocco one year, ten days in Costa Rica another year, and eventually visited the deserts of New Mexico.

Part IV

Out

Chapter 15

Grief

One month after leaving, I mailed a donation for $500 to the Community. I wanted a clean break, without leaving behind any karma. Later, in denial that anything had changed in my relationship to Andrew, I mailed this letter:

Dear Andrew,

Because you are my deepest friend, and because I know you to be insatiably curious, it feels wrong not to share with you more of my life. I am finding that the gifts of God's grace continue. I have no doubt that any understanding of life that I have, I owe to you.

It is a great relief to find that I don't have to stop loving you because I have left. I am glad that even though I have left the Community, I don't have to pull away from you, who opened my heart.

Love from Marlowe

Andrew wrote back to me on a small slip of paper, "It was good to hear from you."

Journal entry:

Thank you, Andrew! A personal note from Andrew himself! I am so touched by his care. Something feels completed. He has freed me up to be fully here now. The past can fall away and I can start from here, and here, and here, forever without shadows. Thank you, Andrew.

I tried to convince myself that I could move on, but I was an open sore. I could not yet grieve.

Three months after leaving, I felt more isolated. It was the darkest time of year; the evenings closed with finality. I drew the

216

kitchen curtains, watching the red fabric fall in folds as I corrected the snag. In that one gesture, I felt the sadness of my generations, daughter, mother, grandmother, making it through interminable winters. I felt our identical satisfaction of drawing family close and shutting out the cold of night.

I regarded the cheap red curtains. I remembered many years ago in Devon how Jürgen and I had picked out curtains for the bay window in the living room. He had been irritated that in provincial Devon the haberdashery store only offered floral prints. I could not relate to the person I was then. She had gone.

I had an hour to spare before 16-year-old Becky would come home from school. Becky had spent her entire childhood in what I would soon call a cult. I had left Andrew but now she no longer needed a full-time parent. Jessica, now 18, was starting her first year of college. Occasionally I would see glimpses of her anger towards me. It would be some years before we could talk about it. Both girls were rapidly gaining strength now they were free of the Community expectations, but I needed more time. They needed me to support their independence, but I wanted to be closer to them in order to redress my loss and guilt.

At the kitchen table, beginning to let in the pain of separation, I wrote in my journal:

> *I am desolate. I feel nothing. I don't fit anywhere.*
>
> *I thought I would find relief out here, but there is none. Out here it is scary.*
>
> *Maybe I need a hobby? What are my hobbies? I can't remember.*
>
> *It feels as if tears have been running down my face all day. Sadness. Loss. Loss of what? Leaving was the right thing to do. Better to leave before I disintegrated.*

One day at power yoga, in a hundred degrees of humid heat, I worked my body till it burned. We were so closely packed that my mat touched that of a tall, strong woman with blond hair. We sweated side by side, aware of each other's effort, each of us knowing the cost to the other of holding the arduous poses.

Afterwards, we talked, sitting on our sweaty yoga mats. She had heard of Andrew Cohen. She asked me what he was like. Glad of her interest, I began, "Andrew is extraordinarily gifted. He has the power to see into a person's soul; he inspires devotion and trust; and he knows how to take people to a perspective beyond the mind."

"I understand that Andrew claims to be perfect," she said softly.

"We were all striving to be a perfect expression of love," I said, sidestepping the question. "Anything less would have been failure."

"Wow," she said. "Tall order! How did it affect you, being his student?" She leaned towards me. "Do you think it strengthened you?" Her gaze was particularly piercing.

My silence spoke for itself.

"How are you doing now?" she asked. I started to put my towel into my backpack and to sponge down the yoga mat. I had thought she was genuinely interested in my story. I had no idea it would draw pity, and I didn't like it. *Surely*, I told myself, *failure in Andrew's Community was failure to reach the highest of all goals. Surely no one could doubt the integrity of my honorable striving.* The thought then crossed my mind that perhaps I was not a failed warrior, but pitiful.

"Look," I said, too sure of my story. "I would never go back in. It was brutal, but I willingly chose a situation for accelerated growth. I don't regret joining Andrew and I don't regret leaving him."

She looked doubtful and afraid.

I regretted talking to her: no one outside the Community could understand. But it was too late. In her eyes I had seen reflected the grandiosity of my story. She had challenged my attempt to hold a cherished belief which sustained my residual narcissism. We rolled up our yoga mats and left the hall.

Seven months after leaving, the girls and I still lived in the expensive house that I was left with when the No Women moved out. I had been offered a job to start a non-profit for children. It paid well and included extensive training, benefits, and tuition for college classes. This opportunity would jump-start my new career as a child psychotherapist. As always, I found work to be an organizing and stabilizing focus.

At home, Becky's steady presence was the most important thing in my life. Her companionship stood between me and depression, which was a heavy burden for a teenager. Becky had always liked shopping for food and cooking. When she was in middle school, I would push the cart in the supermarket in case she spotted a schoolmate and needed to dart away for fear of looking un-cool. Now she was unembarrassed to load the cart with the best combination of cheeses to make ravioli from scratch.

Becky was coming into her own. One of her teachers asked me, "This is an extraordinary young woman. How did you bring her up?" At a teacher's meeting another said, "This is not what we usually get from a single parent." I watched Becky's grades shift from B's to straight A's. Her history teacher said, "This girl brings out the best in those around her. She bridges the divide between races in my classroom."

Andrew used to say that anyone who left him would be haunted for the rest of his or her life. And I *was* haunted. I remembered how in the Community we used to scorn ex-students who would cling to each other once they had left. "Pathetic!" we had said. "Victimized!" "Refusing to take responsibility!" Therefore, I had not spoken to any other ex-Community people, though I knew many lived close by. I hadn't even called Erica, who had shared triumph with me in the Lake, nor Victoria whom I had helped to move out; nor even Missy who had lived with me as a "No Woman."

Instead, I thought of my friends in the Community. I carefully glued the list of Community phone numbers into the back of my address book and duplicated it, in case I lost the book.

I was unable to move forwards or backwards. I was not yet able to grieve the loss in my heart of my leader, my friends, and my sense of meaning in life. I could not say, "Good bye."

Nine months after leaving the Community, I was sleeping long and deep, but it was a hollow sleep without relief.

I wrote, *When my primary drive to change was from fear of Andrew's anger then nothing wholesome could come out of it. The fear amplified not my conscience but my desire to get things right.* I began to suspect Andrew's manipulation of me: *As soon as I surrendered and trusted Andrew, he changed the rules, and I would suddenly find I had made a mistake.*

I had not spoken to a Community person for nine months, yet I saw that I still feared displeasing Andrew. *I am afraid,* I wrote, *because I will make Andrew angry by asking these questions. He still controls me!*

With horror, I saw my irrational fear that I might be punished even now for writing my doubts down on paper. My internal monitor assessing whether my thoughts and actions met with Andrew's approval was still in place. Seeing my ongoing dependence enabled me to begin asking questions that until now had felt unaskable. Very slowly I began to think differently about Andrew.

I had time now to walk around and around Fresh Pond. I was without connections; I needed a friend. My brother John visited during this time. We did not talk much about the Community, but he was very loving. He went out and bought arctic char and asparagus and cooked them for Becky and me. I still remember the flavor. Perhaps it was the first food I had really tasted in months.

One year after leaving, the lease on the expensive No Woman house expired, and I was eager to reduce my rent. I viewed one-bedroom apartments in a safe upmarket area of North Cambridge so that Becky could walk to school. I took a break at the Half Moon café, bought a glass of wine and let the memories flood in. For the first time I became angry.

I remembered arriving, bold and full of fire, on the East Coast after travelling across the country. Andrew welcomed me with warmth and openness, and soon afterwards undermined my independence and trashed my softness. *What gave him the right to play me like a puppet? To herald me like a miracle one minute and banish me as a "No Woman" the next?* I saw how Andrew drew benefit from magnifying and distorting our experience into a world of alternating heaven and hell.

I was angry with Andrew for duping us into believing that he understood love. He must have known that what comes from within is of the greatest value.

I was angry. Angry that Andrew had used his state of contagious luminescence, which blew us away in Totnes, to create a behaviorist hierarchy effective at crushing souls. I was angry with myself for having buried my instincts so deep that I could stand by and witness others' crushing.

I left my third glass of wine on the table and walked out into the summer night needing to be alone. I turned south towards the river.

I was angry with myself for spending so little time with my children, and for neglecting them for almost their entire childhood. My most intense anger was because I only had myself to blame. Why, I asked, did I leave Totnes? Was it for the sake of more bliss at the expense of my entire family? Was it for a spiritual impulse of value or for purely self-serving ends? Had the entire enterprise served my ego?

As my attachment began to loosen, I looked back in disbelief at my gratitude for the one-line comment from Andrew in response to the letter I'd sent him after I left. Andrew Cohen was not my deepest friend: his actions had nearly destroyed me!

It was probably two years after leaving that I began to find moments of meaning in my life. I took classes in woodturning, dance, and creative writing. I made several unsuccessful attempts to relate to men. After the most durable—a 20-month relationship with a man who was good at lying—I would see in therapy the extent to which I had lost myself in this new relationship in search of healing for my years in the Community. I saw that I could lose myself in a blissful romantic connection, but it would take effort to have a healthy balance of power and good communication. The boundaries of my self were so fragile that it would take years before I would be capable of healthy intimacy.

First meetings with Andrew triggered a profound connection with life. I found my own strength and trusted my instincts. This orientation to life recurred when I met the tantric teacher, in the desert in Utah, and when building the meditation center. Now, while valuing support and intimacy with others I determined that I would never again look to someone else to heal me. It would take ongoing attention to accept that I did not need a guru, healer, or lover to be whole.

Chapter 16

Strengthening Relationships

The truth is not unitary or simple, it is vast and multifaceted and complex and confusing.
Bromberg (1998)

Four years after we left the Community, Becky was about to graduate from high school. Jürgen would arrive soon for the graduation. He had visited the children at least once a year for 13 years and now without the disapproval of those around me he would stay with us. We were friends now and without awkwardness, at least on the surface. But this evening Becky and I celebrated alone. We visited the end-of-year art gallery displaying Becky's finest sculptures, then ate at our favorite Algerian restaurant. We sat on tasseled cushions; above us hung an ancient lamp made of colored glass. We ate lamb skewers and smoky baba ganoush served with rosewater-lemonade. Becky, impeccable in a fitted navy-blue spring dress, had lost ten pounds, and regular jogging had built up muscle. High school fears and social insecurities were mostly behind her. Her teachers looked smaller, their foibles more benign. I praised her for the way she systematically planned and worked to get straight A's and a scholarship to a great college. She had forged for herself a robust path toward academic dreams. I was proud of who she had become. I loved how she was growing into a delicate, generous, and successful woman, how she held my gaze, her stiff hugs, her Englishness and her wry smile when she made a joke.

I asked her how she viewed our time in the Community now.

She said, "On the face of it, the way that you adults were with each other gave us the most amazing role models. You did not fight; you negotiated well; you seemed to care about one another. But when I heard recently about the physical abuse and financial corruption, then I am not sure what to make of it all."

I replied, "I know what you mean." Then, thinking out loud, I said, "Did you ever count up how many times we moved house?"

"No," said Becky in a matter-of-fact voice. "But Jane (Victoria's daughter) counted once and said she had moved 26 times in 12 years. But it doesn't matter, Mom. Home is wherever *you* are. "

I asked what had been hardest for her.

She replied cautiously, "I remember our first Community house. Nothing bad ever happened *there*."

But after a pause she continued, "But there was a tension in me all the time we were in the Community. I kept a constant secret: I knew that most people outside the Community would be suspicious of our living arrangements. I had to protect you, so you would not be seen as weird. Worst of all, I was afraid that if I told anyone, the children's protective services would come and send us to a foster home." She looked down, then back at me.

"This is the first time I've told anyone that."

I was devastated to hear that I had caused so much pain and fear in her young life. She had spent her childhood living a double life for fear of losing her family. I asked her when she first had this idea of being taken away. "Very young," she said. "Maybe eight years old."

We were silent for a while. Her longtime pain was too much for me. Finally, I broke the silence, and said, "I am sorry I did not keep you safe. Sorry I did not give you the support you needed."

"Mom, it's all OK."

Becky, who had carried this dark secret all these years, was still protecting me.

Jessica was home from college for spring break. She was studying environmental science, had a tight group of friends, and was loved by a kind young man. She was blossoming into a beautiful, articulate young woman, content with herself. She knew that I loved her. She knew that I would always be there for her. What was I afraid of? *Something needs to be healed, and I am not sure what it is*, I thought. And I did not know where to begin.

We stood on the raised beds in the back garden, preparing them for nasturtium and sweet peas, which would trail over the flowerbeds and be visible from the deck. In the past, she had dreaded having "a talk" with me, suspicious that I would criticize her. Her reticence was understandable: I had often demanded of her an eagerness for change that I could not muster myself.

I told her that I wanted to heal something both inside myself and in how I had treated her. I tried to make the message unladen. I tried not to expect her to respond with gratitude, interest, or even understanding. I told her about my journey over the last few years since leaving the Community, how I had been learning to forgive myself. I told her that I was sorry for all the times I had been harsh or unavailable. Now and then we glanced up at each other, but we continued pulling pieces of weed roots out of the crumbly soil and making little dimples in the friable leaf mold, ready for the seeds.

She responded by opening like a radiant flower.

Later in the day, she accidentally walked in on me naked as I was relaxing in the bath. She hadn't seen me naked for many years. She collected the shampoo that she needed. A few minutes later, she came in again, but not accidentally. This seemed sweet and natural.

And that evening when sitting in the living room after dinner, she was able to talk to me about how angry she still felt about the decisions I had made over and over again each time we moved schools or moved house, disrupting her attempts to build settled relationships. We came closer.

I visited England at Christmas. It was evening. The wood-burning fire was alight, drying my socks which were soaked from a day's work inside leaky Wellington boots. My parents and I relaxed into pleasant tiredness after chopping wood. As we finished eating, the dog scampered excitedly to the kitchen, waiting eagerly for the scraps of fatty roasted Muscovy duck to land in her bowl.

My parents were both 81, slowing but still actively farming a half-acre of vegetables. Dad still smoked an ounce of roll-up cigarettes every day and lived on salt fat pork. The foot that the doctor had sewed back on his leg after the accident with the weed whacker still worked, and he walked without a limp. Tomorrow, he would water the pumpkin seedlings which he hoped would produce the autumn crop.

Mom sighed as she sat down by the fire and added water to the whiskey I had bought at the duty-free.

"I wondered if we could talk a little about when I joined the Community," I began.

Dad was resistant. "It's better that I don't say anything."

Mom said, "It was terribly worrying. I was most worried for the children. I didn't know what would happen to them."

"I am so sorry, Mom," I said. "It was a strange and terrible thing to do to you all."

Mom continued, "The worst moment was when you called from America and told us how unhappy Becky was in school. She was six at the time. Do you remember that?"

I replied, "No. I had forgotten that I had told you that. And you, Dad? What was the worst moment?"

Unable to access intense emotion, he replied, "There's nothing to say."

I continued anyway, "I am sorry for all the hurt and destruction that I caused you. I think I was just riding roughshod over everyone in order to follow my dreams."

Dad said, "I was just so surprised that another person could sway you."

"Why so surprised?"

He replied, "I'd always thought that you were just like me: never listened to anyone, always made up your own mind."

I persisted, "You mean what happens when we give ourselves away."

Dad inhaled a draft of nicotine, "Yes that's it, being swayed by someone."

I said, "I have thought a lot about what made me do that."

My wise mother asked kindly, "Tell me, Marlowe: How else could we have handled it? Was there anything else we could have done? I know some parents who have physically removed their children from cults."

I replied, "There wasn't anything else you could have done. You and Dad have given us a home base ever since we left for America. You never gave up on me."

Mom said, "It was so upsetting when you left Jürgen, he loved you all so much."

I replied, "Yes, he was a good kind husband and I caused him a lot of pain."

"I was devastated by the loss of you all," Mom said. "I mean, the kids are wonderful people, but I will still never get over the fact that you are so far away."

Then Dad surprised me with his insight. "Marlowe needed to do this," he said. "There was something that she needed to learn. It wasn't necessarily a bad thing."

I said, "You are so clever, Dad," glad of a diversion from acknowledging the pain I had caused them.

I was in the process of buying a little cottage in the nearby town, which might, in years to come, be a place for them to retire to. Or maybe I would move back some day.

Back at home in Gloucester, a single candle burned on the low windowsill, though I could still see the trees as I looked out of our living room window. My tawny dog, Dragon, stood outside on a rock staring into the New England forest, every nerve poised. Smells here and there held her attention; then, suddenly, she leapt into the air and bounded into the undergrowth. Her strong forelegs burrowed deep into the snow, throwing up mounds of sandy earth in pursuit of some creature that was long gone.

It was five years since we had left the Community. Becky had come down from Ithaca for the weekend. We looked online for a birthday present for Jürgen. Once a year or so, usually at Christmas, even after we both remarried, Jürgen, the children and I would return to the timeless rhythm of the farm. Jürgen and I had talked a little about the past. I acknowledged the price that I had extorted for the sake of my journey. Mostly we crunched across the shingle beach of Lyme Regis Bay, and even in winter sat at the end of the Cobb while the fog rolled in and the waves crashed at the harbor walls, letting the sour tang of malt vinegar cut the grease of local fish and chips.

Becky settled in to study for her chemistry exam while I typed the following personal ad for the local paper:

I am an intelligent, single woman with a history of spiritual practice. My interests include power yoga, writing, education, traveling, and hiking. I am 53, in great shape, and looking for a companion with whom I might learn, over time, to share laughter, tenderness, and companionable-ordinariness. I am in search of an unusually self-aware man who can meet me in searching for the right balance of intimacy and independence. I am looking for a monogamous, single man with a warm heart, who like myself is both reasonably confident and interested in learning how to give everything to a relationship.

I deleted "everything" in the last line of the ad and inserted "fully" and pressed, "Send."

A few days later I wrote to a psychologist friend, "Poring through the replies in my mailbox makes my head spin! There is one already that catches my eye: from an antique dealer who loves horses, photography, and exotic travel. His name is Julian. We are beginning to correspond."

My friend replied, "Yes, it **is** nerve-wracking, but only when we are so very dependent on the outcome."

I e-mailed her two days later: "Emotions are running high. The force of desire drives my tendency to imbue any likely candidate with gifts from Eros. Is it possible (this time!) to make clear, rational decisions even when fantasy threatens to take control?"

She responded, "Remember you once said to me, 'If he looks REAL good REAL fast, you have to take it slowly and be careful.'"

A week later, I set about writing a report on a five-year-old boy who was regressing at school. The parents had asked me to observe him. At circle time in the classroom, I felt his little body shut down as the teachers plied him with questions which he could not answer. I watched his face go flat with alarm when they tried to force him to imitate the actions of the fish song. I saw his anxiety shoot through the roof to the point of shutdown when they drilled him over and over again to distinguish between pen, cup, and paper. In this highly regimented classroom he had no opportunity to initiate, no moment of joyful connection, and no chance to become a creative human being. I felt desperate to get him out of the situation or change it. But I needed to find a way to write the report which would enable me to build a relationship with the teacher, giving her a way forward to build a relationship with the child. Over the years since leaving Andrew, I had worked hard and without complete success to undo the impulse to tell teachers and parents what they were doing wrong. I knew that only by building a supportive relationship with this teacher would useful change come about.

I took a break to check messages. I had got into the habit of rewarding myself by reading Julian's e-mails. He had written,

"So sorry I missed your call last night. I came home around 8:00 and foolishly laid on my bed to rest... and fell asleep... waking at 2:00am to the punishment of not hearing your voice... As I could not call and disturb your sleep... at that late hour..."

I wondered if the use of ellipses was because he could not spell, but I appreciated the flow of his consciousness.

In search of objectivity, I e-mailed the psychologist instead of him. "Julian's e-mails seem to fuel the fire. I know so well that the most important step is to acknowledge the emotional pulls that are in full flower at times like these. As you know full well, I have never actually succeeded at this, but my goal is that over time, if all goes well, I could grow to know him (and he, me) so that our love can really be about each other."

She e-mailed back, "Wish I had said that! Ahh, well, it seems you have gotten to the heart of the matter."

A few days later, I was at home working through my billing for my business. To procrastinate, I read Julian's latest e-mail. He had written:

Was glad we talked last night... as it makes the distance bearable... hearing your voice and thoughts... when apart from you... In particular... each time we talk of future events (or hopes and dreams)... I feel even closer...! Thank You My Love! Julian

I looked out into the garden. The ground was still frozen, and a light snow covered the outline of the rhododendrons. It would be Valentine's Day next week. I opened Photoshop, searched for a photo of a single white camellia bloom against a dark background, and started working on a card.

Chapter 17

Reunion with ex-Community Members in Costa Rica

The human heart is so delicate, and sensitive, that it always needs some tangible encouragement, to prevent it from faltering in its labor. The human heart is so robust, so tough, that once encouraged, it beats its rhythm with a loud, unswerving, consistency.
Maya Angelou (2009)

Five years after leaving the Community, an ex-senior student, Pasqual, invited dozens of former Community members to a three-week bus tour of Costa Rica. I was intrigued by the prospect but I felt fear rising. I scanned the list of names because I had no intention of sharing a bus with Damian, Shirley, or Stephanie. Even without them, I knew that I might feel ostracized every time I saw a cluster of people. Segregation and ostracism had been a big part of our life in the Community, so how could this gathering be different? But I guessed that we could share an investigation, and promised myself I would leave if I became too uncomfortable.

In 2006, 17 ex-Community members settled into the slow-paced pleasure of Costa Rica. Some had left Andrew very recently; others a long time ago. Some were angry, most reflective and a few appreciative. Some were mourning. All of us were still trying to understand confusing aspects of our experiences in the Community. Dozens more in states of severe depression or PTSD did not come, though later some of them would make contact with us.

We swam off the tropical beaches of the Pacific coast, traveled by dugout canoe to stay with the Bribri tribe in the jungle, and smoked pot among the Rastafarians on the east coast. We did not assume that we knew how anyone else should process their experience or what conclusions they should reach. We were careful not to tell each other what to do or think. We tried to start from scratch, sometimes checking to see which Community values we still wanted to keep and which we did not.

I am not sure what I had expected. I found it most surprising that people were interested in me and my children's experience. They were delighted that Jessica had, at the age of 18, gone round the world by herself and spent some months researching sea turtles in Thailand. She was now married and had a Master's in sustainable business. They inquired about Becky who, when they had last seen her, had dyed-blond hair, was very chubby, and almost never spoke. She was now taking pre-med at Ithaca and spent her vacations skiing in Vermont. I shared the girls' progress with pride and awe for their resilience.

We talked for three weeks. Groups sat outside the cabins, in the dusty light of lanterns, brushing off the mosquitoes. From people who had been senior students for anything up to a decade, I heard that it was systematic for very personal details revealed to Andrew in confidence to be used to humiliate students later. He used rumors that he knew to be untrue to attack people. And I heard descriptions of how he turned on a dime in the middle of a conversation, switching from loving interactions to scathing attacks. He would laugh raucously during stories of his students' shock and pain. His cruelty, even sadism, had been relentless for most of his years of teaching.

During these weeks I listened to many stories much more intense than my own. A woman who had been loyal to Andrew for many years was taken into the basement and four women were ordered to dump buckets of paint on her head as a message of gratitude from Andrew. A man was assaulted and others were threatened with assault. A woman was told that she would be committing spiritual suicide if she left.

I renewed connection with a woman I had not seen in 25 years.

She told me that while her daughter was dying she was systematically intimidated and attacked for not being sufficiently committed to the teachings. The demands on her time for meetings and service were unrelieved. Family loyalties were undermined and her family was treated with terrible cruelty at this time of greatest vulnerability when compassion was sorely needed.

The story that shocked me most was from one of Andrew's most devoted students, a gentle and sensitive man who was forced to make repeated visits to prostitutes over a period of weeks. I was incredulous that Andrew could have justified this to himself in the name of liberation. Andrew requested in-depth notes of these encounters and witnesses reported that he was delighted to read the details. He was unmoved by the man's daily appeals to stop this prescribed "practice."

Andrew was particularly abusive towards women, believing that they were innately flawed.

The friend of a woman who died slowly with her heart broken, after Andrew rejected her as his student, described how, 11 days before her death, a senior student berated her for 45 minutes for her selfishness, telling her that she would "die a miserable old woman." This story is told by Mario Puljiz (2006).

Andrew saw having children as a hindrance to the spiritual path. Women who wanted children sometimes had to choose between motherhood and being his student. The result was that some women felt pressured into having tubal ligations and one woman had an abortion.

As if it had happened yesterday, one ex-student told me that she experienced months of intimidation during women's meetings by formal and senior students. She described her routine defense of leaving her body and observing herself from the ceiling. Then in the middle of a women's meeting she was ordered to leave the premises. With no notice she was banished from the meeting and from her home. She was sent out into the

Boston cold without coat or possessions. She stayed in a motel for a few weeks until her money ran out. For a further week she shared a room at a youth hostel in Everett with drug addicts until two of the No Women came to collect her. Ten years after leaving the Community her nightmares about Andrew continue.

One woman told me that at a retreat in France, she and many other women were interrogated in isolation. Andrew gave instructions to the interrogators to "capture the smiling face of the devil." I imagined the women smiling as a defense mechanism to guard against overwhelming anxiety and confusion. I imagined Andrew laughing at the resulting videos and interpreting them as satanic.

I had always imagined that Andrew was unaware of some of the cruelty meted out by his students. Now I learned from those in his inner circle that he had not only ordered it, but received detailed reports about it. I realized then that his condition was not just a mixed bag of benevolent and cruel; his was, or had become, a pathological condition. Nothing stood in the way of Andrew's demands for control and adoration. There was no check on his abuse of power.

William Yenner had been one of Andrew's most trusted committed students, at the top of the hierarchy. A little older than I, his hair gray, he was lean and fit, still running marathons. He had, under duress, given $80,000 to Andrew's foundation and Andrew refused to return it when William left. He describes his experience in his book *American Guru* (Yenner, 2013). I understood from him that as Andrew became increasingly dissatisfied with his students' progress, he placed increasing pressure on the senior students. As their anxiety and fear increased, they increased the pressure on those lower down like myself. William and I had lived in the same small Community for ten years. I had assumed that he was aloof and unapproachable. Now he had become just an ordinary person trying to make sense of his deep pain.

Early one morning, I was awakened by a thunderstorm's clattering rain on the metal roof of the balcony where I slept. I sat up and watched the multi-textured greens of the jungle soak up the torrents of water. The woman in the sleeping bag next to mine awoke and we chatted. She told me news of Ziggy, my companion in my early days living in California. Ziggy had remained in the Community and had recently been applauded for a miraculous change. She had become a formal student, and had reunited with the love of her life, her former husband. I imagined her joy. A few months later she made a mistake and was demoted and separated from her husband again. I imagined her pain of losing her husband for the second time coming at the same time as group ostracism, and rejection by Andrew. From the pit of my stomach, my gorge rose when I thought of her futile struggle to make amends. It made me angry to hear that she was still in the grip of Andrew's manipulation. My blood boiled to think of Andrew using her love for her husband as a tool to control her.

I could imagine Ziggy saying, "There is no spinning. I am devoted to the teachings and deeply grateful for every part of this precious life. Thank God there is one human being who stands up against the ego." By the end no one needed to spin us because we spun ourselves in accordance with the system.

One day Erica and I walked into the jungle to watch huge, blue morpho butterflies flop lazily around among the flowers. Desiring to reconcile, she apologized for her relentless superiority during the years we lived together. I accepted her apology. She also reminded me of how I had betrayed her during a women's meeting. Her son and his friend had been in a severe car accident. At first I was supportive and caring towards Erica. But when I heard that Andrew was critical of how she had handled the incident, I rearranged my position on Erica. At the next women's meeting, I drew attention to her overly emotional reaction to the situation. I made sure they knew every weakness she had shown. The women turned on her in a unanimous attack, sending her into a crippling crisis of confidence for weeks.

When she reminded me of how I had used her vulnerability to gain purchase in the cutthroat world of the women's meetings, I had a vague memory of it. It was hard for me to see myself in this light and my memory is selective. There were many such conversations during these weeks. Erica and I also acknowledged a friendship and love for each other which had run parallel to the paranoia and exploitation all those years. I wondered how many other acts of my cruelty I had never registered or I had forgotten, and how I might reach out to people whose names I did not even remember.

One morning we sat in a beach shack that served papaya and coffee for breakfast. I talked with an English woman who had shared a house with us in the early days in Mill Valley—happy days for the most part. She told me about the many fractured outcomes of the lives of children who were once in the Community. I broke down in tears. I cried because we had failed the children. I cried for the children. My companion held me warmly. Soon I felt the warmth of other arms around me, and then more, as one after another people stood up, joined and joined us until I was engulfed by a whole group of people. Collectively we had the courage to hold the pain. They said no words, but smiled until I stopped crying and returned their smiles. The love that I had felt in Totnes was rekindled, the barriers once again dropped. We were together again—this time without a leader or dogmatic rules.

The Pacific coast beaches were magical. The waves crashed in a roiling confusion and turmoil of froth. Waves and foam swirled in all directions. We played for half a day; and in the evening, as the sun began to dip, we floated effortlessly in the quiet blackness and watched the crest of every wave highlighted by the last concentrated blaze of sun. Then we pulled ourselves out and sat dripping on the warm sand. Clouds on the horizon were irradiated for a while with red and gold. Behind us, the light bounced off the clouds. A bronze, surreal fire lit up the palm trees on the beach and infused the dense tropical jungle beyond.

William and I were sitting on the beach, ten feet from the water's edge. We must have been in the same room together thousands of times, yet I had never had a conversation with him. I had known the power that senior students had. I wondered whether, even now, I could look him in the eye without fear. I said, "Yesterday, when you said that your friendship with Andrew had been betrayed, you said that it was the people closest to Andrew who were most abused. However, those of us who were less successful suffered too, in a different way. Andrew's ability to spot weaknesses sometimes had devastating consequences for people only peripherally involved."

"What do you mean?" William asked, with a curiosity that surprised me.

"For most of 15 years, I was treated as one of the underclass. I was told on a daily basis that I didn't have much potential. I bought into Andrew's opinion that I was not up to much. Hell! I believed it for 15 years. In fact, I believed it until yesterday. I was oppressed by the elite, and you were part of it. And I am angry that I gave anyone that much power over me."

William said nothing for a moment. I wondered whether he had heard me. I wondered whether I had had reason to keep my distance all those years. I realized that now I did not hesitate to disagree with him.

"I am very touched," he finally said. "I know I was one of the perpetrators of that oppression."

"Yes, you were," I replied, beginning to enjoy this opportunity to get even.

But I was caught off guard by the candor in his voice when he continued, "I wanted to say I am sorry. I think I was getting a lot out of that."

I looked away for a moment to regain composure, and then

looked back at him and said, "Thank you." I felt the hierarchy, which had once seemed so important, crumbling as we spoke. And I understood that Andrew had instituted it as a mechanism for dividing and controlling people. "William!" I exclaimed. "It all looks different now!"

"Yes," he replied. "We have walked out of a shared vision. Or was it shared delusion?"

"Maybe it was both," I said.

"Whichever it is," he said, "I'm grateful that we can talk about all of it and find out."

For me, his apology represented others that might have been. I still felt waves of resentment towards some people in the group. On this trip, I never spoke to most of the women who had been formal students in Boston. Even if they had never done anything to me, I held back as if they were "other." I still had repair work to do.

Someone else on the beach mentioned how those who did not do well in discussion groups failed to thrive. We discussed the misery of competing to be in the top discussion groups and described the humiliation of being at the bottom. Old pain resurfaced. For the first time I remembered the weekend when I'd been removed from the discussion group—a memory previously too painful to be recovered. This memory, with wisdom beyond my perception and control, had kindly remained out of awareness until conditions inside and out might enable healing.

We struggled to understand the nature of Andrew's gifts and his terrible flaws. How can one separate his genuine spirituality from the base human motives which he so often indulged? He had claimed to teach love but was a bully. He taught surrender in an atmosphere of fear; vulnerability in the context of intense competition. He claimed to teach impersonally, yet cultivated favorites in an atmosphere of suspicion. Worst of all were his responses to budding spirituality among his students. In the name of rooting out ego, he crushed the spiritual impulse just as we began to trust our deepest selves. Was there something in him, we wondered, which made him incapable of empathy? Were his moments of apparent gentleness a pretense? Had our adulation changed him from a young man inspired by revelations of love into a corrupt and ruthless egomaniac? Most importantly, was this simply an inevitable consequence of putting him on a pedestal, giving him unquestioned authority, and ignoring or taking upon ourselves every mistake he made?

How do we understand that some of our experiences brought about greater awareness, and some nearly shattered some of us? Could it be that some remarkable things happened in spite of, or sometimes because of, a dangerous and destructive context? And were our experiences tainted because of their context? Together, we tried to figure out what impulses had brought us to his cult ready to both accept and dish out abuse. We had wanted the bliss of Satsang, Andrew's approval, and the safety within the group—and had been ready to do almost anything to achieve it. There were no easy answers. The meaning of my experiences could not be neatly categorized, but I found I spent less energy denying them. We heard one another's stories, threaded with pain and pleasure. We sought redemption from the past by making amends where we could. We supported each other in asking previously unaskable questions and stepping free from the shame of Andrew's judgment.

Chapter 18

Forgiveness

At three in the morning, my head throbbing, I took painkillers. My migraine was back. The pills, if it was not already too late, might enable me to work through the day. Two pieces of toast with curried lentils: eating sometimes helped. A cup of strong English tea: caffeine sometimes helped. I left the bed unmade, left a trail of clothes across the floor, made no attempt to wash the dishes. I reduced energy output to a minimum, thinking I could probably make it through the day on autopilot. Most people probably wouldn't notice, but Becky would. In the mirror, my eyeliner looked coarse, as if it had just been stuck on, but I needed a mask.

Having some time to spare before my first appointment, I stopped in Wellesley, looking for somewhere to spend a quiet moment. I was drawn to the spire of a church, not because I was religious but because I like the energy in some churches. I drove into the church parking lot; then, on foot, I made a circuit around the outside of the church. Unexpectedly, the heavy side door pushed open.

It was dark in the sanctuary; the richly-colored stained glass windows were the only source of light. I paused until my eyes adjusted to the darkness and I could pick out the faint curved lines of the back of the pews. Like a dog twisting around and around, feeling for the best spot in the sun, I drifted around until I found a spot where the energy tingled most strongly up and down my spine. I sat down and was still. Tears welled up in my eyes.

For years, I had been using my breath to practice forgiveness of myself and Andrew. I remembered in the early days at Satsang, when he looked at the furrow in my brow, my chin resting in my hand propped up by my elbow. "That," he said, kindly, "is the pose of a thinker, not a seeker." I had melted inside, feeling a deep love for Andrew, for my children, for my husband, for the people meditating around me. I remembered the times when my soft center had been touched, and I felt tears of surprise that I still had a soft center after so much gritted effort over so long a time. I closed my eyes, imagining a scratched record rotating round and round, the needle digging the scratch deeper until someone lifts the handle. I allowed in memories that I once would have brushed aside as quickly as possible.

I remembered Andrew Cohen standing stony-faced, without a word of acknowledgement, as I walked past him and entered the center that had so much meaning for me. I let the image loose and breathed it outwards into the sanctuary. I remembered the double messages he sent me when I first arrived back from the West Coast, one minute affirming the changes in me, the next sending an insidious wave of rejection towards me. I breathed outwards letting the heat of my anger float towards the roof.

Andrew had orchestrated cruelty all around him, and I had let it trickle down into my actions with my children. He had sent me spiraling away from freedom and towards self-hatred. I breathed the tension in that thought towards the vaulted ceiling. I forgave us both. Again and again, I breathed softly towards my memory of him.

Relieved, I stood up and walked to the back of the church, and there my attention was drawn upwards to a vista of vaulted ceilings. The supporting pillars were broad, smooth swaths of seamless wood. With my eye I followed them high up into the ceiling where the beams interlaced in simple, bold arcs. Here the energy in the church was very strong. I breathed it in, like food feeding my spine. Then, feeling that something was not finished, I walked back and sat in the same pew.

Andrew was my catalyst. He had allowed me to open the door into a spiritual life. I was grateful. He had created the houses in which I learned to communicate. I thanked him for that too.

Opening my eyes, I noticed the ruby red and royal blue of the windows. The stained glass figure of Christ watched me from the center of one of them, his arms outstretched in a gesture of compassion and mercy. I responded for a moment to this image borrowed from the mythology of a vaguely protestant English childhood.

I recalled a dream where dirt was caked on my arm beneath my shirt. I picked at it with a needle until the whole arm bled. When I removed the shirt I saw that it wasn't dirt but a mole. I had mistakenly tried to destroy a part of myself. Is that what I had been doing all those years?

From a very early age I had tried too hard to get it right in the eyes of others. I had been addicted to a life of "shoulds." Recognizing that I was still an addict, I breathed tenderness towards myself. I wondered whether Andrew's judgment of me as "not good enough" coincided with my own judgment of myself. *No more goading myself for not being perfect,* I decided. I took a long, slow breath in and then breathed out, noticing as I did so a jagged hesitation in the breath. Every uneven out-breath was like a stutter. Under my gentled eye, the breath smoothed out in luxurious release. I forgave myself for the actions that I took against my husband, my children and myself. Then I thanked my 30-year-old self for trying so hard to find connection and meaning in her life. I thanked her for her curiosity and spirit in trying to be everything that she could be. As if giving birth, I felt a combination of release and agony. A newborn Marlowe was coming into view.

This breathing—might it take too long? The task seems endless. And what if I have to keep forgiving Andrew and myself for the same things over and over again? Is the task too big? I asked myself. I answered, *No. There will always be more; it may never be finished. I may have to consciously breathe love instead of self-loathing into my own body with every breath for the rest of my life; that is okay.*

Standing up from the pew, I wondered what was still missing. It was the familiar sense of disquiet. I felt around inside; the migraine was still there but instead of contraction, I felt a great expanse, an outward-moving energy that I did not need to conserve. I was ready to begin my day's work. I walked lightly towards the door of the church and took a step out of the dim interior, dazzled for a second by the full sun. I steadied myself with a hand on the stone wall and took in a breath of air.

I thought about my first job of the day, a presentation on play therapy to a group of parents. It was a short distance from the church and I had easily enough time to set up my projector.

Postscript

I experienced so much that was truly profound and transfor-
mative—and that I will forever be grateful for—and also so much
that was really abusive and twisted—and that still deeply saddens
me. The lightest light and the darkest dark. Both. All tangled
together like miles of black and white yarn entwined in a big ball at
the pit of my stomach.
Bridle (2005)

On the bad stuff

Since leaving the Community 16 years ago, I have completed a
Master's degree in counseling psychology which involved taking
courses in the dynamics of group therapy, psychotherapy, and
psychopathology. Doing so has deepened my understanding of
the problems within the Community and of my own partici-
pation in it.

When trying to understand my reactions to the stresses of the
Community, I read Philip Bromberg's essays in which he
discusses the healthy mechanisms of fight/flight/freeze which
enable us to survive in threatening situations. Attacks on our
sense of self or, for some of us, physical assaults were routine in
the Community. The women's meetings and the discussion
groups were classic situations that triggered me to "freeze" and
retreat into fearful silence. Fighting back with explanations or
disagreement was pointless; I would lose. Flight, running away,
trying to escape the Community, was personal failure and was
accompanied by fear of isolation—a crushing blow to be avoided
at all costs. And so I returned to a childhood habit of silently
trying to hide in place by becoming a submissive, dutiful student.
In the Community, signs of fight, flight or freeze were all interpreted as signs of aggression and brought about intensified
assaults, for example when Heidi was attacked during my first

women's meeting.

Bromberg (1998) continues, "What of situations where there are competing algorithms at the same moment? ... when your peer group suddenly becomes a pack of hyenas, stripping you bare while you are still alive? ... The algorithm of flight, fight, or hiding only pertains to escape from predators. What does someone do when there is another strong algorithm already operating such as 'obedience to one's parents,' or 'being accepted by one's peers'?" He states that then the abuse victim may have recourse to a more destructive subconscious survival mechanism—dissociation... When I was abused, Andrew and his students were both the beloved and the attacker. Unable to simultaneously process these drastically conflicting emotions I began to disassociate. It seems that this was the case in "The Discussion Group Weekend." I began to hallucinate that I was a tiger in a pit, attacking my captors as their legs came near the sides of my cage. The situation was analogous to an abusive family in which loyalty, love, and attachment are found inextricably and incomprehensibly bound up with pain, humiliation, betrayal, rejection, and cruelty. My experiences of both spirituality and abuse were less intense than many of Andrew's students. I never experienced the severe abuse meted out to others, yet this story illustrates to some extent the context that was created around Andrew.

A breakdown of our self-identity was an ongoing risk. We were actively trained to not trust our own judgment and to look to Andrew for the answers. This eroded the individual's sense of self and compromised their moral compass. Anti-cult literature describes mechanisms of thought control, hypnosis, and manipulation. The methods used by Andrew were standard forms of control that have been used by power seekers for millennia. The signs are well documented and commonplace, my susceptibility to them not unusual.

In *Prophetic Charisma: The Psychology of Revolutionary Religious*

Personalities (1997), Len Oakes describes the common experiences of people in cults all over the world—experiences common to the Community: "The capriciousness of the guru's reactions is a strategy for keeping you deliberately off balance so that you stop trusting your own intuition." The effect on many of us was not increasing humility but decreasing confidence. In *Deception, Dependency, and Dread* (n.d.), Michael Langone writes, "Threats and punishments occur within a context of induced dependency and psychological alienation from the person's former support network." During my gradual submission to Andrew, my capacity to make independent moral judgments decreased; I relied on the others to tell me what was right. Mechanisms of mind control and my desire for growth blinded me to Andrew's methods of controlling us. It was almost impossible to see his authenticity clearly or evaluate his motives while being his student.

The International Cultic Studies Association has published a list: [*Fifteen*] *Characteristics Associated with Cultic Groups* (Lalich & Langone, n.d.). When I read this list I realized that the experience of Andrew's Community was very similar to that in other cults. All 15 characteristics were endemic to Andrew's Community.

Clearly there was nothing new about our experiences—cults follow well-trodden paths:

- The group displays excessively zealous and unquestioning commitment to its leader and (whether he is alive or dead) regards his belief system, ideology, and practices as the Truth, as law.
- Questioning, doubt, and dissent are discouraged or even punished.
- Mind-altering practices (such as meditation, chanting, speaking in tongues, denunciation sessions, and debilitating work routines) are used in excess and serve to suppress doubts about the group and its leader (sleep

deprivation, chanting sometimes fit in this category).

- The leadership dictates, sometimes in great detail, how members should think, act, and feel.
- The group is elitist, claiming a special, exalted status for itself, its leader(s) and members (for example, the leader is considered the Messiah, a special being, an avatar—or the group and/or the leader is on a special mission to save humanity.
- The group has a polarized us-versus-them mentality, which may cause conflict with the wider society.
- The leader is not accountable to any authorities (unlike, for example, teachers, military commanders or ministers, priests, monks, and rabbis of mainstream religious denominations).
- The group teaches or implies that its supposedly exalted ends justify whatever means it deems necessary. This may result in members participating in behaviors or activities they would have considered reprehensible or unethical before joining the group.
- The leadership induces feelings of shame and/or guilt in order to influence and/or control members. Often, this is done through peer pressure and subtle forms of persuasion.
- Subservience to the leader or group requires members to cut ties with family and friends, and radically alter the personal goals and activities they had before joining the group.
- The group is preoccupied with bringing in new members.
- The group is preoccupied with making money.
- Members are expected to devote inordinate amounts of time to the group and group-related activities.
- Members are encouraged or required to live and/or socialize only with other group members.
- The most loyal members (the "true believers") feel there

can be no life outside the context of the group. They believe there is no other way to be, and often fear reprisals to themselves or others if they leave (or even consider leaving) the group.

A catalogue of some of the abuse within Andrew's Community is documented here:

http://whatenlightenment.blogspot.co.uk/2013/07/the-list-catalog-of-trauma-and-abuse.html

Anti-cult literature exposes mechanisms of abuse and corruption in cults. Andrew Cohen's Community, taken in its entirety, was overwhelmingly destructive to hundreds of people. But to make sense of the controversy surrounding Andrew Cohen we also have to understand the threads of grace and healing that ran simultaneously through his work. I could not dismiss all my experiences as delusional and destructive. I felt that I had experienced both genuine spirituality and craziness. I would never doubt my experience in the Utah canyon that I was nothing more than a bundle of cravings and I would always regard my treatment during the discussion group weekend as abusive. The weakness of some anti-cult writings is that they categorize all forms of spiritual experience as pathological and/or dissociative. In order to do justice to the complexity of human experience we need a model that distinguishes between those experiences that bring about greater awareness and those that shatter us.

On temptation

I conjecture that when Andrew first met his teacher, his transformative experiences radically shifted his relationship to his own mind. As a result he became a powerful catalyst for some people who were receptive to opening their hearts wide. Many of us experienced healing as a result. Perhaps when Poonjaji sent him to "bring about a revolution in the West!" Andrew was doomed to an impossible and self-destructive task: to be the guru. Intoxication by power and corruption was an easy step. But perhaps he could have responded differently to these gifts.

What is clear is that Andrew became too powerful in his self-referential world. When we joined, we implicitly helped to co-create this world, with all its dysfunction. We accepted that his ideas and actions were impeccable, above question, and fed his incipient narcissism, rendering him less and less capable of self-reflection. Andrew used his powers of perception and intuition to manipulate all of us to his own ends. While our relationship with Andrew was supposed to be a vehicle for our spiritual growth, it was surely as much a mechanism for Andrew to control us. As SJ Gelberg (2014) states, "Acquisition of psychological or spiritual insight is one thing—the application of these skills for good or evil is a completely separate matter."

Also, I wonder about my motives after transformative experiences, which brought such strength, clarity and conviction about my next action. The conversion from the sublime to the concrete can be full of ego. In a sudden blissful experience there is a stark discontinuity with previous assessments and evaluations, which shifts us out of our normal frame of reference. The simple truth of the experience leads easily to a slight of hand that makes us think that decisions which affect the people we love are also simple in their implications. It is easy when swept away by the choicelessness of understanding to ignore the consequences to those I hold dear. I have made this mistake over and over again, from the moment that I left my husband to the moment that I followed Andrew to the East Coast. In each case I saw something clearly and made a leap, believing that lack of doubt signified lack of ego. I acted without ego, but selfishly following what I wanted while ignoring the consequences to those I hold dear; I did not weigh the pros and cons or look carefully at the consequences. How easy it is to experience something true, and assume that our very next impulse is the voice of God.

On responsibility

It is very hard to unravel the distinction between the responsibil-ities of the leader and the responsibilities of the followers. The question of why we stayed so long is complex. Anti-cult literature gives us some explanations. And it might seem that to the degree that we were made psychologically dependent, and our innate decision-making was compromised, our moral responsibility was diminished. We found it hard to leave the Community because the system of induced dependency had worked on us. Yet it is also true that we stayed because we were getting something out of it. Perhaps I wanted the growth that comes with freedom so much more than stability that I was willing to risk disintegration. Even worse, I ignored evidence of some of the abuses above for the sake of the benefits that I was getting from being with Andrew. Clearly, I actively participated in a dangerous and destructive cult.

I read with horror about the death of cult members in a sweat lodge in Arizona. Their guru was convicted of three counts of negligent homicide and sentenced to two years in prison. What about me? What would I have done in that lodge? I cannot be sure there was any point at which I would have called a stop to the abuse of others by Andrew or have stood up publicly for myself. What would I have done if asked to stay in a sweat lodge for ten more minutes or to close the door on others? I reflected on my complex reactions to the experience of "The Lake." I actively participated in setting the challenge. Therefore I was part of the collective pressure on other women. After my second attempt to stay in the lake for an hour, I was heralded as a hero for exhorting my companions to succeed. Yet on reflection, if they had collapsed with hypothermia I would have been responsible.

I am responsible because one of the reasons I stayed was willful ignorance about the destructive effect of staying on my friends, children and family. I know now that I can never take for granted the stability of my morality. I intend to never again underestimate my impressionability. I experienced this stark and terrifying reality in Rishikesh: we are all capable of far more good and evil, strength and weakness than we ever dream is possible. If we are to be whole we have to Face Everything and Avoid Nothing from the most ignorant attacks on the sacred life force to the gifts of deepest meditation and intimate connection.

On the current situation

In June of 2013, as a result of demands from his senior students to modify his dictatorial style of leadership, Andrew Cohen stopped teaching and stated that he was taking a sabbatical. He published an apology, which included the following statement:

> Some of my closest students have tried to make it apparent to me that in spite of the depth of my awakening, my ego is still alive and well... when I was being asked to face my own ego by those who were nearest and dearest to me, I resisted. And I often made their lives difficult as a result. I'm aware that many of my students over the years have also been affected by my lack of awareness of this part of myself. And for those of you who are reading this, I apologize. As time passes I intend to reach out and engage in a process of dialogue with those of you who would like to.
> (Cohen, *An Apology*, 2013)

At the time Tomer Persico (2013) described Cohen's stepping down as guru:

> an earthquake took place in the world of New Age. A tectonic shift the likes of which the elders of Rishikesh cannot recall. It was revealed that Andrew Cohen, one of the most famous spiritual teachers in the world, and until a few years ago one

of the most powerful and influential figures in contemporary Western spirituality, is about to step down as guru and resign the leadership of the movement.

Shortly afterwards in private conversation with one of his ex-students, Andrew admitted that he had made a lot of mistakes as a teacher and that during much of his teaching career he had not known what he was doing. At the time of writing he has had no further contact with former members of the Community. This moment of spiritual crisis in the Community coincided with and was perhaps precipitated by a looming financial debacle and one may have fed the other.

It is unclear to what extent Andrew's teachings and the culture that surrounds them are continuing under other names. EnlightenNext, the non-profit created to spread Andrew's teachings, always had separate and independent branches including US, UK, Germany, Denmark, France, Holland, Israel and Australia. Each branch has made its own decisions about whether to close, to continue under the same name and with the same mission statement or whether to transition into organizations with a different approach. Foxhollow lapsed into disrepair and was planned to be sold. The lease on the meditation center was given up. It appears that the US branch of Andrew's Foundation (EnlightenNext) is closed. The EnlightenNext in UK changed its name and in consultation with former students is discussing how to use the residual money in accordance to laws pertaining to non-profits. Several of Andrew's ex-students are currently teaching meditation and spiritual growth.

It is not known if Andrew Cohen will return to teaching.

References

Angelou, M. (2009) *Letter to My Daughter*. New York: Random House Publishing Group

Blacker, H. (2013) *The "A" List: A Catalog of Trauma and Abuse* [online], What Enlightenment??! An uncensored look at self-styled American guru Andrew Cohen. Available from: http://whatenlightenment.blogspot.co.uk/2013/07/the-list-catalog-of-trauma-and-abuse.html (accessed 1 November 2014)

Bridle, S. (2005) *A Legacy of Scorched Earth: Reflections of a former student* [online], Enlightennixt. Available from: http://enligh tennixt.com/ (accessed 6 June 2013)

Bromberg, P. (1998) *Standing in the Spaces*. Hove, UK: Psychology Press

Chödrön, P. (1997) *When Things Fall Apart*. Boston, MA: Shambhala Publications

Cohen, A. (n.d.) *The Five Fundamental Tenets of Enlightenment* [online], Evolutionary Enlightenment: Redefining spirituality for our rapidly changing world. No longer available from www.andrewcohen.org (accessed 17 August 2011)

Cohen, A. (1995) *Enlightenment is a Secret: Teachings of Liberation*. Larkspur, California: What Is Enlightenment? Press

Cohen, A. (2013) *Yoga, Ego and Purification* [online], Evolutionary Enlightenment: Redefining spirituality for our rapidly changing world. No longer available from: http://andrew-cohen.org/yoga-ego-and-purification (accessed 22 September 2013)

Cohen, A. (2013) *An Apology* [online], Evolutionary Enlightenment: Redefining spirituality for our rapidly changing world. No longer available from: http://www.andrewcohen.org/blog/apology (accessed 26 June 2013)

Gelberg, SJ (2007) *Some Things I Learned During My Seventeen*

Years in the Hare Krishna Movement [online], International Cultic Studies Association. Available at: http://www.icsahome .com/articles/some-things-i-learned-gelberg-en6-3/ (accessed 16 June 2014)

Lalich, J. & Langone, MD (n.d.) [*Fifteen*] *Characteristics Associated with Cultic Groups* [online], International Cultic Studies. Available from: http://www.csj.org/infoserv_cult101/checklis .htm (accessed 26 February 2014)

Langone, MD (n.d.) *Deception, Dependency, and Dread* [online], International Cultic Studies. Available from: http://www.csj. org/studyindex/studyconversion/study_recruitconvddd.htm (accessed 8 March 2014)

Oakes, L. (1997) *Prophetic Charisma: The Psychology of Revolutionary Religious Personalities*. Syracuse, NY: Syracuse University Press

Persico, T. (2013) *Andrew Cohen and the decline of the Guru institution*. Available from: https://tomerpersicoenglish.wordpr ess.com/2013/08/ (originally accessed 9 December 2014)

Puljiz, M. (2006) *Not Forgotten — The Story of Caroline Franklyn* [online], What Enlightenment??! An uncensored look at self-styled American guru Andrew Cohen. Available from: http://whatenlightenment.blogspot.co.uk/2006/01/not-forgotten-story-of-caroline.html (accessed 7 February 2014)

Schubert, F. (1839) *Neue Zeitschrift fur Musik*, referenced in Solomon, Maynard, "Franz Schubert's 'My Dream,'" *American Imago* 38 (1981), 137–54. See http://www.williamapercy.com /wiki/images/Franz_Schubert's_my_dream.pdf

Yenner, W. (2013) *American Guru: A Story of Love, Betrayal and Healing—Former students of Andrew Cohen speak out*. Rhinebeck, NY: Epigraph Publishing

Further Reading and Web Sites

Tarlo, L. (1997) *The Mother of God.* New York, NY: Plover/ Autonomedia

van der Braak, A. (2003) *Enlightenment Blues: My Years with an American Guru.* Rhinebeck, NY: Monkfish

http://www.andrewcohen.org
  Andrew Cohen's official website which currently continues to sell books and magazines.

http://enlightennixt.com
  Numerous firsthand accounts of experience within Andrew Cohen's community.

http://www.icsahome.com
  Information on cults is provided by International Cultic Studies Association.

http://shiningworld.com/top/images/stories/pub-pdfs/Articles/ A_Fallen_Yogi.pdf
  "A Fallen Yogi" by James Swartz (accessed July 2015). In this article Swartz offers an analysis of the limitations in Cohen's understanding which enabled him to become an abusive teacher.

http://www.strippingthegurus.com/stgsamplechapters/cohen.ht ml
  In an extract from his book *Stripping the Gurus*, Geoffrey D. Falk described Andrew's career (see chapter titled "Sometimes I Feel Like a God").

"Whatnext?" Facebook group
  This closed group is open to everyone who has been involved with Andrew Cohen.

BOOKS

O is a symbol of the world, of oneness and unity; this eye represents knowledge and insight. We publish titles on general spirituality and living a spiritual life. We aim to inform and help you on your own journey in this life.

Visit our website: http://www.o-books.com

Find us on Facebook:
https://www.facebook.com/OBooks

Follow us on Twitter: @obooks